J I A N G X I N O R M A L U N I V E R S I T Y

江西师范大学博士文库专项资助成果

GLOBALIZATION AND BASKETBALL IN CHINA: GOVERNANCE, MARKET AND CULTURE

Fuhua Huang

中国社会科学出版社

图书在版编目(CIP)数据

全球化时代的中国篮球：治理、市场与文化 =
Globalization and Basketball in China: Governance, Market and Culture/
黄福华著．—北京：中国社会科学出版社，2017.10
(江西师范大学博士文库)
ISBN 978-7-5203-0924-0

Ⅰ.①全… Ⅱ.①黄… Ⅲ.①篮球运动—体育产业—产业发展—研究—中国 Ⅳ.①G841

中国版本图书馆 CIP 数据核字(2017)第 234575 号

出 版 人 赵剑英
责任编辑 郭晓鸿
特约编辑 席建海
责任校对 沈丁晨
责任印制 戴 宽

出 版 中国社会科学出版社
社 址 北京鼓楼西大街甲 158 号
邮 编 100720
网 址 http://www.csspw.cn
发 行 部 010-84083685
门 市 部 010-84029450
经 销 新华书店及其他书店

印 刷 北京明恒达印务有限公司
装 订 廊坊市广阳区广增装订厂
版 次 2017 年 10 月第 1 版
印 次 2017 年 10 月第 1 次印刷

开 本 710×1000 1/16
印 张 18.75
插 页 2
字 数 256 千字
定 价 86.00 元

凡购买中国社会科学出版社图书，如有质量问题请与本社营销中心联系调换
电话：010-84083683

Contents

List of Tables

List of Tables

List of Figures

List of Pictures

List of Pictures

List of Abbreviations

AAU	Amateur Athletic Union
ABA	American Basketball Association
ABC	American Broadcasting Company
ACSF	All – China Sports Federation
AEG	Anschutz Entertainment Group
AHL	American Hockey League
ATV	Asia Television Limited
BAA	Basketball Association of America
BRI	Basketball Related Income
CBA	Chinese Basketball Association
CBAL	Chinese Basketball Association League
CBALC	Chinese Basketball Association League Committee
CBCF	Chinese Basketball Culture Forum
CBCRC	Chinese Basketball Culture Research Center
CBMC	Chinese Basketball Management Center
CCP	Chinese Communist Party
CCTV	China Central Television
CEO	Chief Executive Officer

CFA	Chinese Football Association
CNDSC	Central National Defense Sport Club
CSA	Chinese Streetball Association
CUBA	Chinese University Basketball Association
CUBSL	Chinese University Basketball Super League
CYL	Communist Youth League
DBA	Dongguan Basketball Association
DNT	DuMont Television Network
ESPN	Entertainment & Sport Program Network
FDI	Foreign Direct Investment
FIBA	International Basketball Association
FIFA	Fédération International de Football Association
GAS	General Administration of Sport
GDP	Gross Domestic Product
IABF	International Amateur Basketball Federation
IBSL	Iranian Basketball Super League
IMG	International Management Group
IOC	International Olympic Committee
ISF	International Sports Federation
JBL	Japan Basketball League
KBL	Korean Basketball League
LDS	Labour and Defense System
MLB	Major League Baseball
MNE	Multinational Enterprises
MVP	Most Valuable Player

NBA	National Basketball Association
NBC	National Broadcasting Company
NBDL	NBA Development League
NCAA	National Collegiate Athletic Association
NFL	National Football League
NGO	Non – Governmental Organization
NHL	National Hockey League
NSP	North Star Project
OEM	Original Equipment Manufacturer
PCACSF	Preparatory Committee for the All – China Sports Federation
PLA	People's Liberation Army
PRC	People's Republic of China
SLB	Super Basketball League
SPCSC	State Physical Culture and Sports Commission
TNC	Transnational Corporations
UN	United Nations
WNBA	Women's National Basketball Association
WTO	World Trade Organization
YMCA	Young Men's Christian Association

Chapter 1. Introduction

1.1 Globalization and Sport in China

Every generation faces its own social, economic, or political challenges, and globalization is a powerful combination of all three(Rossi, 2007: 5). Globalization has swept across every corner of the world in the past few decades. It is one of the most formidable forces in human history and is dramatically shaping and transforming the modern world. Under the trend of globalization, the borders of nation states are shrinking, the pace of human life is accelerating, and the world is increasingly interconnecting and being bound together.

China, the most populous country on earth, is rising as a key player in the global community. The move from a state-planned to a market-oriented economy, which began in a small way in the late 1970s and has progressed rapidly since the early 1990s, has heralded China's desire to engage with globalization. Following its escape from the most serious consequences of the Asian financial crisis of the late 1990s, China's accession to the World Trade Organization(WTO) in 2001 marked one of the most significant steps by the Chinese government towards deepening the integration of the Chinese economy with the world economy. Since then, China has benefited from an unprecedented global flow of the capital, human talent, scientific knowledge, and other resources which are required for the country's modernization, and has become the fastest-growing economy in the world with a gross domestic product(GDP) growth rate averaging close to 10 per cent per year. In 2007, China overtook Germany to become the third largest economy in the world. Then, in 2010, China surpassed Japan, taking its place as the world's second largest economy behind the United States.

Coinciding with its meteoric economic growth is China's rising power in world politics. Since the end of the Cold War, Chinese foreign policy has included measures seeking to advance its stature within the international community, increase its global interests, and procure a greater voice for China in its external environment(Lanteigne, 2005: 1). China has become the first developing country and the only contemporary socialist country to gain world power and to hold a chair on the United Nations Security Council. Furthermore, engaging with globalization has paved the way for China's societal transformation and multifaceted integration with the outside world. Thus, since China broke from the bondage of the Cultural Revolution(1966—1976) in the late 1970s, Chinese societal culture has witnessed structural transformations marked by technological innovation, ideological battles, social unrest, and political crises together with economic growth(Yu, 2009: 1). This process has been largely intertwined with fast-paced internal urbanization and modernization, within which globalization continues to influence the social actors due to its liberalizing commercial force.

China's radical and deep societal transit under globalization is shaping the trajectory and momentum of the development of Chinese sport in a profound way. As elsewhere in the world, topics relating to sport globalization inevitably pop up in the public media, daily conversations, and certainly, in academic publications in China. In the broad review and evaluation of the literatures on the topic of globalization and sport published in Chinese undertaken in this study, it is found that a large number of academic works use"globalization"in their titles or as a keyword. However, many of these works fail to centre their discussions on globalization if we consider the term"globalization"more rigorously to mean a set of processes that have increased interconnectedness across the globe, rather than merely a buzz word that points to a historical context for launching research. Apart from this, a good deal of noteworthy works by both Chinese and non-Chinese scholars have been devoted to the research field of globalization and sport in China. These publications were identified and subsequently grouped into four categories. First, works of research on the cultural conflict between tradition and modernity in Chinese sport were considered. Second to be investigated were researches on the institutional conflict between internationalization(for global prestige) and marketization(for internal reformation) in Chinese sport. The third group of works considered were researches on the modernization of Chinese sport through paradigm-assimilation, transnationally and globally. In the fourth category, works of research on the recent introduction or revival of foreign sports in post-reform China were examined.

1. 1. 1 Research on the Cultural Conflict between Tradition and Modernity in Chinese Sport

Most Chinese sport historians retrospect sport globalization in China as having begun with the"Westernization Movement"of the 1860s(e. g. Hong & Hua, 2002; Luo, 2005; Shu, 2006; Shu et al., 2006; Luo & Huang, 2013). With China having suffered successive defeats and a considerable loss of territory to western powers, enlightened politicians in the late 19th century promoted the ideas of "Zhengyan Kan Shijie"(opening the eyes to see the world) and"Shiyi Changji Yi Zhiyi"(learning from the barbarian to defeat the barbarian), policies which advocated the adoption of western-style sports. And so western sports were introduced to and selectively accepted in modern China. At first, western sports, such as gymnastics, were considered new and warlike sports that could be utilized in military training. According to Luo(2005), the goals of"military-enhancing, nation-enhancing, state-enhancing"were key factors in the extensive influence of western sports on the development of modern Chinese sports. Western sports were also rapidly diffused throughout the country via the large number of missionary schools and Young Men's Christian Association(YMCA) societies established in China in the early 20th century(Hong & Hua, 2002; Luo, 2005; Luo & Huang, 2013). As a result of these western influences, Olympism was propagated in China and the connotation of sports was gradually expanded to encompass a form of recreation as well as a means of enhancing the physical fitness and competitiveness of the Chinese people(Hong & Hua, 2002; Luo, 2005; Shu, 2006; Shu et al., 2006; Luo & Huang, 2013). Consequently, Chinese sports teams began to take to the international stage, such as the Far Eastern Championship Games and the Olympic Games. In its early participations in world sporting events, China's performances were relatively poor, and each failure to achieve success for the nation spurred a greater commitment to mastering western sports. In summary, the West-China battle on the sports field ended in the successful transplantation in China of western sport culture, which brought with it"a new conceptualization of physicality and the practice of modern sports"(Hong & Hua, 2002).

For the Chinese, sport globalization in the late 19th and early 20th centuries was undertaken reluctantly, which was a process provoked by western imperial power. However, sport globalization in contemporary China was initiated deliberately with China's "open door" policy since the 1970s. This sudden shift once again gave rise to an extensive discussion on the conflict between sport modernization brought about by westerners and Chinese traditional sports. For some scholars (e. g. Luo, 2005; Shu, 2006; Shu et al., 2006; Song, 2010; Luo & Huang, 2013), over the past century and a half, Chinese sport has been integrated into global sport rationally from passive acceptance in the past. As a result, Chinese sport and world sport have also benefited from globalization, which can be exemplified by the efficient expansion and acceptance of Chinese traditional sport into the Olympic Games. Thus, they consider that sport globalization enhances interconnectedness among the countries of the world. Deng (2007) claims that this process produces cultural heterogenization rather than westernization.

Conversely, some scholars argue that Chinese traditional sports are at risk of being westernized (e. g. Ye, 2007; Li et al., 2008; Lou et al., 2008; Jiang, 2009; Hong, 2010). Luo et al. (2008) point out that a lack of market potential, little governmental support, and inadequate media coverage are the major impediments to the development of Chinese traditional sports. Fang and Wang (2007) hold a negative viewpoint in evaluating globalization's influence on Chinese traditional sports. They contend that western sport is presumed to be "universal" or "core" while non-western sport is seen as "particular" or "periphery". This assumption, Fang and Wang add, has led to an impertinent injection of western values and ideologies into oriental culture, including through the global development of the Olympic Games. Zhang and Zhang (2006) echo that view, stating that sport globalization leads to cultural inequalities between nation states, resulting ultimately in the westernization of sport in less-developed countries, including China.

Some scholars emphasize this challenge to Chinese traditional sports by focusing on the case of Chinese martial arts(e. g. Ye, 2007; Jiang, 2009; Hong, 2010; He, 2011; Xie & Li, 2012). Wang and Qiu(2006) argue that western sports have gradually become dominant in China, challenging the development of Chinese traditional sports and martial arts in particular. Worse still, some of China's traditional martial arts, part of the country's sporting and cultural heritage, have been homogenized by western sport ideology. Jiang(2009) and Hong(2010) add their voices to this argument with evidence of the deformation of Chinese martial arts, which have been dichotomized into performance style and athletic-oriented style practices. For them, the marrow of Chinese martial arts should be harmonious exercise rather than winning or achieving. There are also concerns about the fate of Chinese traditional national minority sports under globalization and the worldwide spread of Olympic culture(e. g. Qu, 2002; Li, 2004a; Ren, 2010; Shi, 2010; Zhu et al., 2010).

The dilemma faced by Chinese traditional sports has provoked a wide range of discussions on the potential benefits of reconsidering the identity of Chinese traditional sports to cope with globalization(e. g. Huang & Ma, 2001; Cui, 2005; Ren, 2005; Song & Zhou, 2006; Xie & Li, 2012). Most scholars acknowledge that sport globalization has brought both opportunities and challenges to Chinese traditional sport culture. Their discussions usually conclude that during this West-China discourse, the Chinese need to ascertain the cultural identity of Chinese traditional sport. Only in this way can the Chinese retrieve national sport culture(e. g. Ouyang et al., 2004; Wang, 2004b; Cui, 2005; Ren, 2005; Zhang, 2012c). Some scholars have been seeking new ways to preserve Chinese traditional sports. For example, Ye(2007) argues that the role of Chinese martial arts in global sport should be reconsidered and that it should be given a voice within the global sport community through its representatives gaining more governance power in international sports organizations. Others consider commercialization a good solution. He (2011) argues that marketization is the only way forward, especially in the post-Beijing Olympics era. Zhu et al. (2009) contend that, from a long-term development perspective, it is important for Chinese traditional sports to work with the media so as to construct a local sports media culture. Furthermore, for some scholars, traditional sports, such as martial arts, should be expanded at grassroots level, especially in middle schools and high schools(Long, 2002; Shi, 2010; Zhu et al., 2010; Hu & Bai, 2011). Li et al. (2008) argue that their capacity for aiding self-improvement could also be significant in preserving martial arts. He suggests Chinese martial arts should place more stress on achieving balance between human beings and nature, between body and spirit, in order to further foster a sense of harmoniousness.

1. 1. 2 Research on the Institutional Conflict between Internationalization and Marketization in Chinese Sport

Notable works in this category include Hong & Xiaozheng, 2002; Luo, 2008; Wang & Fang, 2010; Shu & Shen, 2011; Hong & Huang, 2013. Since the establishment of the People's Republic of China(PRC) in 1949, the main objectives of the Chinese Communist Party(CCP) have been to build China into a strong country and to restore the Chinese nation to its rightful position in the world. Thus began Communist China's use of sport to implement political ideology. As a result, China has been active in participating in international sport competitions. This is witnessed particularly after the implementation of the "reform and opening-up" policy in late 1970s. The *Olympic Strategy* is one of the key tools used by the Chinese government to gain international prestige through sport. The strategy was devised in 1985, a year after China won 15 gold medals and was placed fourth in the

Olympic medals table in Los Angeles in 1984(Hong & Huang, 2013). Thereafter, guided by the *Olympic Strategy*, China has centralized its sport governing power and formed a unique elite sport system called"Juguo Tizhi"(the whole country supports the elite sport system). This sport system has produced many elite athletes to win medals at the Olympics to benefit China's international image and to support the revival of the Chinese nation (Hong & Zhouxiang, 2012). With China's rise in the global community and the further reformation of the market-oriented economy, tension has emerged between the"Juguo Tizhi"and the nascent sports industry. This conflict has drawn the attention of numerous scholars(e. g. Hu, 2002; Hao & Ren, 2003; Li et al., 2003; Wen et al., 2006; Zhang, 2006). According to Hong and Huang(2013), the 2008 Olympics in Beijing proved that the"Juguo Tizhi"has been effective in making China a world sport superpower. However, this power-centralized system has given the government a monopolistic position in dealing with the emerging public investment in sport and is an obstacle for the reformation and commercialization of sport in China. Hong and Huang (2013) further argue that it will be hard for China's market-oriented sports industry to develop unless the government switches its role from steering to leveraging.

1. 1. 3 Researches on the Modernization of Chinese Sport through Paradigm-assimilation, Transnationally and Globally.

For China, globalization is often seen as a double-edged sword that brings both opportunities and challenges, advantages and disadvantages. But most Chinese scholars tend to believe that the opportunities outweigh the challenges, that the advantages outweigh the disadvantages in this global-local interconnectedness. Therefore, a good deal of academic work from a variety of interdisciplinary subjects, especially from sports management, draw lessons from developed countries to put forward proposals for the modernization of Chinese sport. This research widely employs the methodologies of transnational or cross-cultural comparison. Some notable works include discussions of: the state sport system(e. g. Han & Li, 2007; Zhang, 2007; Guo, 2009), sports law(e. g. Fan, 2006; Wu & Zhang, 2009; Tan & Jiang, 2011), sports professionalization(e. g. Amara et al., 2005; Bao, 2011a; Zhang & Cong, 2012), the sports industry(e. g. Zhang et al., 2000; Wong et al., 2004; Chen, 2007), the school sport system(e. g. Feng & Yin, 2004; Gao & Wang, 2007; Wen, 2009), leisure sport(e. g. Sang, 2007; Bao, 2012a), and sporting non-governmental organizations(NGO) (e. g. Wei & Dong, 2009; Qin et al., 2010). Some scholars, however, warn of the hidden dangers that can arise during such a resource exchange with the outside world. For instance, Guo(2009) states critically that"sport globalization has resulted in an inequality of resource flows, such as athletes and sporting goods, between China and western countries. The transnational corporations(TNC) take advantage of China's low-paid and labour-intensive production mode. China should learn from the lesson of the sweatshop and modernize its managerial profession in producing sporting goods".

1. 1. 4 Research on the Recent Introduction or Revival of Foreign Sports in Post-reform China

These sports or sporting entities include: the National Basketball Association (NBA) (e. g. Ding & Wang, 2006; Zhang et al., 2006; Huang, 2008; Li, 2010; Huang, 2013), European football leagues(e. g. Wolfram & Wang, 2003; Wu et al., 2007; Breuer et al., 2009; Zhao, 2010; Zhang, 2012b), tennis(e. g. Ji, 2006; Tian & Liu, 2008; Wang et al., 2008; Wang & Dong, 2008; Yu & Nie, 2008), golf (e. g. Yu, 2005; Zheng, 2006; She, 2012; Wu & Li, 2012), automobile racing (e. g. Chen & Chen, 2004; Chen, 2005; Qin & Li, 2013), taekwondo(e. g. Xin,

2008; Guo, 2012; Jin, 2012), yoga(e. g. Zhao, 2008; Chen et al., 2009; Zhang, 2012d), baseball(e. g. Chen, 1991; Chen & Tan, 2003; Ba, 2005; He, 2005; Liu et al., 2005), extreme sports(e. g. Wang & Shu, 2006), kendo(e. g. Huang et al., 2007; Ma, 2008; Jin, 2011), and rock climbing(e. g. Da, 2001; Zhou, 2007; Mu, 2008). In short, most of these works overlap in focus on the third type of research, aiming to undo the status quo and to come up with strategies to preferably localize these sports, or to modernize the indigenous norms through "learning from the West".

The number of academic works written in English on globalization and sports in the Chinese context is increasing, focusing mainly on football(e. g. Hua, 2004; Jones, 2004; Amara et al., 2005; Manzenreiter & Horne, 2007; Tan & Bairner, 2010) and basketball. In relation to football, for instance, Jones(2004) deals with the business of football in China in the context of both Asian football and global football, examining the design and development of professional football in China. Hua(2004) adds a case study of Chinese football "hooligans" and supporters' culture to Dunning's (2002) compilation of articles on the emergence of "fighting fans" during the on-going footballization of Asian societies. He suggests that age, sex, and place of living are major factors influencing hooliganism in China. But he further points out that media attention on football-related crowd disorder in international games has been amplified by Chinese football fans, who desire to integrate with world football culture.

Academic interest in globalization and basketball in China has continued to grow over the past decade(Morris, 2002; Polumbaum, 2002; Lane, 2004; Oates & Polumbaum, 2004; Wang, 2004a; Larmer, 2005b; Larmer, 2005a; Lavelle, 2006; Huang, 2008; Menefee, 2009; Houlihan et al., 2010; Wolff, 2010; Huang, 2013), particularly after Yao Ming arrived in the NBA. Morris(2002) argues that an absolute and irrevocable link has been created between Chinese basketball and the hegemonic NBA basketball culture, which is loaded with much capitalist import. While he admits that basketball can be called a"national pastime"in contemporary China, he argues that modernity of Chinese basketball is being theorized, shaped, and negotiated by the world around it. Following Morris, the author of this study has written two previous papers which attempted to represent the NBA's diffusion in China from a historical perspective(Huang, 2008; 2013). The earlier paper, published in Chinese, briefly points out:

Since it came to China in 1979, the NBA has taken root in Chinese society over these thirty years alongside the reform and opening-up of China. From the strange eyes on the weird Bullets' jerseys to the developed professional basketball market, the NBA has not only been witness to the solid development of China's reform, opening-up and fast economic growth, it has also infiltrated various aspects of Chinese society and veered the sporting behaviours and values of the Chinese towards those of western culture(Huang, 2008).

The more recent paper is an updated and improved version of this, which was published in *The International Journal of the History of Sport*. Examining the process of the NBA's glocalization in China, it provides the historical groundwork for the current study. By analysing the two contextualizing phases in this process-the reach(globalizing American basketball commodities in the Chinese territory) and the response(reinventing tradition and reconstructing the modernity of Chinese sport) it is argued in this paper that the presence of the NBA in China has greatly remoulded the previous norms of Chinese basketball and sport culture. However, the influence of NBA has not resulted in the homogenization of Chinese basketball, as local resistance from the Chinese Basketball Association(CBA) has risen correspondingly(Huang, 2013).

With regard to the Yao Ming phenomenon, Larmer(2005a) offers a look into Yao's world and more broadly into the transformation in sports, combining an intimate biography of Yao with his own thought-provoking insights into China's sporting politics and society. Lavelle's(2006) dissertation studies the rhetorical construction of Yao Ming, especially how representations of him function to illustrate a clash of cultures and serve as a statement on notions of masculinity in the NBA. He argues that the depictions of Yao in the American media do not evoke the earlier negative stereotypes of Asians but reinforce his position as a model minority, someone who embodies traditional Chinese cultural values and has not assimilated into American culture. Lane(2004) argues while Yao's release to join the NBA demonstrates willingness on the part of the Chinese government to participate in an increasingly globalized sports world, it also highlights the growing pains of a Chinese political system still dominated by the ideology of state control over its citizens. Oates and Polumbaum(2004) maintain that sport can be regarded as a form of entertainment and a distinct place for transnational labour and commodity transactions, and that Yao is playing a significant role in such a celebrity sports market. They point out that "patterns of cultural production and consumption which already have transformed North America are enveloping much of the rest of the world as well". Wang(2004a), however, claims that "Yao and his proliferating cultural economic impact reflects a national-capitalist fantasy that is materialized at the expense of 'stylized' bodies".

1.2 Research Aim and Objectives

In general, Chinese sports are developing under very complex and unique political, economic, and sociocultural circumstances in this global age. This development constitutes an interesting and significant historical phenomenon in globalization studies. However, as previously mentioned, as yet there exists no single work in the literature that has delineated a comprehensive sport globalization process within a Chinese context, or which has provided an answer to the question of how sport globalization is taking place in contemporary China. The process of globalization is not only historical, but also dialectical. Motivated by Rossi's (Rossi, 2007: 2) indication of integrating globalization into one comprehensive framework for cultural, political, and economic processes to extend the frontiers of globalization studies, this study seeks to enhance the body of knowledge in this area within the panorama of the multifaceted and multidimensional sport globalization process underway in China.

Basketball serves as an appropriate lens for this purpose. First, the Chinese have been keen on basketball for more than a century, since it was brought to China by the Tianjin YMCA in 1895. Basketball accommodated the ambitions of both the western imperialists and Chinese nationalists, as well as gaining the acceptance of the Chinese people in the pre-reform era. This unique historical context provides a rich research ground for contemporary sport globalization in relation to Chinese sport. Second, in post-reform China, basketball is in the vanguard, second only to football, of sports globalization through professionalization and marketization. Thus, this reformation and modernization of basketball allows for in-depth examinations of the "global modernity" of Chinese sport (Giulianotti & Robertson, 2012). Third, basketball can better reflect the sporting cultural transformation in the globalizing China than football since basketball is considered an urban game and thus resonates with and is a feature of the fast urbanization of contemporary Chinese society. Fourth, the unprecedented basketball phenomenon taking place in China today, as will be described in section 7. 4. 1 undoubtedly deserves more research attention, regardless of whether it is examined from historical, sociological, or multidisciplinary perspectives.

Therefore, the aim of this study is to investigate the process of globalization in basketball focusing on the Chinese context through an examination of its political, economic, and cultural manifestations. Having examined the multiple definitions of the concept of globalization, this study will align itself with Ritzer's(2003, 2007b) conceptualization of dichotomizing the process of globalization into grobalization and glocalization. On that basis, this study identifies the trajectory of basketball globalization in China as the result of a contextual and competing interplay between the penetration of the NBA and the consequent engagement with Chinese basketball. Drawing upon Ritzer's conceptual foundation of utilizing the theory of grobalization and glocalization to examine the political-institutional, economic, and sociocultural aspects of sport globalization, this study puts forward the following research questions:

- How has the NBA universalized its governance model in China, and how has Chinese basketball adapted and particularized this paradigm?
- How has the NBA expanded its market in China, and how has the Chinese

basketball market integrated with it to create a local market?

• How has the NBA diffused its cultural forms in China, and how has Chinese basketball subsumed them and created cultural hybrids?

1. 3 Thesis Structure

The thesis consists of eight chapters. **Chapter 1.** Introduction, has outlined the existing research on globalization and sport in China. Relevant literatures from both Chinese and foreign scholars were critically reviewed and summarized into four categories according to their research focus: the cultural conflict between tradition and modernity in Chinese sport; the institutional conflict between internationalization and marketization in Chinese sport; the modernization of Chinese sport through paradigm-assimilation, transnationally and globally; and, the recent introduction or revival of western sports in post-reform China. This was followed by the setting out of a research aim to add to the field a comprehensive overview of sport globalization through basketball in China.

Chapter 2. Theorizing the Global-Local Nexus. This chapter spans an intellectual journey, from examining the concepts of globalization to a research inquiry for this study. It will present the various definitions of globalization and the three theoretical positions underpinning them. A picture of sport globalization in its three manifestations (political, economic, and cultural) will also be drawn. Glocalization theory, which is widely used in sport studies, will then be presented in conjunction with an introduction to the complementary concept of grobalization. After explaining why grobalization/glocalization theory is more suitable than glocalization theory for the purposes of this study, this chapter will generate a set of research questions based on Ritzer's grobalization/glocalization theory.

Chapter 3. Methodology. This chapter is about the methodological philosophy behind the study and details how the study was carried out. It will provide a full account of how answering the research questions generated in Chapter 2 was approached: to determine why and how an anti-foundationalist ontological position and a critical realism epistemological position is taken; to consider and explain why and how a qualitative methodological approach rather than a quantitative research approach is employed; and, to introduce and give concrete information about why and how a triangulation of research methods is used, including multiple methods of data collection and data analysis. It will also explain how reliability, validity, and relevant ethical considerations were taken into account during the research. A concentrated blueprint of this study, a research design, is outlined to complete the chapter.

Chapter 4. Historical Overview. This chapter provides two historical contexts for the study. The first covers the development of the NBA and will explicate how American basketball has always been professionalized and commercialized. The second historical context covers the development of sport in the PRC and will elucidate how Chinese sport has been pragmaticized and utilitarianized by the Chinese government since its establishment in 1949. The two sport trajectories ground and contrast the discussion on how the power of globalization is bringing together capitalistic sport and socialist sport in post-reform China.

Chapter 5. Globalization and the Governance of Chinese Basketball. This chapter focuses on the political aspects of globalization and basketball in China. The grobalization of basketball in this realm is embodied within the universalization of the NBA's governance model in China, whereas glocalization is exhibited in the adaptation and particularization of the NBA's governance model by the CBA. An examination of their grobal-glocal interaction is accomplished through a comparison of the governance models used in the two leagues. Following on from this, the governance model for professional team sport is also conceptualized into four segmentations following Borland's(2006) taxonomy: governing authority, product market, capital market, and labour market.

Chapter 6. Globalization and the Chinese Basketball Market. This chapter focuses on the economic aspects of globalization and basketball in China. The grobalization of basketball in this regard is illustrated in the context of the global expansion of the NBA's market in China, whereas glocalization is achieved through Chinese basketball's creation of a local market in response. The examination of this grobal-glocal interaction will be based on the three domains of a sports market: marketing of sports, marketing through sports, and grassroots sports marketing.

Chapter 7. Globalization and Chinese Basketball Culture. This chapter focuses on the cultural aspects of globalization and basketball in China. The grobalization of basketball in cultural terms has occurred with the diffusion of the NBA's cultural forms in China, while glocalization is manifest in the embracement and divergence of Chinese basketball culture. An examination of the transformation of societal sport ideas, cultural identities within the sport community, and the values of individual sport participants will be used to unveil the grobal-glocal interaction. The accounts of relevant basketball governors and participants are used in this examination.

Chapter 8. Conclusion. This chapter ends the study with a reflective discussion. It will present the research findings according to the research questions, followed by discussions on the usefulness of Ritzer's grobalization/glocalization theory in conceptualizing globalization. This chapter will also identify the contributions the research may make, both to subject-area knowledge and theory, and the limitations of the study. Recommendations for future research will also be addressed at the end of the chapter.

Chapter 2. Theorizing the Global-Local Nexus

2. 1 Introduction

The studies of globalization are multiple and varied across and within most academic fields, and sport studies is no exception. Therefore, it is necessary to map out the research terrain in order to conduct the research inquiry for this study. In doing so, this literature review has three objectives. First, it will clarify the definitions of globalization and the major schools of globalization theorists. This is to confirm the theoretical position this study will take amongst the many that exist in the field of globalization studies. Second, it will review the relevant literatures on sport globalization in terms of its political, economic, and cultural dimensions. The aim in so doing is to outline the multidimensionality of sport globalization following Rossi's(2007) suggestion of inquiring into globalization as a historical and dialectical process. Third, this chapter will review the differences between Robertson's(1995) glocalization theory and Ritzer's(2003, 2007b) grobalization/glocalization theory. It aims not only to clarify the theoretical foundations underpinning each theory but also to identify the rationale for selecting the theory which will be applied in this study. The research questions will be generated on the basis of this selection.

2. 2 Definition of Globalization

Globalization is not a new phenomenon. The process of globalization has been on-going throughout human history, but its rate of progress and the effects of certain globalizing actions have accelerated and decreased at various periods in its development(Jarvie, 2006: 98). Held(1999) provides a useful division of globalization into four historical phases. The first phase, pre-modern globalization, incorporates the period from the Neolithic Revolution, between 9, 000 and 11, 000 years ago, to A. D. 1500; the next phase is early-modern globalization, stretching from around A. D. 1500 to A. D. 1850; next comes modern globalization, from A. D. 1850 to A. D. 1945, which is followed by the contemporary period of globalization, from the end of the Second World War to the present day. Robinson (2008: 125) identifies five social developments which have permitted and shaped the current phase of rapid globalization, namely: 1) the emergence of a globalized economy involving new systems of production, finance, and consumption, as well as worldwide economic integration; 2) new transnational or global cultural patterns, practices, and flows, and the idea of a global culture; 3) the political processes, the rise of new transnational institutions, and, concomitantly, the spread of global governance and authority structures of diverse sorts; 4) the unprecedented multidirectional movement of peoples around the world involving new patterns of transnational migration, identities, and communities; and, 5) new social hierarchies, new forms of inequality, and new relations of domination around the world and in the global system as a whole.

Although the word"global"is over 400 years old, in academia, the common usage of words such as"globalization", "globalize", and"globalizing"did not begin until about 1960(Waters, 2001: 2). Globalization studies drew researchers' attention from the 1970s onwards. There have been numerous attempts at defining the term"globalization"since then, each of which can be traced back to a certain theoretical position. Held(1999) has identified three theoretical schools of thought in relation to globalization: the hyper-globalists, the sceptics, and the transformationalists. A summary of the characteristics of the positions held by the hyper-globalists, sceptics, and transformationalists is presented in Table 2 – 1.

Table 2 – 1 The Hyper-globalists, Sceptics, and Transformationalists

Hyper-globalists

- There is a fully developed global economy that has supplanted previous forms of the international economy.
- This global economy is driven by uncontrollable market forces which have led to unprecedented cross-national networks of interdependency and integration.
- National borders have dissolved so that the category of national economy is now redundant.
- All economic agents have to conform to the criteria of being internationally competitive.
- This position is advocated by economic neoliberals but condemned by neo-Marxists.

Sceptics

- The international economy has not progressed to the stage of a global economy to the extent claimed by the hyper-globalists.
- Separate national economies remain a salient category.
- It is still possible to organize co-operation between national authorities to challenge market forces, manage domestic economies, and govern the international economy.

Continued

• The preservation of entitlements to welfare benefits, for instance, can still be secured at the national level.
Transformationalists
• New forms of intense interdependence and integration are sweeping across the international economic system.
• These place added constraints on the conduct of national economic policy-makers.
• They also make the formation of international public policy to govern and manage the system very difficult.
• This position sees the present era as another step in a long evolutionary process in which closed local and national economies disintegrate into more mixed, interdependent, and integrated"cosmopolitan"societies.

Source: El-Ojeili and Hayden(2006) adapted from Held(2000: 90).

Besides the aforementioned three schools of theorists, the definition of globalization is also varied from particular dimensions. Among the wide range of definitions of globalization, some take one particular dimension as the key. A politically centred definition may underscore the decline of the nation-state and the territorically bound societies that formed the basic unit of analysis for modern political science, sociology, and international relations(El-Ojeili & Hayden, 2006: 12). For instance, Held and McGrew(2001) define globalization as the shifting reach of political power, authority, and forms of rule based on new organizational interests which are transnational and multi-layered. An economically centred definition may stress capitalism and the expansion of the free-market system as the key force behind globalizing processes (El-Ojeili & Hayden, 2006: 12). For instance, Prakash and Hart's (2000: 2) definition states that"globalization is the increasing integration of input, factor and final product markets coupled with the increasing salience of multinational enterprises' (MNE) cross-national value-chain networks". A culturally centred definition may emphasize the legitimating cover or ideology behind globalization, a set of ideas that distorts reality so as to serve particular interests(El-Ojeili & Hayden, 2006: 12). Schirato and Webb(2003: 200), for instance, view globalization as"a discursive regime, a kind of machine that eats up anyone and anything in its path". They suggest that"globalization functions as a set of texts, ideas, goals, values, narratives, dispositions and prohibitions, a veritable template for ordering and evaluating activities, which is filled in or inflected with the interests of whoever can access it". A technologically centred definition may view globalization as a much more material reality in the contemporary world (El-Ojeili & Hayden, 2006: 12). Langhorne's(2001: 2) definition is a case in point, stating that"globalization is the latest stage in a long accumulation of technological advance which has given human beings the ability to conduct their affairs across the world without reference to nationality, government authority, time of day or physical environment".

Others give a broader definition of globalization. Building on the phrase "global village", Lechte(2003: 2-7) advocates the use of a progressive term, "connectedness", according to which globalization is to be viewed as an emerging global consciousness. This connectedness, according to Lechte, connotes a number of meanings: communication networks and new technology; the speed at which it is now possible to move around the world; the emergence and contemporary prominence of the multinational corporation; "decontextualization", the idea that place is not as relevant as it once was; an awareness of the finitude of global resources; and, the threat of a standardization of cultural life.

In the work of Held and McGrew(2002: 1), one of the most comprehensive examinations of globalization to date, the definition of globalization highlights the "interconnectedness"and is elaborated as follows: "globalization denotes the expanding scale, growing magnitude, speeding up and deepening impact of interregional flows and patterns of social interaction". It relates to"a shift or transformation in the scale of human social organization that links distant communities and expands the reach of power relations across the world's major regions and continents". In the work of Cochrane and Pain(2000), in this conceptualization, the meaning of globalization is advanced through the following four concepts: 1) stretched social relations, so that events and processes occurring in one part of the world have significant impact on other parts of the world; 2) an intensification of flows, with the increased"density"of social, cultural, economic, and political interaction across the globe; 3) increasing interpenetration, so that as social relations stretch, there is an increasing interpenetration of economic and social practices, bringing distant cultures face to face; and, 4) global infrastructures, which are the underlying formal and informal institutional arrangements required for globalized networks to operate.

In addition, Ritzer(2007a), Robertson(1992), and Scholte(2005) have each given their own definitions of globalization from a transformationalist stance, all of which are widely recognized by other scholars. For Ritzer(2007a: 1), "globalization is an accelerating set of processes involving flows that encompass ever-greater numbers of the world's space and that lead to increasing integration and interconnectivity among those spaces". For Robertson(1992: 8), "globalization as a concept refers both to the compression of the world and the intensification of consciousness of the world as a whole". From Scholte's(2005: 59) point of view, "globalization refers to the spread of transplanetary-and in recent times also more particularly supraterritorial-connections between people. A global relation which can link persons situated at any inhabitable point on the earth. Globalization involves reductions of barriers to such transworld social contacts".

In a way that places more emphasis on the local, Giddens(1990: 64) gives the following definition:

> Globalization can be defined as the intensification of world-wide social relations which link distant localities in such a way that local happenings are shaped by events occurring many miles away and vice versa. This is a dialectical process because such local happenings may move in an obverse direction from the very distanciated relations that shape them. Local transformation is as much a part of globalization as the lateral extension of social connections across time and space.

Waters(2001:5) declares that this definition usefully introduces explicit notions of time and space. Additionally, he outlines three significant contributions of this definition: its emphasis on locality; its acknowledgement of resistance from the local; and, the assertion that the local tends to reflexively reconstruct the community. Broadly consistent with the work of Giddens, Waters therefore defines globalization-a definition that is adopted in this study-as:

> A social process in which the constraints of geography on economic, political, social and cultural arrangements recede, in which people become increasingly aware that they are receding and in which people act accordingly.

2. 3 Globalization and Sport

Drawing upon the work of Robertson(1992, 1995), Maguire(1999: 75-94) outlines five phases in the historical trajectory of sport globalization, which he refers to a complex process of global"sportization"(Jarvie, 2006: 98-99). Phase one refers to an initial sportization phase from about the 1550s to the 1750s; phase two covers the period from about the 1750s to the 1870s, which saw the formation of voluntary associations or sports clubs; phase three refers to the period from roughly the 1870s to the 1920s, when the diffusion of English sports and pastimes in continental Europe also involved the export of the amateur ethos and notions of fair play; phase four, from 1920 to 1960, is when non-westerners began to resist and re-invent western sports and challenge the western domination of global sport; the final phase refers to the period from about 1960 to 1990, when the rivalries between capitalist sport and communist sport were replaced by a truly globalizing sport world with the emergence of the global media and mass consumption(Maguire, 1999: 75-94; Jarvie, 2006: 98-99).

In evaluating the process of globalization, Rossi(2007: 2) presents a framework that analyses globalization as"a multifaceted and conflictual process". He argues that the historical, conflictual, and macro-and micro-perspectives on globalization can be integrated into one comprehensive framework for the study of its cultural, political, and economic processes. Based on this framework, the following sections, with the purpose of providing a brief understanding of sport globalization, will focus on its three dialectical dimensions: political, economic, and cultural.

2. 3. 1 The Political Dimension

The most common debate associated with the literature on political globalization revolves around the assertion that globalization entails the demise of the-nation-state. El-Ojeili and Hayden(2006: 89) provide a broader understanding of this argument, suggesting that"the power and mobility of global finance and multinational corporations, the cultural fragmentation of national populations, the emergence of powerful agents of governance at supra-national and local levels, citizen disaffection from electoral politics, and the growth of global civil society, are all viewed as wearing away at the power or efficacy of the state". Considering the viewpoint of Marx that economics appears to be devouring politics, they further suggest that growing world interconnectedness is bringing with it new and encouraging political tendencies that promise to invigorate democracy and cosmopolitanism.

In the sporting world, the fate of the nation-state is also often linked to the rise of political globalization. Much of the debate focuses on the ways in which global flows or international institutions may undermine the authority of the nation-state. As Jarvie(2006: 97) puts it, the"political globalization of sport refers to the increasing number and power of international sporting organizations that influence or govern international sport". Principal amongst these bodies are the International Olympic Committee(IOC) and the Fédération Internationale de Football Association(FIFA). It is also noted that there are 203 National Olympic Committees affiliated with the IOC, 11 more than the number of countries in the United Nations(UN). For Jarvie(2006: 97), "the very spread of international sports organizations can also be seen as a response to the process of political globalization whereby the types of problems confronting national sports organizations can no longer be addressed locally or nationally, thus political globalization is seen in arrangements for the concentration and application of power in sport".

The question of whether political globalization is or has been in reality curtailing the autonomous sporting power of nation-states has been well explored by sport academics. For instance, Allison's(2005) edited book *The Global Politics of Sport* has presented a broad range of essays examining the emerging global political issues in sport. It focuses on three themes: regime development in the global era; the relationships between emerging global institutions and existing institutions, including states, nationalist parties, and national sports associations; and, the tendencies towards a global culture. There is little evidence in this book that the nation-state's power in sport will diminish with the increasing number of supranational sport organizations and the impact of the U. S. 's hegemonic power. On the contrary, there is further evidence in a wider range of extant literature that indicates that the individual nation-state tends to position itself in the globalizing sporting world to reinforce national identity(e. g. Maguire, 1993; 1994; Houlihan, 1997; Bairner, 2001; Hargreaves, 2002). Sport in some Asian and African countries, particularly in China, is the best case study for revealing how nation-states are centralizing governance power to achieve this goal(Hong & Huang, 2013). Besides centralizing national sport governance power, it is also evident that sport is functional in improving international relationships and formulating foreign policies in some nation-states(e. g. Lowe et al., 1978; Allison & Monnington, 2002; Arnaud & Riordan, 2002; Budd & Levermore, 2004). This can also be seen to support the hypothesis that nation-states are retaining power and identity in an increasingly globalized sport world.

The global spread of sport policy and sport governance models is another major concern with regard to the political globalization of sport(e. g. Green & Houlihan, 2005; Henry et al., 2009; Houlihan, 2009; Houlihan et al., 2010; Houlihan & Green, 2012). Houlihan regards this process as policy transfer and lesson drawing(Houlihan et al., 2010; Houlihan, 2012). Henry et al. (2009) present and evaluate the main approaches to transnational and comparative analysis of sport policy. Their works not only offer theoretical perspectives and methodologies in discussing globalization and sport policy, but also provide case studies of transnational and comparative analysis of sport policy from a variety of countries.

These cases showcase the analytical approaches adopted in dealing with globalization and the governance of Chinese basketball in this study.

2. 3. 2 The Economic Dimension

Economic globalization is the most commented upon, debated, and controversial of topics within the literature on globalization. It is often intimated that economic globalization is the driving force behind the various changes connected with the globalization of culture and politics in the contemporary world, as well as being the principal concern of the alternative globalization movement(El-Ojeili & Hayden, 2006: 49). El-Ojeili and Hayden(2006) suggest that "contemporary globalization is a historical moment in which the economic attains autonomy from, and exerts its weight upon, other spheres such as politics, society, and culture". This view of the primacy of economic globalization has proved popular in the business world. Some scholars, in particular those who adopt a hyper-globalist position, contend that the global flow of capital and labour and the integration of markets will accelerate the processes of globalization.

When scholars discuss economic globalization, "neoliberalism" is a key term to which they often refer. Neoliberalism gained momentum after the fall of the Eastern Bloc in the late 1980s. Miller et al. (2001: 132) argue that neoliberalism describes "a belief system in which the individual pursuit of self-gain is understood to provide maximum benefits to the individual and society". Neoliberalists argue that it is inappropriate for governments to hamper individual decision-making. Thus, market liberalization, restrictive monetary policies, a reduction in tariff levels, the removal of the welfare net, the privatization of government utilities, and outsourcing are all components of the policies of neoliberalism(Miller et al., 2001: 132). Busch(2000: 30) holds the view that globalization assures efficiency and increases welfare throughout the world, and most of all that it is an unavoidable phenomenon.

It is the power of the free-market consciousness under neoliberalism that has pushed sports marketing to a global level. According to Andreff(2008), the relationship between sports and the economy dates back to the first ancient Olympic Games. Gambling on sporting outcomes and the emergence of the first professional sports paved the way for a sports economy in the 19th century. It was not, however, until after the Second World War that the globalization of the sporting economy took off, triggered by the extension of annually paid holidays for individuals, the expansion of television broadcasting of big sporting events, and the emergence of new information and communication technologies such as the internet and mobile phones(Andreff, 2008). Sport has now become a profitable global business. The global market for all sporting goods and services in 2004 was assessed as being in the range of EUR 550-600 billion(Andreff & Szymanski, 2006: 6). The global market for football in the same year was valued at EUR 250 billion, the market for all sporting goods at about EUR 150 billion, and the value of the broadcasting rights related to sports events was estimated at EUR 60 billion, while the global market for sports sponsorship was worth nearly EUR 18 billion(Andreff & Szymanski, 2006: 6).

To further clarify the relationship between globalization and sport economy, Andreff(2008) has sketched out a four-part panorama of the global sport economy. First, the major features of a globalized sports economy, among which, Andreff suggests, sports shows are the most prominent. The increasing number of sports shows has generated two significant economic outcomes: the emergence of a global broadcasting market and the consequent rise of a global sponsorship market (Andreff, 2008). Second, the international economic flows in a global sports economy, which Andreff(2008) further categorizes as: the trades in sports goods internationally, the globalizing market for high-level sporting talents, and the worst-forms of corruption, such as embezzlement, doping, and money laundering(Andreff, 2008). Third, globalization as a geographical spread of the sports economy, which Andreff(2008) categorizes as follows: a number of sport disciplines which fit with development outside their country of origin; sports which settle down from one country to another; and the sports economy itself extending into to new countries. The fourth division of the global sport economy is the globalization of professional sports. Professional sports could be said to fall into the category of sportsshows, but Andreff(2008) claims that professional sports underlie the economic globalization of sports, and that such significance ought to be stressed.

2. 3. 3 The Cultural Dimension

Cultural globalization refers to the growth and exchange of cultural practices between nations and peoples. Many researchers point to the way in which new technologies, such as commercial television, the internet, and other forms of mass communications have created a world that increasingly consumes identical products(Jarvie, 2006: 97). The "3Hs" are often regarded as the ultimate consequences of the process of cultural globalization: homogenization, heterogenization, and hybridization. Homogenization theories see a global cultural convergence and tend to highlight the rise of world music, world cuisines, world tourism, uniform consumption patterns, and cosmopolitanism(Robinson, 2008: 140). Heterogenization approaches see continued cultural difference and highlight local cultural autonomy, cultural resistance to homogenization, cultural clashes and polarization, and distinct subjective experiences of globalization(Robinson, 2008: 140). Hybridization stresses new and constantly evolving cultural forms and identities produced by manifold transnational processes and the fusion of distinct cultural processes(Robinson, 2008: 140).

The cultural globalization of sport has to a great degree resulted from economic globalization. Unlike most other businesses, such as those that produce food, drinks, and clothing, demand for sport consumption is "created" rather than "required". As such, the process of globalization in the sport business is normally integrated with the formation of a global sporting consumer culture, through which transnational media companies and corporate sponsors play a major role in delivering sports products to consumers all over the world.

The media play a leading role in delivering sports products to consumers. Coakley(2003) argues that modern sport and media exist symbiotically. Sport, on the one hand, is primarily interested in the media because of the need for exposure. Exposure is necessary for a sport to attract new recruits, namely fans, consumers, and spectators. This in turn boosts the chances of gaining sponsorship. The media, on the other hand, are interested in sport for three reasons. First, the intrinsic elements of sport mean that it can make for an "ideal" news story. Coakley(2003: 42) argues that "all sports offer a predictable occurrence with an unpredictable outcome and the ideal news story is exactly that". Second, with a few exceptions, sport attracts a predominantly male audience, which most commercially driven media organizations find difficult to reach(Coakley, 2003: 42). Third, sports provide "moments of immense public interest, via the possibility of identification with an absorbing universe of condensed simplicity, which attracts large audiences, boosts reading, listening and viewing figures and can be relied on to produce regular consumers"(Coakley, 2003: 42).

Meanwhile, it is clear that transnational companies now see sports sponsorship as an additional medium for persuasive communication within which they can integrate a marketing mix of advertising, public relations, sales promotion, and personal selling(Boyle & Haynes, 2009: 6). Therefore, sports sponsorship, while dependent on the media, is increasingly a part of the marketing strategy for companies that traditionally have relied upon television, radio, and newspapers to convey their symbolic messages(Boyle & Haynes, 2009: 6). Consequently, the alignment of sports, media, and sponsorship has been forging a global commercial culture. Silk et al. (2005: 4) suggest that sport is now centrally involved in the media-advertising-business relationship, where public space has effectively been colonized for private interests. The result of this commercial spectacle leads to the formation of a sporting consumer life for sports fans. Alongside the emergence of sporting fandom and the consequent consumer culture, it is also crucial to acknowledge the driving forces behind them, sporting stardom and celebrity. Horne (2006) suggests that elite performance sport has become a significant part of consumer capitalism-sports have adopted marketing and promotional strategies suited to the media and have become more spectacular and personality-and star-driven. These interpretations of sport stars' international celebrity status lead to the central theme of the global sport culture: the significance of sport stars' celebrity as a symbol of a diverse acceptance of, resistance to, and ambivalence toward the hegemony of western capitalistic culture(Bairner, 2001; Maguire, 2005).

To sum up, the process of sport globalization is multifaceted and dialectical, and encompasses political, economic, and cultural dimensions, which can be integrated into one comprehensive framework. First, the political globalization of sport refers to the increasing governing power of a growing number of international sports organizations, or the transnational universalization of an isomorphic form of sport governance. This process of globalization may undermine the sport governing power of individual nation-states. Second, the economic globalization of sport refers to the global expansion of sports business. Neoliberalism is the major force leading this process. Third, the cultural globalization of sport refers to the global alignment of sports, media, and sponsorship, which resultantly creates modes of sport consumption. This process may result in cultural homogenization, heterogenization, and hybridization.

2.4 Grobalization/Glocalization Theory and Sport Studies

2.4.1 Glocalization Theory and Its Application to Sport Studies

Glocalization theory was developed by Robertson(1995) and is a landmark concept which is widely applied in sport studies. Robertson first introduced the term in the mid-1990s, drawing on the Japanese word *dochakuka*, meaning "global localization" or "indigenization". In his view, much of the talk about globalization that had arisen in various parts of the world in the previous years had tended to abrogate issues of locality. Therefore, he suggested replacing the concept of globalization with that of glocalization(Robertson, 1995). In advocating the theory of glocalization, Robertson(1995) seeked to blur the boundaries between the local and the global. Challenging former views which saw globalization as a contrast between the local and the global, Robertson instead proposed the local itself as one of the aspects of globalization.

For Robertson(1995), claims of homogeneity of culture under globalization are inadequate. Even though intercultural ties are increasingly being fastened throughout the world, Robertson does not believe that we are heading for a united or uniform human culture. He argues that in glocalization these ties and influences are selected, processed, and consumed according to the local culture's needs, tastes and social structure. In short, glocalization means that trends of homogenization and heterogenization coexist throughout the global age(Robertson, 1995).

Over the past two decades, a growing number of theoretical and empirical studies in a wide variety of academic disciplines and research fields have applied the conceptualization of glocalization. These fields include: sociocultural theory, human geography and urban studies, marketing and business, anthropology, social network analysis, cultural studies, literature and translation studies, migration studies, and media studies(Giulianotti & Robertson, 2012). Glocalization theory is also widely in use in sport studies, and Giulianotti and Robertson (2012) argue that sport provides one of the most salient representations of the glocalization process. They have also published a series of essays and books on globalization and football in which they have adopted glocalization theory (Giulianotti, 2004; Giulianotti & Robertson, 2006; 2007a; 2007b; 2007c; 2009). Their book *Globalization & Football* demonstrates how the world's most popular sport has been influenced by a range of complex global processes and flows. They again highlight the strengths of the concept of glocalization, which they claim enhances "the possibilities of transnational convergence, divergence and interrelations among social groups and societies, and the making and remaking of the local, regional, national, international and transnational realms" (Giulianotti & Robertson, 2009: 172). Cho(2009) uses the lens of glocalization to explore how the expansion of U. S. sports in South Korea since the late 1990s has influenced the de/reconstitution of the national among local sports fans.

Amara and Henry(2004) reveal"a transformative process which encompasses the response of Algerian society to the imposition of western modernity and other secular and non-secular ideologies by synthesizing the history of modern sport in Algeria, particularly football".

A series of papers applying glocalization theory to research on Asian sport were published in a recent special issue of the *Sociology of Sport Journal* entitled "Glocalization of Sports in Asia". In one of the papers, Giulianotti and Robertson (2012) develop their prior work to examine how glocalization may be applied to examine Asian sport. They begin by discussing the different usages of glocalization in the social sciences and the role of Asian scholars in developing and applying the term. They then set out their sociocultural understanding of glocalization, drawing on Robertson's(1995) work and their subsequent conception of the"duality of glocality". They go on to consider in detail how the study of glocalization processes in Asia may be most fruitfully developed with reference to four lines of research inquiries: the broader aspects of Asian sport and the duality of glocality; sport business and commerce; sport mega-events; and, sport and identity. They conclude by suggesting that future research investigate "multiple modernities" through glocalization theory. Silk and Manley's(2012) paper brings together an amalgam of the applications of glocalization theory and the simultaneous reinscription of the importance of global growth rationalities in aiding understandings of contemporary Pacific Asian sporting spectacles. Their conclusions are centred on the structural inequalities embedded within these processes and transformations. Gilmour and Rowe(2012) address professional sports in the Malaysian context, where the nation-building process has been problematized by the complex racial, cultural, and religious make-up of the country's population. They analyse the obstructive tension between the local sporting developmental agenda and the orchestrated intrusion of global sports commodities. Merkel(2012) explores the impact of globalization on sport and physical culture in North Korea. He argues that although North Korea categorically rejects globalization, its response to the globalization of sport is more differentiated, multifaceted, and state controlled, and ranges from stubborn resistance to wholehearted acceptance. He further argues that North Korea's historical trajectory, national needs and interests, and the ethnic nationalism prevalent in that society shape this reaction to globalization. TzuHsuan (2012) examines both the general narratives of baseball in Taiwan and New York Yankees-related narratives in particular after Taiwanese player Chien-ming Wang joined the team in 2005. Having reviewed newspaper coverage and TV ratings data, he demonstrates a nationalistic undertone to the reports in the Taiwanese mass media. However, following Wang's departure from the Yankees in 2009, the Yankees were removed from Taiwan's nationalistic narratives and returned to being New York's team. He concludes that "as the relationship between athletes and their teams change, team-related national narratives can also change". All these works have provided sufficient evidence that glocalization theory is suitable for application in a study on globalization and sport culture.

2. 4. 2 Grobalization/Glocalization Theory and Its Application to Sport Studies

The concept of "grobalization" is proposed by Ritzer(2003) to complement the idea of glocalization. For Ritzer, glocalization can be defined as the interpenetration of the global and the local, resulting in unique outcomes in different geographic areas. This view emphasizes global heterogeneity and tends to reject the idea that "forces emanating from the West in general and the United States in particular are leading to economic, political, institutional, and cultural homogeneity"

(Ritzer, 2003) . Thus, he points to the need for the companion concept of "grobalization". Grobalization, he argues, encompasses the "imperialistic ambitions of nations, corporations, organizations, and other entities and their desire and need to impose themselves on various geographic areas"(Ritzer, 2003) . Table 2-2 presents a systematic contrast between the ideas of grobalization and glocalization.

Table 2-2 Essential Elements of Two Globalization Theories

Grobalization Theory	Glocalization Theory
The world is growing increasingly similar.	The world is growing more pluralistic.
Grobalization theory tends to minimize differences within and between areas of the world.	Glocalization theory is exceptionally sensitive to differences within and between areas of the world.
Individuals and groups have relatively little ability to adapt, innovate, and manoeuvre within a grobalized world.	Individuals and local groups have great power to adapt, innovate, and manoeuvre within a glocalized world.
Grobalization theory sees larger structures and forces tending to overwhelm the ability of individuals and groups to create themselves and their worlds.	Glocalization theory sees individuals and groups as important and creative agents.
Social processes are largely one-directional and deterministic.	Social processes are relational and contingent.
Grobalization tends to overpower the local and limits its ability to act and react, let alone act back on the grobal.	Globalization provokes a variety of reactions-ranging from nationalist entrenchment to cosmopolitan embrace-that respond to and transform grobalization, producing glocalization.

Continued

Grobalization Theory	Glocalization Theory
Commodities and the media, arenas and key forces in cultural change in the late 20th and early 21st centuries are seen as largely coercive.	Commodities and the media are not seen as(totally) coercive but rather as providing material to be used in individual and group creation throughout the glocalized areas of the world.
Core concepts include capitalism, Americanization, and McDonaldization.	Core concepts include hybridization, creolization, and heterogeneization.

Source: adapted from Ritzer(2007b: 21).

Shor and Galily(2012) have provided a good example of the application of grobalization/glocalization theory in sport studies in their examination of the case of Israeli basketball. Their paper notes that the tension between grobal and glocal processes is also evident in other Middle-Eastern and East-Asian countries. They first discuss the process by which American basketball practices, ideology, language, culture, and players came to dominate Israeli basketball. They then move on to examine the glocal responses to this process, which combine adoption and acceptance with local resistance to the increasing domination of American players and culture. In summation, they argue, as many scholars have already demonstrated, that grobalization rarely penetrates localities without tension or resistance, and that it is important for empirical studies to move beyond simply trying to show that glocalization exists. Instead, future research should focus on examining the various manifestations of the grobal-glocal interaction in different settings and should make an attempt to understand the similarities as well as the differences that characterize these intricate dynamics as they occur in various locations.

2. 5 Theoretical Framework and Research Questions

In answer to Shor and Galily's(2012) call, this study attempts to use grobalization/glocalization theory to examine the various manifestations of the grobal-glocal interaction between the NBA and Chinese basketball. The considerations of this study also rest on the implications of Ritzer's(2007b: 18) grobalization/glocalization theory, which makes possible an examination of this process of the globalization of basketball from a variety of perspectives, in contrast to Robertson's (1995) glocalization theory which focuses more on the cultural aspects. The ability to inquire the case of the NBA in China beyond the cultural is extremely important for this study, since a preliminary literature review suggests that discussion of the capitalistic dimension of the NBA is both needed and worthwhile. It is also hoped that the approach adopted will help avoid the shortcoming observed by Andrews and Ritzer(2007: 136) in some contemporary sport studies, which"falsely polarize the global and the local, in a manner that tends to privilege, and indeed romanticize, expressions of the sporting local".

According to Ritzer(2007b: 18), the ideas of grobalization and glocalization can be used to analyse not only the cultural realm but also the economic, political, and institutional realms. First, in the realm of culture, he suggests that grobalization can be seen as a form of transitional expansion of common codes and practices, whereas glocalization involves the interaction, and the implosion of many global and local cultural inputs to create a kind of"pastiche", or a blend, leading to a variety of cultural hybrids.

Second, he argues that with grobalization, economic factors tend to emphasize their growing importance and homogenizing effect throughout the world. Globalization is generally seen as the spread of the neoliberal market economy throughout the many different regions of the world. Glocalization also exists at the margins of the global economy. Globalization is then seen in the interaction of the global market with local markets, which leads to the creation of unique glocal markets that integrate the demands of the global market with the realities of the local market(Ritzer, 2007b: 19) .

Third, Ritzer(2007b: 19-20) argues that grobalization in the political domain is focused on the worldwide spread of models of the nation-state and the emergence of isomorphic forms of governance throughout the globe; in other words, the growth of a more or less single model of governance around the world. Glocalization in the political domain, on the other hand, tends to be associated with an intensification of nationalism and is therefore apt to lead to greater political heterogeneity throughout the world. This interaction of governance models at the local level may produce unique, glocal political formations that integrate elements of both the former and the latter.

With the employment of Ritzer's ideas to examine the multiple manifestations of sport globalization, it becomes clear the NBA is an agent of the converging grobal power which brings about universality, uniformity, and homogeneity, while Chinese basketball(in the form of its officials and participants) represents the diverging glocal power which brings about particularity, dissimilarity, and heterogeneity. On this basis, the research questions for this study are set out as:

- How has the NBA universalized its governance model in China, and how has Chinese basketball adapted and particularized this paradigm?
- How has the NBA expanded its market in China, and how has the Chinese

basketball market integrated with it to create a local market?

• How has the NBA diffused its cultural forms in China, and how has Chinese basketball subsumed them and created cultural hybrids?

2. 6 Conclusion

Globalization is not a new phenomenon but one which can be traced back to the Neolithic Revolution. The progress of globalization has accelerated rapidly since the end of the Second World War. However, the process of globalization rarely drew the attention of researchers until the 1970s. The field of globalization studies is still developing, though researchers tend to assign omnibearing definitions to globalization on the basis of their alliance with one of three theoretical schools of thought: the hyper-globalists, the sceptics, and the transformationalists. This study adopts Waters' (2001) definition, which is developed from Giddens' (1990) conceptualization with an emphasis on local transformation across time and space.

The phenomenon of sport globalization is also historical and is generally accepted as dating back to the initial emergence of sportization in the 1550s. The globalization of sport has also progressed rapidly in its various dimensions since the end of the Second World War, and especially since the late 1980s. The political globalization of sport has seen increasing governing power accorded to a growing number of international sports organizations and the transnational universalization of an isomorphic form of sport governance. This process of globalization may undermine the sport governing power of nation-states. Sport globalization in economic terms has seen the global expansion of the sports business. Neoliberalism is the major forces which have led the advance of sport globalization. Sport globalization from a cultural perspective has seen the global alignment of sports, the media, and sponsorship, which have resultantly created increased and global means of sport consumption. This process may result in issues related to cultural homogenization, heterogenization, and hybridization.

Although there has not yet been advanced a single theory of either globalization or sport globalization, the conceptualization of glocalization advocated by Robertson(1995) is one widely employed in sport studies. Robertson's glocalization theory suggests that global ties and influences are selected, processed, and consumed according to the local's needs, tastes, and social structure. Ritzer(2003, 2007b) has criticized this conceptualization, arguing that it emphasizes global heterogeneity and tends to reject the imperialistic ambitions of western entities and their desires to impose themselves on various geographic areas. Thus, he proposed grobalization to complement the idea of glocalization. Moreover, while Robertson's glocalization is constrained in that it highlights primarily the cultural aspects of globalization, Ritzer's grobalization/glocalization theory is more suitable for this study as it offers a more balanced theoretical basis for examining the multi-dimensional process of sport globalization. The theory of grobalization/glocalization thus constituted the theoretical keystone for the formulation of this study's three research questions, outlined in section 2. 5 above.

Chapter 3. Methodology

3.1 Introduction

This chapter documents the methodological procedures adopted in order to answer the research questions detailed in the previous chapter. It consists of five sections. The first section, Ontology and Epistemology, reflects on the philosophical considerations underlying knowledge and research. Following the assumption of ontological and epistemological positions for this study, the second section, Methodological Considerations, deals with the selection of one of the two major methodologies for researchers, namely, the quantitative approach and the qualitative approach. The third section, Research Methods, covers the process of data collection and the methods of analysis employed during the research. It is followed by a discussion of how issues of reliability, validity, and the relevant ethical considerations have been dealt with to maximize the scientific nature of research and to achieve an ethical standard for the research detailed in the third section. The final section, Research Design, presents the executive procedures used from start to completion in conducting this study.

3.2 Ontology and Epistemology

Discovering answers to questions is the purpose of research. Grix (2002: 179) suggests that our ontological and epistemological positions shape the very questions we might ask in the first place, how we pose them, and how we set about answering them. Therefore, ontology and epistemology are considered the two foremost issues to be clarified in the current research. Ontology and epistemology are philosophical concepts key to the pursuit of knowledge and research. Ontology is the starting point for all researches, and refers to the philosophy of existence and the nature and categories of being. Basically, ontology asks: "What is out there to know?" Epistemology is a philosophical inquiry into the nature of knowledge, what justifies a belief, and what we mean when we say that a claim is true (Alcoff, 1998: 3). Epistemology thus basically asks: "What can we know about it and how?" According to Gratton and Jones (2004: 14), the ontological and epistemological positions that researchers take have important implications for the way that their research is approached, notably in the type of data that is collected, how such data is collected, the ways in which the data might be interpreted, and the conclusions that can be drawn as a result.

With regard to ontology, there are two major positions: foundationalism and anti-foundationalism. Foundationalism is based on empirical science and implies that there is a real world "out there" that exists independently of our senses. Foundationalists observe the world, collect evidence, measure, and calculate in order to depict the patterns and regularities they find (Moses & Knutsen, 2007: 50-52).

They believe that the universe is deterministic. Foundationalism also maintains that social phenomena, along with the categories we use in everyday life and their meanings, have an existence independent of social actors(Bryman, 2004: 16-17). Anti-foundationalists doubt whether the"real world"really does exist independently of our knowledge of it. They do not consider the world to be as"fixed"as foundationalists believe, and think that it is more likely to present itself in a variety of forms(Moses & Knutsen, 2007: 142-149). Anti-foundationalists also maintain not only that social phenomena and categories are produced via social engagement with social actors, but also that they are in a constant state of revision(Bryman, 2004: 16-17).

Epistemology focuses on knowledge-gathering processes, and epistemological affiliation ties in with one's ontological position. There are three principal epistemological positions: positivism, interpretivism, and critical realism. Positivism develops from the foundationalist ontological position that there is a social reality to study that is independent of the researcher and the research subjects(Matthews & Ross, 2010: 27). The positivist approach is traditionally taken by natural scientists, but a growing number of social scientists have argued that this approach can be applied to the study of social phenomena. A positivist approach has a number of distinct features: knowledge is defined as that which can be observed by the senses; knowledge of a social phenomenon is based on what can be observed and recorded rather than on subjective understandings; usually, data are gathered to test a hypothesis which has been generated from an existing theory; the researcher is independent of and has no impact on the data, i. e. the researcher is objective (Matthews & Ross, 2010: 27). This approach implies that objectivity is possible, so positivists usually use quantitative methods as research tools as they are objective and the results are generalizable and replicable(Marsh & Furlong, 2002).

Interpretivism is an antithetical position to positivism that prioritizes people's subjective interpretations and understandings of social phenomena and their own actions, and develops from an anti-foundationalist ontological position. Thus, interpretivists suggest that the nature of a social phenomenon can be identified in the understanding and meanings ascribed to the phenomenon by the social actors (Matthews & Ross, 2010: 28). An interpretivist approach has the following features: 1) knowledge gathered includes people's interpretations and understandings; 2) the main focus is on how people interpret the social world and social phenomena, enabling different perspectives to be explored; 3) the researcher is interpreting other people's interpretations in terms of the theories and concepts of the social researcher's discipline-studying the social phenomenon as if through the eyes of the people being researched; 4) the researcher works with the data gathered to generate a theory(Marsh & Furlong, 2002: 26). With no possibility for objectivity, interpretivists usually employ qualitative research methods. Unlike positivists, they look to understand social behaviour rather than explain it, and focus on its meaning(Marsh & Furlong, 2002: 26).

Critical realism lies between the diametric positions of positivism and interpretivism. Its proponents believe that the social sciences can use empirical methods to measure and observe causal explanations while maintaining the need to adopt an interpretive understanding of that which is being studied(Grix, 2010: 86-87). In the words of Matthews & Ross(2010: 29), critical realism "suggests that the apparent social reality is underpinned by invisible but powerful structures or mechanisms. These mechanisms are not directly observable but their effects are apparent so these can be gathered and used to provide evidence of the underlying structures or mechanisms". Thus, a critical realist approach prioritizes "identifying structures or mechanisms that result in inequality or injustice and thus offers the opportunity for social change by changing or negating the structural mechanisms that are identified as having these impacts"(Matthews & Ross, 2010: 29). This position does not develop from a foundationalist or an anti-foundationalist ontological position as it focuses on the identification of knowledge that is real but unobservable. Therefore, a critical realist approach to social research typically incorporates: revealing hidden structures and mechanisms; uncovering power relations and dominant ideologies; research that leads to action; collecting qualitative and/or quantitative data(Matthews & Ross, 2010: 29-30).

Within sport studies, these three epistemological approaches are considered to have their own relative strengths and weaknesses. Gratton and Jones(2004: 16) state that positivists assume that the sports environment is relatively stable across different times or settings. Within such a stable context, the precise measurement and analysis of"facts" allows for the development of theories which can then be tested through further measurement and used to predict future behaviour. As such, a positivist approach is advantageous in terms of precision, control, and objectivity, and it dominated in the early years of sports-related research, particularly in the natural-scientific areas(Gratton & Jones, 2004: 16-17). However, the positivist approach is often criticized by interpretivists for not paying enough attention to the meanings and effects of social actors in the sport world. As Gratton and Jones(2004: 19) argue, "sport is a social phenomenon, that is those who participate in, watch or manage sports are acted upon by a number of external social forces, but also have free will to respond to such forces in an active way, and are not inanimate objects, whose behavior can be understood in terms of causal relationships". In this consideration, the interprevist approach is strengthening in that the social aspects of sport studies can be taken into account. This study aims to analyse globalization and basketball in the Chinese context and focuses on the relationship between structure(globalization) and agency(organizations and individuals). A critical realist approach, which lies between a positivistic approach and an interprevistic approach, is therefore the most suitable epistemological position to adopt since it allows us not only-from a positivistic position-to identify the deep structure and mechanism of the process of globalization that is shaping the diffusion and transformation of basketball in China, but also-from an interpretivistic position-to interpret basketball globalization phenomena by taking into account the engagement of social actors such as those from the relevant basketball organizations and individuals.

3. 3 Methodological Considerations

There are, in general, two main methodological approaches that may be adopted by a researcher: the qualitative approach and the quantitative approach. Quantitative methods are mostly employed by positivists, who try to produce causal explanations or even scientific laws. They not only refer to the notion of natural science in their ontology and epistemology, but also employ the corresponding methods. Typical methods of quantitative research involve surveys and/or statistics because the nature of the collected data allows them to be manipulated using statistical analysis techniques(Walliman, 2006: 54). As such, typical examples of quantitative data include census figures(population, income, living density, etc.), economic data(share prices, gross national product, tax regimes, etc.), performance data(e. g. sport statistics, medical measurements, engineering calculations, etc.), and all measurements in scientific endeavour(Walliman, 2006: 54). Ultimately, the aim of quantitative research is to make no or little interpretation in the analysis but to identify direct and exact causations which are irrefutable. The great advantages of this approach are that the data is usually easy to replicate, which is also a very important factor for ensuring scientific naturein research in the natural sciences, and, especially, that the results can easily be generalized (Walliman, 2006: 54). Therefore, quantitative research is widely used in certain research areas of sport studies, such as sports psychology and sports biomechanics. In these fields, controlled experiments are undertaken in laboratory settings to measure human behaviour and develop proposals for physical enhancement(Gratton & Jones, 2004: 23).

However, there is a lot of useful information in the social world that cannot be accurately measured or counted or reduced to numbers. Qualitative researches, therefore, focus on developing an understanding of how the world is constructed through words and texts. They are usually undertaken by interpretivists, corresponding with their ontological and epistemological position. According to Denzin and Lincoln(2005: 53), qualitative researchers attempt to make sense of, or provide an interpretation of, observed phenomena, which are relative to the meanings attributed to these phenomena by individuals involved in specific incidents or situations. As such, typical examples of the kind of data collected for qualitative analysis are literary texts, the minutes of meetings, observation notes, interview transcripts, documentary films, historical records, memos and recollections, etc. (Walliman, 2006: 55). Some of these are records taken directly or very close to the events or phenomena whereas others may be remote but highly edited interpretations. Silverman(2001: 32) argues that researchers who use the qualitative method for their work commonly believe that they can provide a deeper understanding of social phenomena. In sport studies, qualitative researches have been increasingly undertaken and acknowledged over the last few decades, and have evolved into"an eclectic mix of research ideologies and viewpoints that seek to critically investigate the role, effects and position of sport within broader society"(Gratton & Jones, 2004: 23). Table 3-1 summarizes the distinct features of the quantitative and qualitative approaches to research.

In consideration of the nature of these research questions outlined in 2. 5 and of the characteristics of the quantitative and qualitative approaches outlined in Table 3 - 1, a qualitative methodological approach was considered the most suitable for this study. First, numeric conclusions such as those that result from quantitative researches may lack the detailed understanding and explanations needed to answer these questions. Second, the opinions, feelings, ideas, values, experiences, and traditions of social actors in the basketball sphere are crucial data for answering these questions(Gratton & Jones, 2004: 54). Third, a qualitative research setting will allow us to understand and provide an in-depth analysis of the basketball globalization phenomena through the gathering and representation of multiple sources of data. Although it is argued that a qualitative research approach is the most suitable for this study, it is nonetheless important to acknowledge the inherent weaknesses of this methodology, namely, issues of reliability, validity, and ethics(e. g. , consent, personal bias, etc.). Bearing this in mind, every effort has been made to generate qualitative research that is as scientific as possible. These issues will be examined again in the Research Methods section below and are further discussed in Reliability, Validity and Ethical Considerations of this chapter.

Table 3-1 Features of the Quantitative and Qualitative Approaches to Research

Quantitative	Qualitative
Ontological and epistemological approaches are positivist(the assumption that the social world is real).	Ontological and epistemological approaches are interpretivist(the assumption that reality is a social construct).
Research questions may be set out as testable hypotheses.	Research questions may be developed using subsidiary questions.
The research question can be answered(or a hypothesis tested) by counting events and using statistical analysis.	The research question can be answered by describing and explaining events and gathering data on participants' understandings, beliefs, and experiences.
The researcher normally knows what s/he is looking for.	The researcher may only have a general idea of what s/he is looking for.
Research design/strategy is usually fixed before data collection.	Research design/strategy may be fluid and evolutionary.
Objectivity(the researcher is not part of the research).	Subjectivity(the researcher is involved as a social being).
Often makes use of tools(such as surveys or questionnaires) to collect data.	Usually involves no use of tools: the researcher can be seen as the main instrument for collecting data.
Data is often represented by numerical or named codes.	Data may be in any form.
It may be possible to generalize from the data.	It is not usually possible to generalize from the data.

Source: adapted from Matthews & Ross(2010: 142).

3.4 Research Methods

This section details the process of data collection and the methods of analysis used in the study. The technique adopted in this research was that of "triangulation". This term was coined by Denzin (1978) to refer to the use of multiple methods of data collection and data analysis which, as a result of their complementarity, may be employed to correct for their respective shortcomings (Mouton & Marais, 1988: 91; Yin, 2010: 81). It is generally accepted that the inclusion of multiple sources of data and multiple methods of data analysis in a research project is likely to increase the reliability and validity of the research. For this reason, two data collection methods were employed in this study: semi-structured interviews and documents. Two data analysis methods were also adopted, namely, thematic analysis and narrative analysis.

3.4.1 Data Collection

Semi-structured Interviews. Interviewing is one of the principal data collection methods used by social researchers since it provides the opportunity for direct interaction between the researcher and the research participants. The most distinctive feature of interviews is that they facilitate direct communication between two people, either face-to-face or at a distance via telephone or the internet, which enables the interviewer to elicit information, feelings, and opinions from the interviewee using questions and interactive dialogue (Matthews & Ross, 2010: 219). Depending on the degree of control exercised by the researcher, interviews can be divided into three types: standardized structured, semi-structured, and unstructured interviews. Standardized structured interviews follow a common set of questions for each interview. The questions are asked in exactly the same way, i. e. using the same words and probes for each interview, and participants are presented with a set of answers to choose from(Matthews & Ross, 2010: 221). Unstructured interviews focus on a broad area for discussion, enabling the participant to talk about the research topic in their own way(Matthews & Ross, 2010: 221). Semi-structured interviews follow a common set of topics or questions for each interview, but may introduce the topics or questions in different ways or orders as appropriate for each interview. They also allow the participant to answer the questions or discuss the topic in their own way using their own words(Matthews & Ross, 2010: 221).

Semi-structured interviews were employed for this study for the reason that both the content of the interview, such as the participants' experiences, behaviour, values, and understandings, and the way the participants express themselves were considered pertinent for answering the research questions. As indicated by May (2001: 93), this type of interview better allows people to respond on their own terms than the standardized interview. Bearing in mind that semi-structured interviewers can control the quality of the result, I had formulated and rehearsed the interviewing process before beginning the interviews with a view to increasing reliability and ensuring validity.

The most important considerations were the selection of the interviewees and the determination of the criteria for selection. I identified four groups of interviewees to contact according to the themes of the study(governance, market, culture): 1) policy-makers who have been involved, preferably directly, for at least five years, in the decision-making processes of the NBA's operation in China and/or those of the Chinese Basketball Management Center(CBMC) and its local administrators, which is the governing body for Chinese basketball; 2) staff from professional basketball clubs who are deemed to have had direct experience or knowledge of Chinese professional basketball and preferably had at least five years' working experience; 3) basketball participants who have been involved in basketball for at least five years and for at least ten years for the members in the selected fans community, whose experience, behaviours, and values in relation to basketball-playing and/or basketball consumption demonstrate their cultural identities relating to basketball; and, 4) basketball experts, who are close to the basketball scene or have at least 10 years' experience in the research of basketball and as a result can provide further insights into globalization and basketball in China.

In addition, I drafted different sets of questions for each group in advance of the interviews. For instance, in interviewing the CBMC officials, I mostly started with the questions I came up in their speeches at important meetings. Questions were related to the policy-making process in conducting professionalization, marketization and culturalization for Chinese basketball to cope with the NBA's expansion in China. For those local basketball administrators, I concerned about the policy implementation process from the CBMC and the development of local basketball, professional basketball and mass basketball participation in particular. For the staff of NBA China, questions were related to the NBA's global strategies, marketing strategies in China, strength and weakness of its marketing in China. More general and open questions about globalization, sport globalization and basketball globalization in China were given to the basketball experts. Interviewing diverse groups of social actors, from governmental officials to basketball participants, can be time-consuming and pose difficulties in terms of operability. Fortunately, the Chinese Basketball Culture Forums(CBCF) provided a favourable platform from which to enhance operability and efficiency. These forums are jointly organized by the CBMC, the Sport Culture Development Center of the General Administration of Sport(GAS), and Soochow University. The School of Sport Studies in Soochow University, where I was a Master's student from 2006 to 2009, is responsible for administering the executive affairs of the forums. The CBCFs are held more often than academic events and are substantial gatherings of the relevant governmental officials from the GAS and the CBMC, as well as club managers, media and sponsors, and academics in sport studies and marketing. The reformation(professionalization, marketization, and culturalization) of Chinese basketball is discussed and advanced at these gatherings. During the 2007 CBCF, I worked as a coordinator and receptionist for the forum, which provided the opportunity to get into touch directly with some important attendees.

From 26 November to 7 December 2011, I went back to Soochow University and took part in the organization of the 3rd CBCF. Through my previously established network and with help from the convener of the CBCFs, I conducted my first round of interviews in Suzhou. This included interviews with three senior CBMC officials, two senior staff in the Chinese Basketball Association League (CBAL) clubs and six professors. With respect to interviewing the policy-makers in the NBA, I thought that a visit to the NBA headquarters might prove useful for the research. Unfortunately, my visa request was denied so this was not possible. My contacts at the NBA headquarters later suggested, via e-mail, that I should contact NBA China instead, their overseas office in China which is in charge of the NBA's business in the Chinese market. However, when I contacted NBA China by e-mail with a request to carry out academic interviews, I was told that they were unwilling to comply with the request for reasons of commercial confidentiality. Finally, with the help of one senior CBMC official, I made contact with three members of staff at NBA China who agreed to be interviewed on the condition that their identities were not revealed.

The second round of interviews took place between 23 December 2011 and 4 January 2012 in Beijing. First, I conducted three interviews with the three members of staff from NBA China. They were fairly open in talking on the NBA's global strategies and their marketing strategies in China and in particular the development of basketball in China as well as the NBA's grassroots marketing. However, they were not willing to give out accurate marketing statistics of their Chinese market and tended to avoid commenting on the NBA's strength and weakness in competing with the CBAL. The best offer from these interviewees was that they promised to verify the data I had collected from the CBMC, NBA. com and other media sources. Following this, I interviewed one club manager from the CBAL, whom was recommended by interviewees I had talked to in Suzhou. With assistance from ChinaPacers. com, I then interviewed eight basketball participants during a gathering of Indiana Pacers fans in Beijing. The Pacers fan community was chosen not only because it covers the trajectory of the NBA's diffusion in China since it began to take shape in the mid-1990s, but also because its members are relatively constant participants, unlike other fan groups whose memberships causally change with the coming and going of superstars. Interviewing Indiana Pacers fans served the purpose of obtaining a deep understanding of the story of the NBA's Chinese fans and their community behaviours. I also noted that focus group interviews are widely used in such a research environment as the interviewees have something in common. Even before undertaking this research, I had been observing and personally involved with the Pacers fan community through ChinaPacers. com for more than 10 years and had participated in several of their fan-gatherings, so I had a moderate understanding of the fans' general behaviours. Undertaking face-to-face interviews, rather than focus group interview, was considered useful for providing more in-depth information and insight from the respondents, and should also help to further ensure the reliability and validity of the research.

The third round of interviews took place from 17 to 28 July 2012 in Dongguan. The purpose of this round of interviews was mainly to gather data on the transformation of local basketball culture under the culturally homogenizing influence of the NBA. Dongguan is an important industrial city located in the heart of Pearl River Delta of Guangdong Province. On the one hand, it is one of the most urbanized cities in post-reform China and has been subject to considerable western cultural influence, including from the NBA. On the other hand, Dongguan has been named a"Basketball City"by the GAS and was the first Chinese city to have a professional basketball club. Basketball is also a popular amateur sport in Dongguan. Thus, basketball in Dongguan can be seen as a quintessential representation of Chinese basketball culture. For this reason, Dongguan was considered an ideal location for investigating how Chinese basketball culture has reacted to and integrated with that of the NBA. In this round, I interviewed two officials respectively from the Dongguan Sport Administration and Dongguan Basketball Association(DBA), and one club manager, all of whom were also recommended by interviewees I had talked to in Suzhou. I also interviewed 22 basketball participants, ranging from high school students to elderly basketball supporters. APE teacher at Changping High School, helped me to target and get into touch with these interviewees. Zhang has more than 10 years' experience in school basketball teaching, amateur basketball development, and professional match refereeing. His insight and social network proved a great help in getting to the heart of Dongguan basketball. Please see Appendix for detailed list of interviewees.

Documents. Documents are written records about people and things that are generated through the process of living(Matthews & Ross, 2010: 277-278). They are more than a bundle of papers and can contain very different sorts of data depending on their type, purpose, and medium. This can range across but is not limited to: news items and commentary; numerical data(such as population censuses and surveys); qualitative data, such as reports and the findings of research projects; policy documents, such as government and other official documents; personal information and interpretations, such as diaries, letters, or shopping lists; visual material like films, photographs, or videos; audio material, etc. (Matthews & Ross, 2010: 277-278).

Documents are important to researchers for a number of reasons: 1) they are often readily available and often contain large amounts of information; 2) they can be used to triangulate data gathered from other sources; 3) they are long-lived, so they can be researched across time; and, 4) they are useful for providing context for research(Matthews & Ross, 2010: 278). Depending on their origins, documents are generally grouped into three categories: primary, secondary, and tertiary documents. According to Matthews and Ross(2010: 279), primary documents are those created by the person who observed or participated in the events described, while secondary documents are reports of things seen or recorded by others and tertiary documents are compilations based on secondary documents and other data.

The primary documents used in this study are official documents of the NBA and the CBMC, mainly key policy documents, annual reports, and minutes of key meetings. With regard to the official documents of the CBMC, the Chinese Basketball Culture Research Center(CBCRC), the CBCF's secretarial office based in the School of Sport Studies in Soochow University, provided access to a considerable amount of useful data. The official documents of the NBA were obtained from its official website, NBA. com, which hosts some important policy documents. NBA China and the Indiana Pacers also generously offered me access to some useful documents. The secondary documents employed in this study were academic publications and media articles(printed and online). However, these documents have some obvious weaknesses as sources of data. First, a number of the academic publications referenced in this study were written by Chinese scholars. In China, an academic paper is usually required to undergo political censorship before publication, which can lead to a certain bias on the part of the author(s). To mitigate for this weakness, I conducted a critical examination of such documents before deciding whether or not to use them. With respect to media documents, there are simply too many such articles available online or in print and the process of selection can be extremely time-consuming. The solution was to try to target the most important and relevant articles from the official websites of the NBA and the CBA, or from other reliable web portals, such as Entertainment & Sport Program Network(ESPN) and Xinhua News. After selecting the secondary data from the media, I double-checked their credibility via another data source or the internet. In addition to these primary and secondary documents, some tertiary documents, such as statistics and indexes, were also used in this study.

3. 4. 2 Data Analysis

Thematic Analysis and Analytical Framework. To answer the research questions set out for this study, an analytical framework was constructed according to the research aims and objectives. This process was informed by a brief review of the existing research on globalization, sport and governance, on globalization, sport and the market, and on globalization, sport and culture. This framework(see Table 3-2) divides the research questions into two key themes, three subthemes and nine indicators. According to these themes and indicators, ideal sources of data were identified and collected. Follow, the collected data were indexed and coded. This also helped me to develop some further ideas in answering the research questions. I recorded the thoughts at this stage. Then I started to draw charts on a notebook to link these thoughts and ideas with the themes and indicators. After that, I began to interpret the data with the assistance of the charts.

Table 3-2 **Analytical Framework for the Study**

Key Themes	Subthemes	Indicators
		NBA's universalization of its governance model.
	Governance	CBA's negotiation and particularization of this model.
		Current degree of paradigm assimilation.
Grobalization		NBA's market expansion.
	Market	CBA's negotiation of this and existence at its margins.
Glocalization		Current degree of market growth.
		NBA's cultural diffusion.
	Culture	CBA's negotiation of this and cultural heterogenization.
		Current degree of cultural homogenization.

Narrative Analysis. Narrative analysis in the social sciences refers to "a family of approaches to diverse kinds of texts, which have in common a storied form"(Riessman, 2004). In some disciplines, such as social history, the term "narrative"can refer to an entire life story, woven from the threads of interviews, observation, and documents(Riessman, 2004) . According to Riessman(2004), what makes such diverse texts"narrative"is sequence and consequence: events are selected, organized, connected, and evaluated as meaningful for a particular audience. Storytellers interpret the world and their experience in it, and sometimes create moral tales, to show how the world should be. Thus, narratives represent storied ways of knowing and communicating(Hinchman & Hinchman, 1997). Four models are included in Riessman's taxonomy of narrative analysis: thematic analysis, which emphasizes the content of a text, i. e. "what" is said more than "how" it is said, and what is "told" rather than the "telling"; structural analysis, which shifts emphasis to the telling, the way a story is told; interactional analysis, which emphasizes the dialogic process between teller and listener; and, performative analysis, which "extends the interactional approach, [and in which] interest goes beyond the spoken word and [in which], as the stage metaphor implies, storytelling is seen as performance"(Riessman, 2004).

This study attempts to explore the extent of the NBA's penetration into the Chinese basketball market and Chinese basketball's consequential negotiation of that. The stories of the agents-from officials to individuals who exert grobal/glocal power in the realm of basketball-reflect the process of the globalization of basketball in China. Thus, this study adopts narratives as an analytical tool. Given the themes identified and outlined in Table 3-2 above, a thematic narrative analysis was considered the most appropriate choice since, as Riessman(2003) points out, "language is a direct and unambiguous route to meaning".

3. 5 Reliability, Validity, and Ethical Considerations

Reliability and validity are two key concepts used to assess how truthful and accurate a piece of research actually is(Gratton & Jones, 2004: 85). In qualitative research, reliability and validity are seen as measures of the quality, rigor, and wider potential of a research work, and are achieved through adherence to certain methodological and disciplinary conventions and principles (Mason, 1996: 21). Reliability refers to the capacity to produce consistent results. As Matthews and Ross(2010: 479) argue, "reliability is a measure of research quality, meaning that another researcher would expect to obtain the same findings if they carried out the research in the same way, or the original researcher would expect to obtain the same findings if they tried again in the same way". Yin (2003) suggests that documenting the procedures adopted during previous work or establishing several steps which are as simple as possible in order to make them operational are ways of achieving higher reliability. To accomplish this during this study, I elaborated a discreet procedure before setting about each research phase(see section 3. 6 below). I also consulted multiple works on research methodology in order to ensure the adoption of the correct and most reliable approach(e. g. Yin, 2003; Bryman, 2004; Gratton & Jones, 2004; Maxwell, 2009; Matthews & Ross, 2010). Moreover, the data collection process for this study was based on unambiguous research and interview questions, and on deliberate considerations, such as selecting appropriate conversation sites and using ice-breaking words before beginning the interviews. Voice recording was carried out during the interviews.

Validity is an important term in research and refers to the conceptual and scientific soundness of a research study(Graziano & Raulin, 2004: 158). Matthews and Ross(2010: 480) state that"validity is a measure of research quality, meaning that the data we are planning to gather and work with to address our research questions is a close representation of the aspect of social reality we are studying". In other words, the primary goal in taking validity into account is to increase the accuracy and usefulness of findings by eliminating or controlling as many confounding variables as possible, allowing for greater confidence in the findings of a given study(Marczyk et al., 2005). Yin(2010: 78) notes that a valid study is one that has properly collected and interpreted its data, so that the conclusions accurately reflect and represent the real world that was studied. Based on his own work as well as numerous other qualitative studies, Maxwell(2009) has offered a seven-point checklist to be used in combating threats to validity: 1) Intensive long-term(field) involvement, to produce a complete and in-depth understanding of field situations, including the opportunity to make repeated observations and interviews(Maxwell, 2009). In addition to participating in the CBCFs in Soochow University, I have been involved in the field in a variety of roles. I have been playing and"consuming" basketball since childhood, and observing the development of Chinese basketball through newspapers, magazines, television, and later through the internet, as well as the growth of the NBA's presence in China. Like many of my interviewees, I rate myself a"close insider"in the field. Since my obtaining my Master's degree in 2006, one of my principal research interests has been basketball. Apart from working part-time for the CBCRC in Soochow University, I also completed a 6-month internship as a part-time reporter covering NBA games for SOHU Sports in 2007. Given this experience, I consider myself a competent observer of the field. This long-term field involvement has also brought benefits in terms of Maxwell's(2009) second point: 2) "Rich"data-to cover fully the field observations and interviews with detailed and varied data. Furthermore, the vast number of images and visual data gathered during the field involvement has provided a solid foundation for putting into practice Maxwell's(2009) third point: 3) triangulation-to collect converging evidence from different sources. For the purposes of triangulation, multiple methods of data collection and analysis were adopted. The remaining four points suggested by Maxwell(2009) were also taken into consideration(Maxwell, 2009): 4) Respondent validation-to obtain feedback from the people studied to lessen the misinterpretation of their self-reported behaviours and views; 5) Search for discrepant evidence and negative cases-to test rival or competing explanations; 6) Quasi-statistics-to use actual numbers instead of adjectives; and, 7) Comparison-to compare explicitly the results across different settings, groups, or event(Maxwell, 2009).

Ethics is an important issue associated with any academic research and refers to the question of whether the research is socially and morally acceptable(Gratton & Jones, 2004: 110). The study follows the UCC Social Research Ethics Committee guideline. First, it should be noted that the research for this study was gathered strictly on the basis of informed consent. Before commencing the interviews, each participant was presented with a copy of my PhD student ID and an introductory letter on headed paper from the School of Asian Studies in University College Cork that was signed by the head of the department. Each participant in the research was informed about the nature of the study and how data supplied would be used. This was done before the data was collected from them and consent was obtained from each participant. Two of the participants were in high school and under the age of 18 at the time of interviewing. Consent was thus obtained from their PE teachers. ① All participants were also informed that the conversation could be stopped at any time if they wished to do so. Second, all the participants were told that a voice recording would be taken of the conversations and that they could ask to stop the recording at any time. Third, all participants were guaranteed anonymity and told that only my supervisor and I would have access to the research data after the interviews and after use in the thesis. In addition, I created a protected folder to store the digital data, while all paper-based data was locked away.

3. 6 Research Design

According to Yin(2003: 20), a research design is a logical blueprint for getting from here to there, where"here"is defined as the initial set of questions to be answered, and"there"is some set of conclusions or answers to these questions. Between here and there are a number of major steps, including the collection and analysis of the relevant data(Yin, 2003: 20). The following research phases created the"logical blueprint"for conducting this study.

Phase 1: Identification of Research Topic. During this phase, a preliminary literature review was conducted in relation to the research topic of globalization and sport in China, as well as for the research field of globalization studies. This desk study enabled me to familiarize myself with the research topic and to address the research aim of integrating the globalization of basketball into one comprehen-

① In China's high school, the headteacher is the general legal guardian of the students in the campus, while the on-duty teacher is the legal guardian during the classes.

sive framework in order to examine its cultural, political, and economic processes.

Phase 2: Clarification of Concepts. After broadly deciding what to study in the field of globalization and sport, I conducted a more selective and rigorous literature review of globalization theories. This not only enabled me to clarify the various definitions of globalization and identify the three foundational theoretical schools, but also guided me towards adopting Ritzer's grobalization/glocalization conceptual framework to analyse the multi-dimensional process of the globalization of basketball in the Chinese context, and consequently aided the generation of a set of research questions and the selection of the methodology to be used for this study.

Phase 3: Construction of Analytical Framework. During this phase, a broad review was undertaken of the extant literature review on the political, economic, and cultural globalization of sport, as well as of literature on the historical background of the NBA and Chinese basketball, the governance models of professional sports leagues, the expansion of professional sports markets, and cultural convergence through sports. This literature review not only enabled me to position the research questions into a specific analytical framework by refining the subthemes and indicators, but also helped me to identify the ideal source of data and methods of analysis.

Phase 4: Collection of Data. After identifying the ideal source of data for answering the research questions, I drew up a detailed schedule for data collection. During this phase, I went to China twice to conduct interviews and to collect documents. On the first trip, I attended the 3rd CBCF in Suzhou, where I conducted the first round of interviews and collected most of the official documents I needed. I then went to Beijing for the second round of interviews. The second visit was to Dongguan, where I conducted the third round of interviews and collected more documents after a preliminary process of data analysis.

Phase 5: Data Analysis and Interpretation. During this phase, I began to analyse the data and to interpret the results with the guidance of the analytical framework previously constructed. At the same time, I looked for any additional documents that might be useful for the research and referred back to some of the interviewees by phone and email for feedback.

Phase 6: Drawing Conclusions. In this phase, I revisited the research questions and elaborated the findings. I also established whether or not the research objectives had been met, noted the strengths and weaknesses of the study, and made some recommendations for further research.

3. 7 Conclusion

Research is an established means of making a contribution to a body of knowledge by discovering the answers to questions. Ontology and epistemology are two philosophical concepts that underpin our understanding of knowledge and research. Ontology refers to the philosophy of existence, while epistemology refers to the philosophical inquiry into existence. Foundationalism, which proposes that there is a real world independent of the senses of social actors, and anti-foundationalism, whereby the world presents itself in a variety of forms with constant revisions by social actors, are the two major ontological positions. In general, researchers may determine their epistemological and methodological positions by following their ontological assumptions. Foundationalists usually adopt a positivist epistemological position and use quantitative methods as research tools as they believe that objectivity is possible and that the results of researches are and should be generalizable and replicable. Anti-foundationalists usually take an interpretivist epistemological position and use qualitative methods as research tools. They prioritize people's subjective interpretations and understandings of social phenomena and their own actions. However, there is a third epistemological position, critical realism, which forsakes the polarity of positivism and interpretivism. Critical realists are neither foundationalist nor anti-foundationalist but adopt an inbetween ontological position and focus on the identification of knowledge that is real but unobservable. Therefore, critical realists can employ either or both quantitative and qualitative research tools. This study adopted a critical realist epistemological position because it permitted taking into account not only the identification of the fixed structure and mechanisms of globalization, but also the engagement of social actors in the realm of basketball. A qualitative research approach was selected in order to produce a more in-depth study using qualitative data from social actors.

To answer the research questions in a detailed and rigorous way, the method of triangulation was adopted during the research, aiming to increase the reliability and validity of the study. Two data collection methods were used-semi-structured interviews and documents-as well as two data analysis methods, thematic analysis and narrative analysis. With regard to the semi-structured interviews, four groups of people, namely, policy-makers, practitioners, basketball participants, and experts, were identified and interviewed in three rounds that took place between December 2011 and July 2012 in Suzhou, Beijing, and Dongguan, China. Regarding documents, key policy documents, annual reports, and the minutes of important meetings were collected from both the NBA and the CBMC. Secondary documents including academic publications and printed or online media articles, as well as some tertiary documents such as statistics and indexes, were also collected and used. Thematic analysis was employed to construct the analytical framework for the study. Narrative analysiswas used to facilitate the examination and incorporation in the data of the stories of relevant social actors. As reliability and validity are important considerations in research, every step of the research process was carefully considered and Maxwell's(2009) seven-point checklist was followed in an effort to increase the validity of the results. Ethical issues-such as those relating to informed consent, willingness, and confidentiality-were also taken into consideration. Structurally, the study was undertaken in six phases: identification of research topic, clarification of concepts, construction of analytical framework, collection of data, data analysis and interpretation, and drawing conclusions.

Chapter 4. Historical Overview

4.1 Introduction

Globalization has been blurring the boundary between capitalist sport and socialist sport over the course of the past few decades(Maguire, 1999: 94; Jarvie, 2006: 99). This study focuses on how globalization has brought together the capitalist basketball of the American NBA and Chinese socialist basketball. Prior to the proper examination, this chapter provides an overview of two trajectories of sport development which comprise the historical context for this research topic. One is the development of the NBA, which demonstrates how a typical capitalist sporting entity is formed. The other is sport development in the PRC, which reveals how a typical socialist sport institution took shape in China.

4. 2 Development of the NBA

4. 2. 1 The Early Years of American Professional Basketball (1891—1945)

Basketball is a game played by two teams of five players who score points by throwing a ball through a basket mounted at the opponent's end of a rectangular court(A. & C. Black Publishers, 2006). The origins of many popular sports today are unclear, and in some cases they remain unknown. However, basketball is one of the few ball games for which the invention process has a relative accurate record. The inventor of basketball, Dr James Naismith, held multiple degrees in theology, sport science, and medicine. In 1891, Naismith was a teacher in the International YMCA Training School(now Springfield College) in Massachusetts, U. S. At that time, students at the school were not permitted to perform outdoor exercise during the state's long, cold winter, even though most sports were outdoors-based. Insufficient opportunity for the students to exercise during the winter led to a lot of discord and disorder on campus. Therefore, the head of the sports department assigned Naismith to invent an indoor game that would be interesting, easy to learn, and easy to play in winter. Thus, Naismith invented basketball with the idea of combining characteristics of several sports: baseball, football, hockey, and soccer, as well as a game call"duck on a rock", which was children's game played in Naismith's youth(Jordan et al., 2000: 50-51; LaFeber, 2002: 33-40; Kirchberg, 2007: 7-12; Rob et al., 2009: 42-64).

Naismith's invention gained popularity throughout the country almost immediately. Within a few weeks, basketball had spread rapidly to many university campuses in the Northeast and then to other major American states thanks to the influence of the YMCA. Basketball appealed to the ordinary people because it was easy to play, involved moderate physical demand, and required teamwork. It was soon played extensively by Americans in both urban and rural areas, as well as by a large number of the growing immigrant population(Jordan et al. , 2000: 50-51; LaFeber, 2002: 33-40; Kirchberg, 2007: 7-12; Rob et al. , 2009: 42-64). Basketball was introduced to other countries as well. In 1892, basketball was brought to Mexico City, making Mexico the first country outside the U. S. where basketball was played. Shortly thereafter, in 1895, the YMCA brought basketball to China, and then to India in 1901 and Persia in 1904. In 1905, it was introduced to Japan, Germany, and Russia. On 18 June 1932, the International Amateur Basketball Federation(IABF) (originally Fédération International de Basketball Amateur, FIBA) was established. Basketball then debuted as an official competitive event in the 1936 Olympic Games. Naismith was present at the Games and awarded the first Olympic gold medals for basketball to the Team USA in Berlin(Cunningham, 2009: 1-27; Rob et al. , 2009: 151-161; Wolff, 2010).

The first professional basketball game in sports history is recorded as having been held on 7 November 1896. The Trenton Basketball Team(formerly Trenton YMCA Basketball Team) in New Jersey rented a local church for USD 25(EUR 18. 75)[①] to host a game against the Brooklyn YMCA Basketball Team. They charged entrance fees and shared the revenue after the game. Each player received roughly USD 15(EUR 11. 25). Fred Cooper, a key player and the coach,

① Approximately, 1 US Dollar = 0. 75 Euro

was rewarded for his efforts with the surplus USD 1(EUR 1. 25) and thus became the first star player. Thereafter, there emerged not only more and more basketball teams that played for money all over the U. S. , but also basketball equipment manufacturers, such as Spalding. With the growth in basketball's popularity, and the increase in the number of local basketball teams and basketball fans, it became increasingly exigent to establish professional basketball leagues. In 1898, the first professional basketball league was set up in the area around Philadelphia and New Jersey, and was named the National Basketball League (NBL, est. 1898). Even though the NBL(est. 1898) was soon dissolved, the initial modality of American professional basketball can be seen as having been clearly established(Jordan et al. , 2000: 42-51; LaFeber, 2002: 41- 48; Batchelor, 2005: 177-188; Kirchberg, 2007: 13-46). This means that the transformation of basketball from its invention to a professionalized sport took less than a decade. Originating in United States' industrial capitalism era, basketball seems to have been fated to become a commodity.

The NBA has dominated American professional basketball for most of the time since its invention, but attempts and efforts to set up professional basketball leagues in the U. S. had occurred even before the Second World War. The first half of the 20th century saw the emergence of a number of regional American professional basketball leagues, for instance, the Philadelphia Basketball League in the New England region and the Mid-Atlantic, the Hudson River Basketball League, the New York Basketball League, and so on. However, most of these leagues did not last long. The American Basketball League and the National Basketball League(NBL, est. 1935) were the two most successful basketball leagues in the pre-NBA era(Jordan et al. , 2000: 42-51; LaFeber, 2002: 41-48; Batchelor, 2005: 177-188; Kirchberg, 2007: 13 – 46). Barnstorming teams were also popular at that time. They travelled around the country, competing with local basketball teams. Most of them were professional teams but they tended not to join professional leagues or stayed in them only for a short time. The Harlem Globetrotters was the original barnstorming team, a concept which remains popular throughout the world today. The four most famous barnstorming teams at that time also included the Original Celtics, the Renaissance Five (The Rens), and the Buffalo Germans. All of these teams are now honoured in the Naismith Basketball Hall of Fame (Jordan et al., 2000: 52-57; LaFeber, 2002: 41-48; Batchelor, 2005: 177-188; Kirchberg, 2007: 13-46).

4. 2. 2 The Birth of the NBA (1946—1949)

Americans' enthusiasm for physical activities continued to increase after the Second World War. This can be largely attributed to the fast development of the tertiary sector, which allowed the middle class more leisure time. At this time, baseball undoubtedly remained the first sport as it still held the largest part of American sports market. In contrast, professional American football had encountered some difficulties and had not yet got a firm foothold in the market. Many star football players had joined or been enlisted in the armed forces during the Second World War, and a great number of elite football players had moved to college teams after the war. Professional hockey still occupied the northern sports market even though their territory had shrunk to only two Canadian cities and four American cities during wartime. The other two major professional sports were boxing and horse racing, which had experienced little change since the pre-war era. Professional basketball had low competitiveness in the American sports market since college basketball was attracting the majority of American basketball fans. In addition, the professional teams often did not have home venues and games were usually held in the stadia of other professional sports(Jordan et al., 2000: 38-41; Jay, 2006: 9-44; Kirchberg, 2007: 47-66).

After the Second World War, a few hockey stadia were vacant for two or three nights a week when they were not being used for professional hockey, boxing, and college basketball matches. The college basketball season was short, normally from November to March. Therefore, there were frequent discussions on establishing a new professional basketball league to fill the vacant stadia. These hockey stadia mainly belonged to the owners of teams in the National Hockey League(NHL) and the American Hockey League(AHL), which spanned 11 big cities, including New York, Boston, Chicago, and Toronto. On 6 June 1946, the 11 stadium owners met in New York and came up with a project for establishing a new professional basketball league, the Basketball Association of America(BAA) (Jordan et al., 2000: 38-41; Jay, 2006: 9-44; Kirchberg, 2007: 47-66; Rosen, 2008).

The BAA's first season was a failure. Reports on BAA games could only be found in some local newspapers, with little radio and no television coverage. The second season did not progress much further and the BAA incurred severe financial losses. The Board realized the significance of star players and shifted their efforts to attracting elite players from the NBL(est. 1935). After the 1947—1948 season, the BAA President, Maurice Podoloff, persuaded two of the NBL's(est. 1935) best teams, Fort Wayne and Indianapolis, to join the BAA. Following in their footsteps, the Minneapolis Lakers, with their superstar George Mikan, and the Rochester Centrals decided to join the BAA. As a result, the NBL(est. 1935) was forced to disband after the 1948—1949 season and the other six NBL(est. 1935) teams were absorbed into the BAA. In this way, the BAA finally monopolized the American professional basketball market, with its territory covering 17 American cities and spanning from the east coast to the west coast. On 6 June 1949, the BAA changed its name to the National Basketball Association(NBA) (Bjarkman, 1992: 10-29; Jordan et al. , 2000: 38- 41; Jay, 2006: 9- 44; Kirchberg, 2007: 47-66; Rosen, 2008; Nelson, 2009) .

4. 2. 3 The NBA's Struggle to Survival(1950—1976)

Between the late 1940s and 1970s, the NBA experienced considerable difficulties. The league survived in this period for four main reasons. The first was the emergence of superstars. In the 1950s, American society was relatively harmonious and prosperous. But by the 1960s and 1970s, radical social and political upheavals greatly influenced the values of the younger generations. Sports thus became a way for them to find relief from their disappointment with society and to look for heroes they could rely on. George Mikan, the first superstar in the NBA's history, dominated the basketball games with the ground-breaking skills he displayed throughout his career. The Boston Celtics swept up eight consecutive NBA championships between 1959 and 1966 under coach Red Auerbach, creating the so-called Celtics Dynasty(Bjarkman, 1992: 30-75; Jordan et al. , 2000: 26-35, 38-41; Jay, 2006: 9-44; Kirchberg, 2007: 47-66; Rosen, 2008; Schumacher, 2008) .

Second among the reasons for the survival of the NBA was the acceptance of African-American players. Although racial segregation had been abolished in the 1950s, racial discrimination was still widespread in American society in the NBA's early years. Due to the prejudices in the labour markets, African-Americans rarely had a chance to participate in professional sports. This situation began to change when an African-American baseball player named Jackie Robinson debuted as a professional player in the Major League Baseball(MLB) , playing for the Los Angeles Dodgers against the Brooklyn Dodgers on 15 April

1947. This event was a landmark in the history of professional sports as well as in the history of the United States' civil rights movement. The first African-American NBA player was Earl Lloyd, who played in a game for the Washington Capitols on 10 October 1950. After that, more and more African-American basketball athletes were selected by NBA teams, which greatly enriched their rosters. The fancy dribbles and flowery moves of the African-American players were a part of their body culture and an expression of egoism. But they were initially rejected as mainstream basketball skills. However, these moves were more attractive to audiences and thus gradually gained acceptance. By 1970, more than 50 per cent of NBA players were African-American athletes. Therefore, working hard to become a professional player and integrating into white society became the dream of many African-American youths. In addition, the NBA's interfusion of African-American and white players has greatly contributed to breaking down the long-standing racial barriers within American society (Bjarkman, 1992: 52-75; Ashe, 1993: 22-52; Jordan et al., 2000: 58-61; Batchelor, 2005: 177-188; Jay, 2006: 45-78; Kirchberg, 2007: 31-38).

The third reason for the NBA's survival in the 1960s and 1970s was the modification of gaming rules. In the early 1950s, most NBA teams lost money due to the tedious nature of the games and very low attendance. When one team was leading the game, players often held the ball without attacking until the game ended. This often meant that the other team had to make intended fouls to ensure turnovers. As a result, the basketball games were essentially free throwing contests. To eliminate this problem and increase the pace of the games, the Board of the NBA decided to introduce the 24-second rule (24s Rule) from the 1954—55 season, which restricted attacking time for each team. In the next season, the average scores for NBA games increased to 93.1 points, compared to 89.5 in the previous season. Implementation of the 24s Rule is considered to have been the most effective measure in ensuring the survival of the NBA. Furthermore, the NBA's introduction and implementation of three-pointers also helped ensure the continued vivacity of NBA games. This rule extended the defence zone to a wider scoring line, so that attacking sills, such as cut in and pick and roll, were easier to accomplish. The three-pointer leads to a lot of clutch games and has been behind many great moments in NBA history. Another useful innovation is Spirit Shooting and Slam Dunk, which are the two most popular programmes at the annual NBA All-Star Weekend. In summary, these reforms contributed significantly to making NBA games more attractive and lively and have thus helped ensure the continuance of the league(Bjarkman, 1992: 52-75; Jordan et al., 2000: 98-101; Kirchberg, 2007: 67-85).

The fourth factor in the NBA's endurance was its commercial development through franchises mergers, expansions, and relocations. The NBA began to expand its territory to cities in the western U. S. For instance, in 1960, the Lakers decided to move to Los Angeles from Minneapolis where they had been located for 13 years. Two years later, the Philadelphia Warriors moved to San Francisco, which was a revolutionary move because of California's large population, potentially a big market for sports consumption(Bjarkman, 1992: 76-95; Jozsa, 2006: 81-105; Kirchberg, 2007: 59-66; Jozsa, 2011). The NBA's expansion was simultaneously a strategy designed to help it win in its competition with another professional basketball league, the American Basketball Association(ABA). The ABA was founded on 1 February 1967. Former superstar George Mikan was hired as the ABA's first president. Most of the ABA's teams were located in those western cities that the NBA had deserted or not yet gained a foothold in, such as Denver, Indianapolis, Dallas, and Houston. Compared to NBA games, ABA games placed more emphasis on freestyle and fast breaking. However, for geographical reasons, the ABA could not compete with the other major professional sports leagues, i. e. the MLB, the National Football League(NFL), and the NBA. As a result, after nine years' competition with the NBA, the ABA was dissolved due to increasing deficit. By contrast, the NBA now owned 18 teams in most big cities throughout the country. On 18 June 1976, the Board of the NBA put through a solution for a merger with the ABA. The Denver Nuggets, the Indiana Pacers, the New York Nets, and the San Antonio Spurs, as well as most of the star players from other teams, joined the NBA(Bjarkman, 1992: 76-95; Jordan et al., 2000: 62-75; Jozsa, 2006: 81-105; Kirchberg, 2007: 59-121; Jozsa, 2011).

4. 2. 4 David Stern Made the Money Kingdom(1977—Present)

Although television had been an important part of American's daily lives since the early 1950s, broadcasters did not put many sports games on their schedules at first. The DuMont Television Network(DTN) first began broadcasting professional football, professional basketball, and professional baseball in the late 1950s. However, NBA games were only televised on a trial basis in the 1950s. In fact, some team owners believed that television broadcasting would actually bring down attendance. In 1962, Walton Kennedy took office as President of the NBA and signed a long-term contract with the American Broadcasting Company (ABC). NBA television broadcasting achieved unprecedented success in the 1960s. In the 1970s, however, television coverage of the NBA declined sharply, and the 1979—1980 NBA Finals were televised as a"tape delay"broadcast(Bjarkman, 1992: 30-95; Sarmento, 1998; Jordan et al., 2000: 36-37, 98-101; Kirchberg, 2007: 39-66; Jozsa, 2011).

Worse still, even though there was a wider marketing territory and more brilliant basketball players in the league, the NBA encountered financial difficulties in the 1970s and early 1980s. First, overexpansion of the league had resulted in an excessive number of games and a lower quality of play. Second, tensions between the league and players grew as players' salaries were increasing even though most teams were still losing money. Third, the organizational structure was incapable of managing the league. In 1980, there was a staff of 40 working in the NBA Headquarters, among whom just one person was responsible for public relations and three were in charge of media distribution and marketing. The staff were not large enough to cope with the growing business, especially its market expansion. Fourth, the worst impact came from the negative image associated with violence and drug use among the increasing number of African-American players, who accounted for 75 per cent of all NBA players in the 1978—79 NBA season (Bjarkman, 1992: 96-117; Sarmento, 1998; Jordan et al., 2000: 30-37; Kirchberg, 2007: 39-108).

Under these circumstances, the league needed an injection of new life and new direction, both of which were provided by David Stern, a graduate of Columbia University Law School who had been working for the NBA since 1978. In 1980, Stern became the NBA's executive vice-president and earned his chair as its fourth president on 1 February 1984. After taking office, Stern began to reform the league. He advocated a series of innovative management rules and regulations, including the introduction of free agency system, anti-drug agreements, and the Collective Bargaining Agreement. In addition, he established NBA Properties and NBA Entertainment (Bjarkman, 1992: 118-139; Jordan et al., 2000: 30-37; Kirchberg, 2007: 132-161). Another of David Stern's masterstrokes was the introduction of star promotion. He worked towards a reimagining of the league with his new "spokesmen", "Magic" Johnson and Larry Bird. This plan proved to be successful and saw the rise of a new generation of NBA stars like Michael Jordan and Patrick Ewing. NBA All-Star Weekends provided a useful platform, especially after the dunk contest of 1984 and three-pointer shootout of 1986. Stern's star-promotion strategy was an immediate success in terms of media exposure, and television ratings increased by 12 per cent between 1981 and 1983, whereas these figures for other major American professional sports leagues continued to drop. In the 1989—1990 season, more than 700 regular games were broadcast by local television stations, 35 per cent more than that in the 1985—1986 season. Cable television broadcasts during that period also increased by 39 per cent(Bjarkman, 1992: 118-165; Jordan et al. , 2000: 20-25, 30-37; Batchelor, 2005: 243-254; Jay, 2006: 180-216; Kirchberg, 2007: 162-201) .

Commercial sponsors were important participants in Stern's star-promotion strategy. For example, in 1985, Nike launched Air Jordans, a new line of sneakers named after Michael Jordan. This was the first time in sport history that sports shoes had been given a player's name. Nike also hired the renowned film director Spike Lee to make the advertisements for Air Jordans. Lee used an alien theme to highlight Jordan's basketball skills as he flew across the screen with his Nike sneakers. Endorsements with Jordan doubled sales of Nike shoes between 1987 and 1989, which reached USD 1. 7 billion(EUR 1. 25 billion) . In the early 1990s, 40 per cent of all sportswear in America was produced by Nike(Bjarkman, 1992: 118-165; Jordan et al. , 2000: 20-25, 30-37; LaFeber, 2002: 75-188; Batchelor, 2005: 243-254; Jay, 2006: 180-216; Kirchberg, 2007: 162-201) .

Since David Stern's revolution of the league, the NBA has enjoyed a period of significant prosperity with NBA merchandise sales, advertising revenue, and television agreements making huge profits. The NBA dominates American professional basketball and is one of America's four major professional sports leagues alongside the MLB, the NFL and the NHL. As one of the most successful sports leagues in the world, since the late 1980s the NBA started to expand its business to other countries.

4. 3 Sport Development in the PRC

4. 3. 1 Red Sport and the Centralized Sport System(1949—1976)

The Features of Sport Development. In the PRC, sport has always been associated with pragmatism and utilitarianism. The ambition of Communist China to use sport as a means of implementing political ideology began as early as its establishment in 1949. The All-China Sport and Physical Education Congress took place on 26 and 27 October, immediately after the establishment of the new republic in 1949(Hong, 1999; Fu, 2007: 6-125; Hong, 2008; Wei et al. , 2010; Hong & Huang, 2013) . Zhu De, the commander-in-chief of the People's Liberation Army(PLA) and vice-chairman of the central government, outlined the role that sport ought to play in the future:

> Sport is a significant component of education and health. The central government must give it its place in building socialism...and it should serve the people, and the purposes of national defence and health. Chinese people, including students, peasants, workers, citizens, and soldiers, should all participate in physical exercise and sport activities of all kinds. (Zhu, 1950)

The Preparatory Committee for the All-China Sports Federation(PCACSF) was established at the conference and Feng Wenbin, secretary of the Communist Youth League(CYL), was elected as its first director. He announced three tasks for the PCACSF at his inauguration, one of which was to establish a national sports organization (Feng, 1950). In 1952, the PCACSF formally changed its name to the All-China Sports Federation(ACSF), a semi-governmental organization which functioned under the leadership of the central government and the CCP. It followed the"Common Program of the Chinese People's Political Consultative Conference", and helped the government to organize and promote physical education and sport. The objective was to improve people's health, and to serve the purposes of national defence and state-building. Zhu De was elected as the honorary president of the ACSF (ACSF, 1952; Hong, 1999; Fu, 2007: 6-125; Hong, 2008; Wei et al., 2010; Hong & Huang, 2013).

Soon after its establishment, the general secretary of the ACSF, Feng Wenbin, wrote to the IOC and the International Sports Federations(ISF) to inform them that from then on the ACSF would represent China in international sport affairs (Tan, 2005: 416). In 1954, the IOC formally recognized the ACSF. In the same year, the Central National Defence Sport Club(CNDSC) was established under the ACSF. This semi-governmental system played a significant role in the development of Chinese mass sport and military sport in the early 1950s. Some 30,505 local sport associations were established throughout the country and memberships reached 915,150 by 1956(Hong, 1999; Fu, 2007: 6-125; Hong, 2008; Wei et al., 2010; Hong & Huang, 2013).

However, China's political dispute with Taiwan and the Soviet Union's victory over Western Europe and the U. S. at the Helsinki Olympic Games in 1952 demonstrated that the ACSF was unable to meet the central government's political needs in terms of utilizing sport to restore the nation's prestige in international politics. After the Helsinki Olympics, Rong Gaotang, head of the Chinese Olympic delegation, visited the Soviet Union to learn about its centralized sport system, and reported his findings to the Chinese Communist Party Central Committee in April 1952 (Hong, 1999; Fu, 2007: 6-125; Hong, 2008; Wei et al., 2010; Hong & Huang, 2013).

In September of the same year, Ma Xulun, the Minister of Education, submitted a similar report to the Government Administration Council. The two reports came up with the same proposal. It was argued that the ACSF was merely a semi-governmental organization which did not have enough power to lead sport development and physical education in China. In order to further promote sports in China and to win recognition on the international sports stage, an influential sports organization with authority, like the Ministry of Sport in the Soviet Union, was needed. Both reports suggested that the central government should establish a national governing body for sport under the Administration Council of the Central Government and that Marshal He Long should be appointed its leader(Hong, 1999; Li & Zhou, 2002: 52; Fu, 2007: 6-125; Hong, 2008; Wei et al., 2010; Hong & Huang, 2013).

The proposal was approved by the central government. In November 1952, the State Physical Culture and Sports Commission(SPCSC) was formally established following the Soviet Union model. It was a governmental ministry with the same status as other ministries like Education, Finance, and Commerce, all directly under the leadership of the State Council. At the same time, local sport commissions were established successively at provincial, municipal, and county levels throughout China. These sport commissions were governed by the SPCSC in terms of sport policy making and implementation, but under the direct leadership of local government in terms of human resources, budgeting, and general operation. Thus, a top-down governmental system took shape. It soon took over from the ACSF as the dominant power in governing Chinese sport(Hong, 1999; Fu, 2007: 6-125; Hong, 2008; Wei et al. , 2010; Hong & Huang, 2013) .

Under SPCSC system, mass sport developed rapidly in the late 1950s, particularly during the Great Leap Forward and following the implementation of the *Ten-Year Guideline for Sports Development* issued by the SPCSC in 1956. This Guideline aimed to promote mass sport and competitive sport simultaneously and to reach world levels within a decade. The major target was to "have four million people achieve the standard of the Labour and Defense System(LDS) , and to cultivate eight million active athletes and five thousand elite athletes in ten years' time"(SPCSC, 1958) . By mid-1958, inspired by the booming campaign in agriculture and heavy industry, the SPCSC believed that "the goal of surpassing the capitalist West has stimulated the development of sport ... [and that] the old Guideline no longer suits the current situation and will reduce people's enthusiasm" (Fu, 2007) . Therefore, the SPCSC revised the Guideline in September 1958, and now required "150-200 million people to achieve the standard of the LDS, and aimed to cultivate 50-70 million active athletes and 10-15 thousand elite athletes"(Fu, 2007) . The revised T*en-Year Guideline for Sport Development* was approved by the CCP Central Committee in September 1958 (Hong, 1999; Fu, 2007: 6-125; Hong, 2008; Wei et al. , 2010; Hong & Huang, 2013) .

In 1960, the CCP changed its slogan to "Readjustment, Consolidation, Replenishment, and Raising Standards". In 1961, the SPCSC revised its policy on producing elite sports players(SPCSC, 1982: 60, 72) . The government determined that its limited resources should be used to provide special and intensive training for young athletes with the potential to compete on the international sporting stage. Under this policy, a centralized sports system which aimed to produce a few elite sports stars took shape. In 1963, the SPCSC issued its *Regulations for Outstanding Athletes and Teams* in an effort to improve the system. Following instructions from the Ministry, a search for talented young athletes took place in every province(SPCSC, 1982: 102). Meanwhile, 10 of 43 sports were designated key sports: athletics, badminton, gymnastics, swimming, football, basketball, table tennis, shooting, weightlifting, and skiing(SPCSC, 1982: 103). This marked a key turning point in the Chinese sport ideology and system, changing the sport system's focus from"two legs walking"(elite and mass sport) to"one leg walking" (elite sport only), as the Chinese saying goes(Hong, 1999; Fu, 2007: 126-296; Hong, 2008; Wei et al., 2010; Hong & Huang, 2013).

The advent of the Cultural Revolution, however, heralded a tumultuous period for Chinese sport. This was a political movement initiated by CCP leader Mao Zedong. Mao believed he was losing control of the party and that his revisionist enemies had changed the colour of the Party from red(communism) to black(capitalism and revisionism). His aim for the Cultural Revolution was to regain and consolidate his power and to prevent China changing its colour(Hong, 1999). In matters of sport, the focus ultimately turned to the relationship between elite sport and mass sport. The former was regarded as the representative of bourgeois and capitalist ideology and the latter as communist and proletarian. Mass sport thus survived and maintained a steady pace of development(Hong, 1999; Fu, 2007: 297-386; Hong, 2008; Wei et al., 2010; Hong & Huang, 2013).

As a result, the SPCSC, which had regarded elitism in sports as a promising solution for building China's international image within a shortest possible time in the planned economy system, broke down. The Revolutionary Communist Central Committee, the State Council, and the Central Military Commission(which took over the top governing chair from the SPCSC) jointly issued a *Military Order* on 12 May 1968 disbanding the SPCSC, including the CNDSC, and the provincial and local sports commissions. He Long, the Sports Minister, was accused of neglecting mass sport and of supporting a revisionist and capitalist sport policy. He was condemned, jailed, and died in prison in 1975. PLA officers and soldiers were sent to replace sport administrators. More than 1,000 sport administrators from the SPCSC were sent to a May Seventh Cadre School in Shanxi Province to be "re-educated" through physical labour. The administrators and coaches of provincial and local sports commissions were also sent to the countryside to be re-educated (Hong, 1999; Fu, 2007: 297-386; Hong, 2008; Wei et al., 2010; Hong & Huang, 2013).

The whole elite sport training system in China was dismantled. Sports schools were closed down. Provincial and local sports teams were disbanded and national squads stopped participating in international competitions. Sports facilities were destroyed by the Red Guards and revolutionary rebels. Sports stadia became venues for denunciation meetings. Top athletes, renowned coaches, and sports scientists and scholars were condemned as counter-revolutionaries, capitalist-roaders, and rightists and suffered mentally and physically. Some of the athletes even died in the violent revolutionary storm of the Cultural Revolution. For example, three famous world-class table tennis players, Rong Guotuan, Fu Qifang, Jiang Yongning, committed suicide in 1969 as they could no long endure the torture they had been subjected to by the revolutionaries (Hong, 1999; Fu, 2007: 297-386; Hong, 2008; Wei et al., 2010; Hong & Huang, 2013).

The situation began to change after the "Ping-Pong Diplomacy" of the early 1970s, which developed for political and diplomatic reasons when China felt threatened by the Soviet Union and sought to cultivate the U. S. as a new ally. Sport was used to open the channels of communication with the western powers.

In February 1973, the SPCSC was restored to power to govern Chinese sport under the State Council. The provincial and municipal sport commissions were rebuilt accordingly to implement the political strategy and sports policy of the central government and the SPCSC(Hong, 1999; Fu, 2007: 387-417; Hong, 2008; Wei et al., 2010; Hong & Huang, 2013).

The Features of Basketball Development. Basketball had been a very popular sport in China since its introduction in the late 1890s and remained so after the establishment of the PRC. "Fazhan Tiyu Yundong, Zengqiang Renmin Tizhi"(to promote sport and enhance people's body) was the slogan for mass sport adopted by the new communist Chinese government. Basketball soon emerged as a national game, and was practiced at all levels. He Long once claimed, "San Da Qiu Bu Fanshen, Wo Si Bu Mingmu!"(I won't die with peace without the booming of football, basketball, and volleyball), which demonstrated the Chinese government's determination to promote basketball, among other sports (Zhong, 1989: 47-60; Li et al., 1991: 91-96). In fact, basketball soon became one of the sports utilized by the CCP for building the country's reputation on the international stage. Even before the formal announcement of the new government on 1 October 1949, a basketball team was assembled by the CYL to attend the World Student Games in Hungary from 14 to 28 August. The team was coached by Mou Zuoyun. During the six years from 1949 to 1955, Chinese basketball teams participated in 16 international games, helping the CCP to establish mutual relationships with other countries, as well as impressing the world with its active enthusiasm in joining world sport, even though the teams generally performed quite poorly in these games(Zhong, 1989: 47-60; Li et al., 1991: 91-96).

The Chinese government began to place particular emphasis on elite basketball as one of the sports with the potential to gain international prestige for the country. The ACSF turned to the Soviet Union to learn about their model. In 1950, a basketball delegation from the Soviet Union, including 21 expert coaches and prominent players, was invited to share their experience in promoting basketball. The visit lasted for more than two months, and 33 games were performed in eight cities, including Beijing, Shanghai, Guangzhou, Wuhan, Shenyang, Tianjin, Nanjing, and Harbin. After the tournament in Beijing, the ACSF held four symposia on developing basketball in Beijing and invited the Soviet Union delegate to introduce their sport system and training methods in basketball, particularly in relation to the formation of an offense and defence system. The delegate was also asked for suggestions on the further development of Chinese basketball. In addition, the ACSF sent the Bayi army team to Bulgaria, Poland, and Romania to learn from their training models in 1954. The national teams were sent to the Soviet Union to be trained under soviet coaches in the same year(Zhong, 1989: 47-60; Li et al., 1991: 97-100).

The 1950s saw a nationwide debate on improving Chinese elite basketball based on the lessons learned from the Soviet Union. At the First National Athletic Training Conference, held in Tianjing from 21 to 31 March 1955, the director of the Competition Department of the SPCSC, Li Menghua, stated that training in Chinese basketball should focus on "positivity, initiative, and speed". This sparked an extensive debate among basketball coaches throughout the country. Following Wang Yongfang, who published a review of the Beijing Basketball Games in the *Evening Post*, Xu Li wrote an article for *New Sport* that focused on the fast-breaking system displayed during basketball games. Other basketball instructors, such as Wang Shan, Guo Shouting, Zhang Zipei, and Wu Chengzhang, shared their own viewpoints in *New Sport*, emphasizing the development of basketball tactics, especially fast-breaking, which greatly informed Chinese basketball training in the coming decades(Zhong, 1989: 47-60; Li et al., 1991: 110-122).

Furthermore, as part of the government's focus on elite basketball, domestic basketball competitions of all levels were held extensively by the ACSF(and later the SPCSC) in the 1950s. In May 1951, the first National Basketball and Volleyball Tournaments were held in Beijing, featuring eight basketball teams from North China, East China, Northeast China, Central China, Southwest China, Northwest China, the PLA, and the railway company. The first ever National Basketball Tournament took place in Beijing between 25 October and 10 November 1955. Fourteen men's teams and 9 women's teams took part in the tournament and the best players were selected for the national teams(Zhong, 1989: 47-60; Li et al., 1991: 97-100).

In order to win more international games and improve domestic basketball competitions, the SPCSC and local commissions also set up basketball teams at every level in the 1950s, as well as setting up basketball departments in sports colleges. Training courses for the national men's and women's teams, called Central Training Course Basketball Teams, were established in 1952. The men's teams were coached by Mou Zuoyun, who had studied athletic training methods in America. The women's teams were coached by Wu Xuanzhao, who was born in Guangzhou and had taught basketball to female players in Hong Kong for many years. In the same year, the SPCSC established six sports colleges in Beijing, East China, Central China, Northwest China, Northeast China, and Southwest China, each of which contained a basketball department responsible for instructing local basketball teams and recruiting and training elite basketball players for national matches. Basketball teams were formed in the military at roughly the same time. By the end of 1952, there were 16 basketball teams with about 200 players in the military(Zhong, 1989: 47-60; Li et al., 1991: 97-100).

As a result of these efforts, the number of provincial and military regional teams participating in the National Jiaji(Premier) Tournament rose to 20 in 1956, with a further 54 teams taking part in the National Yiji(Secondary) League Competition. In 1959, 29 basketball teams took part in the 1st National Games. To further improve China's elite basketball from grass-root level to the national team, the SPCSC instituted a postgraduate basketball course in Shanghai Sports College in 1957. Renowned Soviet Union basketball player Laguna Vista was hired to chair the course with the assistance of veteran Chinese basketball coach Li Zhenzhong. Most of the 25 attendees later became important figures in Chinese basketball history(Zhong, 1989: 47-60; Li et al., 1991: 97-100).

A decade after the debut of the Chinese national basketball team on the international stage in Hungary, another series of matchup games between the two countries were held in 1959. It marked the first roll out of China's elite basketball teams. The Hungarian national team was one of the strongest team in Europe and had ranked fourth in the last European Championship Games. The Chinese national team, the Bayi team, and the Beijing team, however, won all four games over the visitors in Beijing, Tianjing, Shanghai, and Shenyang. Another series against the Czechoslovakian national team in the same year also saw the Chinese national team win five out of eight games(Zhong, 1989: 47-60; Li et al., 1991: 97-100).

However, as with other sports, the Chinese basketball system, particularly at the elite level, broke down during the Cultural Revolution. During this disastrous political movement, all basketball competitions, both national and international, were abolished by the red power(Hong, 1999). A number of basketball athletes, coaches, referees, and other contributors to elite basketball were sent to May Seventh Cadre Schools in the countryside to be re-educated(Li et al., 1991: 161). The early 1970s saw the overall recovery and consolidation of the basketball system, a development that occurred as the result of two significant events. One was Comrade Jiang Qing granting an interview to visiting American basketball players in 1972(Li et al. , 1991: 161) ; the other was the attendance of CCP's central leaders, including Prime Minister Zhou Enlai, at the 1972 Five Ball Games Meeting. In the same year, the SPCSC set out a three-year plan for basketball, volleyball, and football. According to the plan, the men's national team should contend for a spot in the top ten teams in the world and aim to be first in Asia within one year, and then for a position in the top eight in the world within two years. The women's national team should strive for a place in top five in the world and be first in Asia within one year, then to be in the top 3 in the world within two years (Zhong, 1989: 86-99; Li et al. , 1991: 154-158). Although this aim seemed to overestimate the national teams' competence and skills, the plan drove the development of Chinese basketball for more than a decade. By the end of the year, the SPCSC had assembled the national teams and six top-level basketball teams in Beijing, Shanghai, and Jilin. In early 1973, a further eight teams were established in Jiangsu, Liaoning, Hebei, and Tianjin. National basketball games, basketball competitions in the National Games, and army games began to take place again from 1973(Zhong, 1989: 100-175; Li et al. , 1991: 211-237).

In summary, sport development in pre-reform China was organized, both at Party and state administration level, in a vast hierarchy with power flowing down from the top. Between the late 1940s and the late 1970s, the national governing body, the ACSF/SPCSC, was responsible for the formulation and implementation of sport policy, the administration of national sports programmes and organizations, training elite athletes, and organizing national and international competitions. The model for the Chinese sport administrative system reflected the political and diplomatic strategies and wider social system in China. In this period, sport was seen as a useful tool for the government to improve the country's international image, as is reflected in the development of basketball(Hong, 1999; Hao, 2008: 5-70; Hong, 2008; Wei et al. , 2010; Hong & Huang, 2013) .

4. 3. 2 "Juguo Tizhi"and the Paradoxical Sport Reformation (1977—Present)

Mao's death in 1976 brought an end to the Cultural Revolution. The Third Plenary Session of the 11th Central Committee was held in September 1978 and marked the beginning of a new era for China. The Maoist"class struggle-oriented" political policy was replaced by economic reform and an"open-door" policy. It was hoped that, through economic reform and communication with advanced countries in the west, China would catch up with the west and again become a strong, modernized country. Sport administration in Chinese sport also underwent institutional transformation in the new era, highlighting the importance of public involvement in governing China's mass sport. Meanwhile, government leadership was retained in elite sport. According to the *Decisions about the Reformation of the Sports System(Draft)* issued by the SPCSC in 1986, the proposed structure of China's sport governance was that mass sport should be promoted by a variety of public organizations in different sectors with support from the sports commissions, but that elite sport should continue to be managed by the state but in co-operation with some public organizations. The purpose of this strategy was to transform the state-centralized sport governance model to a mix of state centralization and public involvement-a new model. (Hong, 1999; SPCSC, 2006: 92; Fu, 2007: 387-417; Hong, 2008; Wei et al. , 2010; Hong & Huang, 2013)

There was only mediocre progress in mass sport due to the lack of public interest but the reform in elite sport began apace. The SPCSC held a national sports conference in 1980 and officially established its strategy for the future development of sport. Wang Meng, then Sports Minister, stated that, on the one hand, China was still a poor country and was restricted in terms of the amount of money it could invest in sport. On the other hand, elite sport was an effective way to boost China's new image on the international stage. Therefore, the solution was to bring elite sport into the existing planned economy and administrative system, which would assist in the redistribution of the state's limited resources towards medal-winning sports(Wang, 1982). It was hoped that the international success of Chinese athletes would in return bring pride and hope to the nation, which were badly needed in the new era of transformation(Rong, 1987; Hong, 1999; Hao, 2008: 5-70; Hong, 2008; Wei et al., 2010; Hong & Huang, 2013).

In 1982, the SPCSC started to reallocate its governance power within the committee to carry out this strategy. Previously, three major departments had operated under the SPCSC on the general management of athletes, military sports, and ball games(both team sports and individual sports). However, in 1982, this structure was reorganized into six departments named Competition Sport Departments One to Six. Each was responsible for certain sport events(Hong, 1999; Hao, 2008: 5-70; Hong, 2008; Wei et al., 2010; Hong & Huang, 2013).

The purpose of this was to cover all the Olympic sports and to centralize all resources to ensure victory in international competitions. It was a successful strategy which brought immediate success at the 1984 Los Angeles Olympic Games. After a 32-year absence from the Olympics, China won 15 gold medals and was placed fourth in the Olympic medals table. Although the success in Los Angeles was partly attributed to the absence of the Soviet Union and the Democratic Republic of Germany, it nevertheless excited many in China, from government officials to ordinary citizens. (Hong, 1999; Hao, 2008:

5-70; Hong, 2008; Wei et al., 2010; Hong & Huang, 2013). In addition, this centralized training system prompted the Chinese national basketball teams to secure a dominant place in Asian basketball and has made them competitive worldwide since the late 1970s. The national women's team achieved third place at the 9th Basketball World Championship for Women in 1983 in Brazil. The men's team came ninth in the FIBA World Championship in Spain three years later(Zhong, 1989: 100-175; Li et al., 1991: 211-237). "Develop elite sport and make China a superpower in the world" became both a slogan and a dream for the Chinese people.

The Chinese government had captured the national competitive spirit and wanted to capitalize on the inspiration of the Olympic victory for the Chinese people. The Society of Strategic Research for the Development of Physical Education and Sport produced the *Olympic Strategy* for the Sports Ministry in 1985. This strategy clearly stated that "elite sport is the priority". It aimed to use the nation's limited sports resources to develop elite sport in order to ensure that China would become a leading sports power by the end of the 20th century. The strategy was the blueprint for Chinese sport in the 1980s and 1990s and the target was primarily the Olympics(Hong, 1999; Hao, 2008: 5-70; Hong, 2008; Wei et al., 2010; Hong & Huang, 2013).

Wu Shaozu, the Minister of Sport from 1990 to 2000, claimed that "the highest aim of Chinese sport is success in the Olympic Games. We must concentrate our resources on it. To raise the flag at the Olympics is our major responsibility" (Wu, 1999: 64). To achieve this goal, the government had to channel much of its limited resources into providing special and intensive training for potential gold medallists. Chinese athletes benefited from both the "whole country support elite for the sport system" and the *Olympic Strategy* and achieved very satisfactory results(Hong, 1999; Hao, 2008: 5-70; Hong, 2008; Wei et al., 2010; Hong & Huang, 2013).

The turning point from purely politicization to the commercialization of sport came in 1992 when a major reform policy was initiated by Deng Xiaoping (1904—1997). On his South Patrol in February 1992, Deng urged the central and local governments to speed up economic reform at all levels of Chinese society. In response, the SPCSC held a conference in Zhongshan City, Guangdong Province, in November 1992 to discuss how to speed up the reformation of Chinesesport. At the conference, Wu Shaozu pointed out that the major objective of sport reformation was to further transform the sport system, which was still based on a planned economy, to a new system, which would be based on the market-oriented economy. Sport, he maintained, should stand on its own feet (Hong, 1999; Cao, 2008: 46-152; Hong, 2008; Wei et al., 2010; Hong & Huang, 2013).

Based on the principles espoused at the Zhongshan Conference, the SPCSC issued *The Proposal of Moving Ahead of Sport Reformation* on 24 May 1993, which officially announced a market-oriented reform policy. In this policy document, the SPCSC, for the first time, publicly advocated the commercialization of sports and the promotion of a sports industry. Wu Shaozu claimed:

> The Chinese sport system must reform without delay. The strategy for the reform is to commercialize sport and to integrate sport into people's daily life. This includes people paying for sports and exercise, privately sponsored sport, the club system, and promotion of a commercial sports market. (Hong, 1999; Wei et al., 2010)

Later the same year, the Third Plenary Session of the 14th Central Committee was held and the establishment of the socialist market economy was approved. Soon thereafter, in the sport field, the SPCSC set out the framework for the future development of Chinese sport and three decrees were issued in June 1995: the *Olympic Strategy*, the *National Fitness-for-All Programme*, and the *Development of Sports Industry and Commerce Outline*. These decrees were designed to be integrated, and were expected to support each other to form a new model for sport policy and practice in China (Hong, 1999; Cao, 2008: 46-152; Hong, 2008; Wei et al., 2010; Hong & Huang, 2013).

The implementation of the three decrees simultaneously legitimized the involvement of the public, who would exert power in the form of non-governmental federations, and indicated that the role government played in the Chinese sport system should be transferred to leveraging, rather than commanding or direct control. Therefore, the SPCSC changed its name to the GAS in 1998. With the change of the name, a new administrative structure for Chinese sport was introduced as part of the wider reformation towards a market economy (see Figure 4-1). At the same time, 14 sports management centers were set up to work with 41 national sports federations to manage 56 sports under the GAS (Hong, 1999; Cao, 2008: 46-152; Hong, 2008; Wei et al., 2010; Hong & Huang, 2013).

However, as is depicted in Figure 4-1, non-governmental sports federations did not yet preside over sport administrations. There was a slow transference of power, and the practical power in governing Chinese sport was effectively old wine in a new bottle. Nevertheless, there has been a tendency and trend away from direct government control of sport. This reflected the globalizing trends in sport in which the market actor plays an active role. In the Chinese context, the shift has been gradually taking place but with "Chinese character".

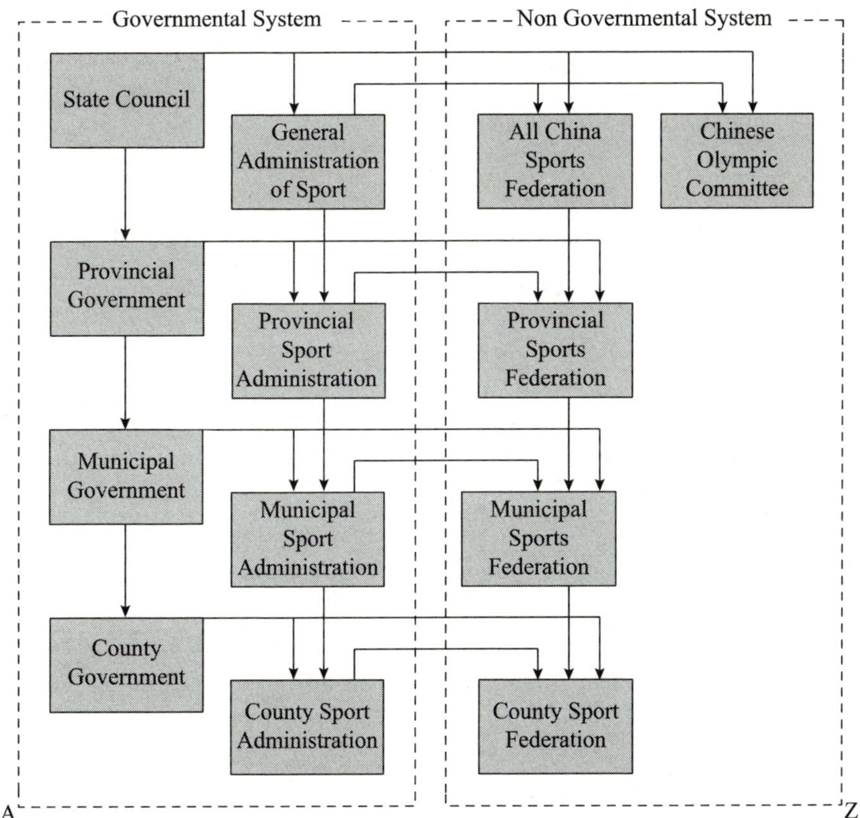

Figure 4-1 The Current Administrative Structure of Chinese Sport Governance

4.4 Conclusion

This chapter has provided a historical overview for this research. It covers two parts: the development of the NBA and of sports in the PRC. Basketball, which was invented by Naismith in 1891, has been professionalized since 1896. A number of professional basketball leagues and barnstorming basketball teams operated throughout the U. S. before the Second World War. Since the late 1940s, the NBA has implemented an array of strategies and regulations to produce the highest-quality professional basketball games in the world. Between the late 1940s and 1980s, the four NBA Commissioners and the league's team owners primarily concentrated their marketing efforts and financial investment on the development and growth of professional basketball in the North American market(Jozsa, 2004: 103) . Therefore, the NBA has gradually come to dominate the basketball market in North America. Since the late 1980s, NBA Commissioner David Stern has activated an international campaign to energize and transform his organization and thereby expanded the league's business and market power into nations across the global, including China(Jozsa, 2004: 103) .

In the PRC, sport has always been associated with pragmatism and utilitarianism. The Chinese government's determination to achieve a global presence and reach first place in the international sports tables has resulted in the centralization of sport governance power since 1949 in order to get elite athletes into world competitions. Although a reformation in sport has been undertaken to combine government power and public investment since the early 1980s and the determination was made in the early 1990s to promote the establishment of a sports industry, public power still has to give way to government interest under the"Juguo Tizhi" and the *Olympic Strategy*. The decisive power in governing Chinese sport is still in the government's hands.

Despite this paradoxical relationship between state and private interests in sport policy-making, the Chinese sports industry and demand in sports consumption are steadily growing with the deepening of the market economy. Meanwhile, it might be argued that sport has gradually become detached from national affinity for Chinese people. This is to a great extent a result of the explosive promotion of western sports commodities, including the NBA, under the trend of sport globalization. This unique sport environment raises an interesting question about the interplay between the NBA and Chinese basketball in the era of globalization which will be examined in the coming chapters.

Chapter 5. Globalization and the Governance of Chinese Basketball

5. 1 Introduction

This chapter examines the interplay between the grobalization of the NBA in China and the glocalization of Chinese basketball from a political and institutional perspective. McDonaldization, a concept that Ritzer(1998; 2007b; 2002, 2010) derived from Max Weber's work on rationalization, is the major process of his grobalization theory in this realm. He considers that the fast-food restaurant, especially the pioneering and dominant McDonald's chain, is the contemporary paradigm of the rationalization process and thus he terms this process McDonaldization. Fundamentally, McDonaldization involves"an increase in efficiency, predictability, calculability and control through the substitution of non-human for human technology"in the fast-food chain(Ritzer, 1998: VII; 2002; 2007b; 2010) . Supported by the increasing number of scholars who are applying this conceptualization to various social structures and institutions, such as higher education(McUniversity), politics(McCitizens and McFascism), and religion(Ritzer, 2002), the applicability of McDonaldization has been expanded to a global level, and beyond the scope of the fast-food chain. In short, McDonaldization accounts for the growing power of a specific form of governance and its increasing influence throughout the world.

This chapter looks at how McDonaldization is taking place in basketball in China. The chapter firstly depicts how this process set off with the NBA's grobal power. The second section looks at how Chinese basketball has been McDonaldized. The third section, with the purpose of looking for evidence of glocalization, explicates the extent to which Chinese basketball's governance model has been McDonaldized by the NBA, and the extent to which the NBA's governance model has been de-McDonaldized in the Chinese context. To establish this, a comparison is conducted. Elements included in the comparison are adapted from Borland's(2006) taxonomy of the stakeholders and infrastructure of a professional sport league, namely: governing authority, product market, capital market, and labour market.

5. 2 The Grobalization of the NBA and the Internationalization of Basketball

Since the Second World War, the sport world has been changing more rapidly and profoundly than ever before. Most significantly, it has been commercialized to a great degree following the collapse of amateurism across western countries. Furthermore, this trend has been reinforced by certain historical forces since the late

1980s: the collapse of Cold War Olympic politics between capitalist countries and socialist countries following the collapse of the Soviet Union(Jarvie, 2006: 99) ; the evolution of free market economies in many countries; and the emergence of new cable and satellite systems and television networks that supply their broadcast services throughout the world(Jozsa, 2004: 109) . As a result, capitalist sports are aggressively seeking profits and markets domestically and globally and have consequently accelerated the pace of sport globalization. The NBA is a typical capitalist sporting entity.

5. 2. 1 The NBA-FIBA McDonald's Tournament

The strategy behind the NBA's first global appearance was to showcase its superiority in world basketball. The Olympic Games and the FIBA World Championships seemed two natural channels via which to do this. NBA President Stern had to put considerable effort in generating publicity before the IOC allowed NBA players to compete. A couple of months before the 1988 Summer Games got under way in Seoul, the NBA sent the Atlanta Hawks to the Soviet Union to participate in a basketball exhibition with the soviet Olympic team (Kirchberg, 2007: 200) . A few weeks later, the NBA sponsored a pickup game at the Civic Center in Rhode Island between the U. S. Olympians and a group of NBA stars including Michael Jordan, Magic Johnson, Larry Bird, Isiash Thomas, and Patrick Ewing. This game was won by the Olympians with a score of 90-82 (Kirchberg, 2007: 200) . However, the NBA did not push FIBA to let NBA stars participate in the Olympics. As Russ Granik, Deputy Commissioner of the NBA from 1985 to 2006 and a principal figure in U. S. basketball throughout the 1990s, stated:

> Though in 1987 the NBA did have talks with FIBA, those talks were not about the Olympics. We were never engaged in any conversations of any kind about the NBA playing in the Olympics until FIBA had actually adopted it. Playing in the Olympics was not something we aspired to or thought about much. (Cunningham, 2009: 289)

In the summer of 1987, Gary Bettman, vice-president and general counsel of the NBA, acknowledged that the NBA would be delighted if the Olympic opportunity arose, but he also made clear that the NBA was not pushing for it(Cunningham, 2009: 289). What David Stern and FIBA's Secretary General Boris Stankovic focused on was how FIBA's international rules would fare against the NBA's style in actual game play(Kirchberg, 2007: 201).

Thus, the McDonald's Open was born. This annual international basketball tournament, sponsored by McDonalds', was the first substantial platform linking the NBA to world basketball. On 23 October 1987, the Milwaukee Bucks defeated Tracer Milan of Italy 123-111 in the opening game of the first McDonald's Open held at the Milwaukee Arena. Then the Bucks defeated the Soviet Union National Team, 127-100, in the championship game of the tournament (NBA China, 2011a). In the next year, the tournament's name was changed to the McDonald's Championship and was held in Madrid, Spain. The Boston Celtics defeated Real Madrid 111-96 at the Palacio de Deportes to win the championship(NBA China, 2011a). In its third year, the McDonald's Championship moved to Rome, Italy. This time, the Denver Nuggets represented the NBA against the Spanish champions, F. C. Barcelona, the European champions, Jugoplastika Split, and Philips Milan. The Nuggets defeated Barcelona in the tournament opener and went on to defeat Jugoplastika Split 135-129 to capture the title(NBA China, 2011a).

Although NBA teams continued to win the McDonald's Championship titles in the early 1990s, it had also become clear that the NBA teams' superiority was no longer a given. The reason was that, to a great extent, basketball's global popularity on a pro level had spread substantially, aided by the migration of former NBA players to Europe in order to continue their careers. These players also influenced the style of their European teammates(Kirchberg, 2007: 202). For instance, the New York Knicks, led by NBA All-Star Patrick Ewing, played in a thrilling overtime in the opening game to beat the Scavolini Pesaro in the 1990 McDonald's Championship, which took place in Barcelona, Spain(NBA China, 2011b). The 1991 McDonald's Championship saw the Los Angeles Lakers travel to Paris, France, to compete against the host team CSP Limoges, as well as Joventut Badalona and Slobodan Dalmacija Split of the former Yugoslavia. With Magic Johnson at the helm, the Lakers defeated Joventut Badalona to gain the title with a close win of 116-114 on the scoring board(NBA China, 2011b). As a result and in order to safeguard its winning record, the NBA announced in 1995 that in future the winner of the NBA Finals would represent the league in the McDonald's Championship. In the late 1990s, NBA teams continued to win first place thanks to the participation of the NBA champions(NBA China, 2011b).

5. 2. 2 The American Dream Team

The principal figure pushing for the acceptance of NBA players into the Olympics and World Championships was FIBA's General Secretary, Boris Stankovic. In 1984, the IOC passed legislation allowing individual sporting federations to determine eligibility guidelines. Since then, international sporting bodies have tended to let professionals participate in the Olympics. In fact, the idea of allowing professional basketball players to compete in the FIBA games and the Olympics had been floating around since the 1972 Olympic Games in Munich, when the Soviet team shocked the U. S. by winning the gold medal. At that time, some countries had been spending years training their national teams for the Olympics while the U. S. teams were still composed of college students(Kirchberg, 2007: 200; Cunningham, 2009: 209) . Unfortunately, the dominance of American basketball players at the professional level and the commercial impact that NBA players might have on the Olympics remained a concern for some FIBA committee members, who ultimately voted against allowing NBA players to compete in the 1988 Summer Games(Kirchberg, 2007: 200; Cunningham, 2009: 209) .

However, the opposing votes did not put a halt to Stankovic's efforts, and he continued to express his desire to see NBA players at the Games. In his opinion, allowing NBA stars to participate in the Games would raise the quality of the Olympic basketball competitions(Kirchberg, 2007: 200; Cunningham, 2009: 210) . He predicted that it would be only a matter of time before FIBA made NBA players eligible:

> Our executive board suggested to our full congress in July that all basketball players should be allowed into our world championship and the Olympics. It went to a vote of 31 opposed, 27 in favour, and 14 abstentions. So it is shelved until after 1988, but we will introduce it again, and by 1992 the new rule will exist, I think. All pros will be welcome. (Cunningham, 2009: 210)

The poor performance of the 1988 U. S. Basketball Olympians, who finished the Games in third place, served as an instant catalyst to make Stankovic's prediction come true. On 7 April 1989, the FIBA committee finally voted to drop restrictions on professional basketball players competing in international events. The NBA's response to FIBA's decision was prompt this time. At the end of the same year, the NBA joined the ABA/USA, the United States' representative in FIBA, who changed its name immediately to USA Basketball(NBA China, 2011b). On 21 September 1991, USA Basketball announced the roster of the "Dream Team"for the 1992 Olympics: Charles Barkley, Larry Bird, Patrick Ewing, Magic Johnson, Michael Jordan, Karl Malone, Chris Mullin, Scottie Pippen, David Robinson, and John Stockton. USA Basketball added Christian Laettner and Clyde Drexler to the team on 12 May 1992. Except for Christian Laettner, who was a top college player at that time, all the team members were superstars from the NBA (NBA China, 2011b).

The"dream"really started from there. When the 1992 U. S. Olympic basketball team arrived at the luxurious Hotel Ambassador in Monte Carlo a week before the Barcelona Games, the hotel's managers scoffed at suggestions that they might need to enhance security, assuring all that their experience hosting rock stars and kings and princesses had sufficiently prepared them for the task at hand(Cunningham, 2009: 318). Needless to say they were wrong. The experience in Monte Carlo gave Olympic officials an indication of the enormous response the team would receive in Spain. So, when the American players journeyed from Monte Carlo to Barcelona, Olympic officials flew them first to Reus and then had them driven to Barcelona. This allowed the team to avoid the 3, 000 to 4, 000 fans who had gathered at the host city's airport in anticipation of its arrival(Cunningham, 2009: 318). Still, once the players made it to the Olympic Village to get their accreditations, a mob enveloped them. Rather than shield the players from the onslaught of people, security guards angled for autographs, as did many of the other Olympic athletes(Cunningham, 2009: 318-319).

5. 2. 3 Commercialism and the New Order of World Basketball

The changes the Dream Team wrought on basketball went far beyond the basketball court where NBA superstars won the gold medal with an average of 43. 8 points over other teams. It brought the relationship between the Olympics and advertising to a new level. The following illustrates clearly Dream Team and NBA stars' potential to draw sponsors' interest:

> Forty different companies, spending an estimatedUSD 40 million [EUR 30 million], emerged as promotional partners of the squad. Fourteen of those went through USA Basketball, paying USD 750, 000 [EUR 563, 000] apiece. Twenty-six others aligned themselves with the team using separate licensing agreements. These figures do not even count the money spent by corporations like Nike, which circumvented official association with USA Basketball by making its own ads featuring the stable of six Dream Team players it had under contract: Jordan, John Stockton, David Robinson, Charles Barkley, Scottie Pippen and Chris Mullin. These Nike men were featured in commercials depicting them as larger-than-life cartoon characters smashing everything in their path. Also excluded from the figures is the spending of numerous publications like *Sports Illustrated* and *USA Today*, which, in an effort to increase readership, set up games and gift promotions centered on the Dream Team. Sponsors, official and otherwise, hocked everything from posters to peanuts, hats to pins, shoes to trading cards; if you could imagine it, you could probably find it. (Cunningham, 2009: 319)

Within four years of the Barcelona Olympic Games, the NBA, whose marketing division USA Basketball had been hired to market its gear, made U. S. Olympic basketball team apparel available in 17 countries, compared to seven in 1992. By 1996, the league's total global merchandise sales amounted to roughly USD 3 billion (EUR 2. 25 billion), up from USD 1 billion(EUR 0. 75 billion) in 1990(Cunningham, 2009: 319).

Since the early 1990s, American basketball's growing dominance in world basketball and the overwhelming globalizing commercial force enveloping the NBA stars have jointly contributed to the reconstruction of a new world order in basketball. Soon after the Barcelona Olympic Games, the world witnessed the NBA's aggressive expansion beyond the U. S. borders. Canada was naturally the first territory the NBA targeted because of its unique advantage in terms of geographical proximity and the well-established mutual co-operation between North American countries in other professional sports leagues. On 4 November 1993, the NBA Board of Governors awarded an expansion franchise to Toronto, Canada. After that, the Board awarded another expansion franchise to Vancouver, increasing the total number of NBA teams to 29. The Toronto Raptors and the Vancouver Grizzlies started playing in the NBA in the 1995—1996 season (Jordan et al., 2000: 289). Since then, no NBA team from outside the U. S. has been awarded membership. Instead, the NBA has set up a number of overseas offices to expand and administrate its local business throughout the world. On 10 March 1992, the first ever NBA office outside North America, NBA Asia, was established in Hong Kong. Within the five years from 1992 to 1997, ten overseas offices had been set up outside the U. S. (Jordan et al., 2000: 187). Table 5-1 lists the overseas offices the NBA set up between 1992 and 1997.

Table 5-1 List of NBA Overseas Offices Established between 1992 and 1997

Date	Office	Location	Continent
March 1992	NBA Asia	Hong Kong	Asia
June 1992	NBA Australia	Melbourne, Australia	Oceania
July 1993	NBA Europe, S. A. Geneva	Geneva, Switzerland	Europe

Continued

Date	Office	Location	Continent
January 1994	NBA Japan	Tokyo, Japan	Asia
March 1995	NBA Canada	Toronto, Canada	North America
April 1995	NBA Latin America	Miami, United States	North America
January 1996	NBA Europe S. A. London	London, United Kingdom	Europe
August 1996	NBA Europe, S. A. Paris	Paris, France	Europe
August 1997	NBA Europe, S. A. Barcelona	Barcelona, Spain	Europe
August 1997	NBA Taiwan	Taipei, Taiwan	Asia

Source: adapted from NBA China(2011b).

Furthermore, the NBA's commercial success and global impact has provided an example to basketball governing bodies around the world. Since the late 1990s, an increasing number of countries have begun to learn from the NBA's governance model in running their own professional basketball leagues. For instance, Mexico adopted the NBA's franchise system with the establishment of the National Professional Basketball League in 2000. This type of North American sports league model is also becoming more and more popular in Asian countries. The major professional basketball leagues in Asia employ this governing model, including the Korean Basketball League(KBL, est. 1997), the Iranian Basketball Super League(IBSL, est. 1998), The Super Basketball League(SLB, est. 2003) in Chinese Taipei, the Chinese Basketball Association League(CBAL, est. 2003), and Japan Basketball League(JBL, est. 2005). The next section will focus on the CBAL's adoption of the NBA's governance model.

5. 3 Glocalization and the Professionalization of Chinese Basketball

5. 3. 1 The Jiaji League Period(1995—2003)

Participation in international sports competitions and organizations has long received the approval of the Chinese government, but to pursue internationalization by conducting internal reformation is pioneering. Three forces enabled the CBA to undertake the breakthrough reformation aimed at achieving professionalization and marketization in the mid-1990s: the emergence of China's market economy, the *Olympic Strategy*, and the ruling accepting professional players into FIBA Championships and the Olympics.

Football was at the forefront of the professionalization of Chinese sports in 1990s. Compared to football, the possibilities for the professionalization of Chinese basketball were even brighter since it had been much more competitive internationally and reputable nationally since the late 1980s. In the 1990s, the national teams finally achieved high world rankings. The women's team won second place in the 1994 FIBA World Basketball Championship while the men's team gained eighth place. In addition, basketball was the most played sport in the country at that time. A report based on the *Fourth Survey on the Statistics of China's Playgrounds*, conducted by the Planning and Financing Department of the SPCSC in 1995, showed that the number of basketball grounds was higher than that of any other sport(SPCSC, 1995) . Nevertheless, basketball was facing cutbacks due to the *Olympic Strategy*. As a result, and following in the footsteps of the Chinese Football Association(CFA) , on 20 December 1994, Yang Boyong, Deputy Chairman and General Secretary of the CBA, announced at the annual meeting for basketball training that the nationwide basketball tournament would be arranged"professionally"from 1995 so as to be self-supporting and internationalized(Yang, 1994) .

The primary approach of the CBA was to reformat the traditional premier nationwide competition, the Top-Eight Basketball Tournament, into a professional basketball league called the Jiaji League(1995—2003) . The research literature tends to refer to two dominant models of sport governance for professional team (the North American and European models) though such a characterization may actually mask the level of heterogeneity that exists particularly in Europe. A European model is characterized by a tiered structure adopting a promotion and relegation system to determine participation in a hierarchy of leagues or divisions, which is also known as an"open"league. A North American model is characterized by its use of franchises and limited membership, which is also known as a "closed"league. The CBA picked the former. Under the European model, which is used in European football, the ultimate objective of major European clubs is to qualify as often as possible for international or Europe-wide contests. Thus, this model is often regarded as a"competitiveness maximized"model. The European model was adopted by the CBA in the league's first decade. During this period, the league was divided into two conferences, North and South, with four to eight teams in each conference. The two lowest performing teams in each conference were required to compete in an extra elimination tournament. The highest performing team in one conference competed with the bottom team from the other conference. The two winning teams are retained in the league while the two losing teams would be relegated to the lower division league, the Yiji League(Secondary League). The top two teams in the Yiji League in each season would be promoted to the Jiaji League in the next season. Table 5-2 lists the team changes in the Jiaji League from the beginning of the league in 1995 to 2003.

Under this model, however, the Jiaji League remained a sports tournament rather than a professional sports league except for the fact that it operated a home-and-away system. The 1995 season, which was also called the Top-Eight Tournament or "Initial Season", lasted for only two months, from February to April. Participating teams included the top eight teams from the 1994 national tournament. Before the 1995—1996 season started, the CBA made a number of changes to the league to allow it to be further professionalized. For instance, the CBA issued three regulations on league management, player-transfer methods, and club management. However, the league was still far from"professionally"run. At the 1999 National Routine Meeting for Basketball, Xu Chuan, vice-director of the CBMC①, pointed out that: 1) financial support for the league was insufficient and that they should develop new ways to open the games up to the market; 2) under the strict promotion/relegation system, some clubs focused only on short-term interest, while the long-term development of the clubs was being ignored; 3) marketing of the games should be emphasized so as to attract more basketball fans; 4) the quality of the games was low and young players did not have enough chances to compete in the contests; and 5) the players' salaries, particularly those of international players, were going up too fast, resulting in some clubs having to scramble for players and using improper methods to ensure their participation in the league (Xu, 1999).

① The CBMC was set up in 1998. The Competition Department under the CBMC has been in charge of the professional league since then.

Table 5-2 Team Changes in the Jiaji League

Season	Team No.	Teams Promoted	Teams Relegated
1995	8		Jilin Province, Guangzhou Army.
1995—1996	12	Shandong Province; Shenyang Army; Zhejiang Province; Jiangsu Province; Guangdong Hongyuan Basketball Club; Air Force Army.	Nanjing Army; Qianwei Army.
1996—1997	12	Sichuan Province; Shanghai Municipality.	Zhejiang Province; Jinan Army.
1997—1998	12	Zhejiang Province; Jinan Army.	Shenyang Army; Sichuan Province.
1998—1999	12	Beijing Aoshen Basketball Club; Sichuan Lanjian Basketball Club.	Jinan Army; Sichuan Lanjian Basketball Club.
1999—2000	12	Nanjing Army; Qianwei Army.	Hubei Province; Nanjing Army.
2000—2001	12	Shuangxing Jijun Basketball Club; Shenbu Anshan Basketball Club.	Jinan Army; Shenyang Army.
2001—2002	13	Shanxi Dongsheng Basketball Club; Shenzhen Runxun Basketball Club; Xinlang Lion Basketball Club.	Beijing Aoshen Basketball Club; Shenzhen Runxun Basketball Club.
2002—2003	14	Xinjiang Guanghui Basketball Club; Beijing Aoshen Basketball Club; Hong Kong Feilong Basketball Club.	Xinlang Lion Basketball Club. Hong Kong Feilong Basketball Club.

Source: adapted from the Jiaji League's schedule from 1995 to 2003.

5. 3. 2 The North Star Project and the Emulation of the CBA since 2004

Inspired by the speech of Xu Chuan, Li Yuanwei, then vice-director of the CBMC, turned his attention to alternative league models. He led a group of officials to Japan and Korea in 2011 to learn how the JBL and KBL were run. When Li Yuanwei took over as first chair of the CMBC in 2003, he decided to further restructure the league's organization and launched a commercialization reformation for the proposed CBAL①, drawing upon the North American professional sports leagues model. Later in the same year, he led another group of officials to the U. S. to learn how the NBA and the National Collegiate Athletic Association (NCAA) were run. In Li Yuanwei's opinion, the NBA's approach to running a professional basketball league held some useful insights for the Chinese. From his examination of the NBA, Li Yuanwei contended that there were some major problems that the CBA needed to address(Li, 2004b): 1) the property rights and investment systems of the Jiaji were ambiguous, and an incentive system was needed to attract market investment; 2) the league and the clubs had not yet formed an interest incorporation; 3) the league lacked marketing strategies and managerial professionals; 4) sponsors were not loyal enough to the league; and 5) clubs and players were not loyal enough to the fans so younger fans tended to follow the NBA.

In order to solve these problems, in September 2003, the CBMC set up the Research Group for the Operation of Basketball Professionalization. The members of the group included: Liu Yumin, vice-president of the CBA and a famous basketball player for the women's national team; Dr Bao Mingxiao, a renowned professor in the field of sport economics and industry in China; Xu Jicheng, a senior corre-

① The name of Jiaji League was changed to CBAL in the 2003-2004 season.

spondent for Xinhua News who was familiar with the NBA's operation and a part-time interpreter for the national basketball teams; Yan Xiaoming, a graduate of Tsinghua University who had served as general manager of the Liaoning Panpan Basketball Club for eight years. The group hired Shanghai Qianrui Sports Business Consultancy Co. Ltd to conduct a comprehensive market survey. After the six-month survey of basketball-related sponsors, fans, clubs, players, venues, and media had been completed, the research group and Qianrui Co. came up with a detailed market report. In addition to this report, the CBMC looked at the governance models of 13 professional sports leagues, including the NFL, the NBA, and England's Premier League. On 5 April 2004, the CBMC put forward its proposal for the North Star Project(NSP).

The aims of the NSP were to: 1) make the CBAL the best professional sports league in Asia and a world-class professional basketball league; 2) develop the CBAL into a sound brand; 3) make the CBAL a cradle for the development of high-level basketball players; 4) have CBAL teams win more international basketball competitions; and 5) make the CBAL a persistent and profitable sports league (CBA, 2004b). The Project was set to be carried out in three stages: 1) Stage I. Initialization(2005—2008): to improve the league and its clubs' capabilities in managing, operating, and developing the CBAL. This stage aimed to build a normative model(closed-membership, franchise system) for the professional sports league; 2) Stage II. Development(2009—2012): to clarify the property of the CBAL and attract long-term marketing partners; 3) Stage III. Consolidation (2013—2015): to conclude the works of the two previous phases and to come up with further strategies to aid in running the league. It was also emphasized that the aims of the NSP should be accomplished in this phase(CBA, 2004b).

Despite the fact Li did not agree that the implementation of the NSP amounted essentially to cloning the governance model of the NBA, he admitted that his reformation was applying "NaLai ZhuYi" from(selectively emulating) the NBA. He stated:

> We always encourage the values of openness. Chinese professional basketball is in its infancy. We should learn something useful from the NBA and also take into account our national characteristics. That is why I strongly advocate' NaLai ZhuYi'. The useless [experience and practice] from the NBA which is not suitable for our country should be rejected. (Li, 2007)

5.4 Conflicting Globalization: A Professional Sports League with Socialist Characteristics?

In this section, I will examine to what extent the NSP has emulated the NBA's governance model, and to what extent Chinese basketball has generated heterogeneity in the Chinese context, through the method of transnational comparison. To begin with, it is necessary to introduce the stakeholders and infrastructure of a professional sports league. Borland(2006) suggests that production of a sporting competition incorporates at least three main components: 1) the set of players able to be chosen to participate in the sporting competition; 2) the clubs that will organize players into teams to participate in the sporting competition; and 3) a sporting league or association[①] that will have responsibility for the design and management

① The term league has many different meanings in different areas around the world. Usually, a league is a group of teams that play each other during the season. It is also often used for the name of the governing body that oversees the league. To avoid confusion, the author will use the term "association" to indicate the governing body that oversees the league since both the NBA and the CBA use this term.

of the sporting competition(Borland, 2006: 22). These components, according to Borland, frame the production of team sports into four segments: governing authority, labour market, capital market, and product market(see Figure 5-1). This section will go through each of these segments in turn.

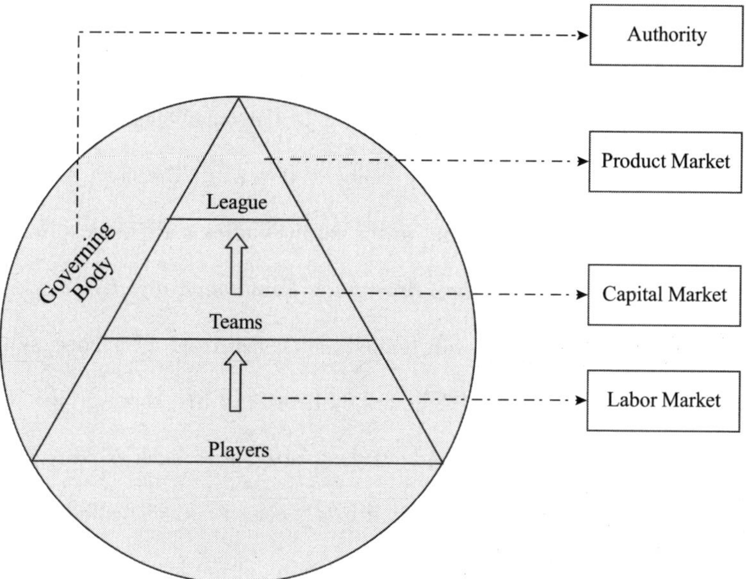

Figure 5-1 Stakeholders and Infrastructure of a Professional Sports League

5. 4. 1 Governing Authority

The two fundamental issues concerning governance of a sports league pertain to the power structure of the league and teams and the extent to which an independent authority plays some role in the operations of the league(Noll, 2003). It is no secret that Chinese sports are under the tight control of the government. For Li, the major objective of his reformation of the CBAL in terms of governance was to weaken the government's power and pass the power to the market. To achieve this, the NSP would establish a government-independent company(CBA Company) with a Chief Executive Officer(CEO), a governing authority like the NBA's Board of Governors, and a commissioner(CBA, 2004b).

The Board of Governors and the Commissioner of the NBA. The NBA is a typical North American closed-membership professional sports league, under which member teams are independently owned and managed, and collectively create the league as a joint venture for co-ordinating their league activities(Noll, 2003). In these leagues, a commissioner or president is the chief operating officer of the league, while team owners make up the board of directors. The chief executive may have considerable expressed authority in the league's rules and policies(Noll, 2003). According to the *National Basketball Association Constitution and By-Laws*, the NBA is"an unincorporated association with limited membership and a franchise system, not organized or operated for profit"(1989 cited by Lentze, 1995). However, the NBA also conducts some business through its independent subsidiaries, such as NBA Properties, Inc. Owners of the 30 teams are organized in a common council, called the Board of Governors, which oversees and controls the operation of the league. A meeting of the Board of Governors is usually convened in November every year. However, interim meetings may be held for unexpected events(Lentze, 1995).

The NBA Commissioner is elected by the owners and possesses disciplinary power, dispute resolution authority, and decision-making authority, including the power to appoint other officers and committees, unless the collective bargaining agreement renders specific powers to other authorities(Lentze, 1995). By comparing the role of Commissioner of a North American sports league to a CEO in a corporate-governance company, Lentze (1995) points out that even though the Commissioner in a sports league is the chief executive officer and an employee of the league structurally, which is the same as a CEO in a corporate company, the scope of his/her authority goes far beyond the authority typically set out under the usual corporate governance model. In particular, he argues, the Commissioner does not act under the control of the league. Rather, the league owners, as the Commissioner's factual employer, are actually themselves subject to the disciplinary power of the Commissioner(Lentze, 1995). In short, the employed NBA Commissioner represents an autonomous authority within the internal structure of the league, uncontrolled by its principal team owners. The reason for this power allocation, according to Lentze(1995), is that the sole power of the commissioner in the league may decrease interference in relation to judicial issues.

It can be concluded that governance power of the NBA is centralized in a Board of Governors, who are the team owners, and a selected, independent Commissioner. In contrast, power allocation in Chinese basketball is more complicated. Therefore, the relationship between the governmental and non-governmental basketball systems that are both involved in the governance of the CBA, the CBMC, and the Chinese Basketball Association League Committee(CBALC) needs to be clarified. Figure 5-2 shows the relationship between them.

The CBA. The CBA was established under the leadership of the ACSF in June 1956. Although the CBA had claimed jurisdiction over all Chinese basketball activities from late 1950s, it was not until 1978 that the CBA was endowed with power in administrating Chinese basketball when it was granted an official charter. The CBA was finally recognized by the FIBA while Taiwan's membership was successfully exempted in 1976. According to its current structure, the CBA is defined as a nationwide non-governmental sports organization with independent juridical qualification and a non-profit association comprising a hierarchical system of associations in the provinces, autonomous regions and municipalities, and basketball associations or corresponding sports departments in the PLA. It is a member of the ACSF, an Olympic organization recognized by the China Olympic

Committee, and the only legitimate Chinese organization qualified to participate in the FIBA and the Asian Basketball Confederation(CBA, 1998b) .

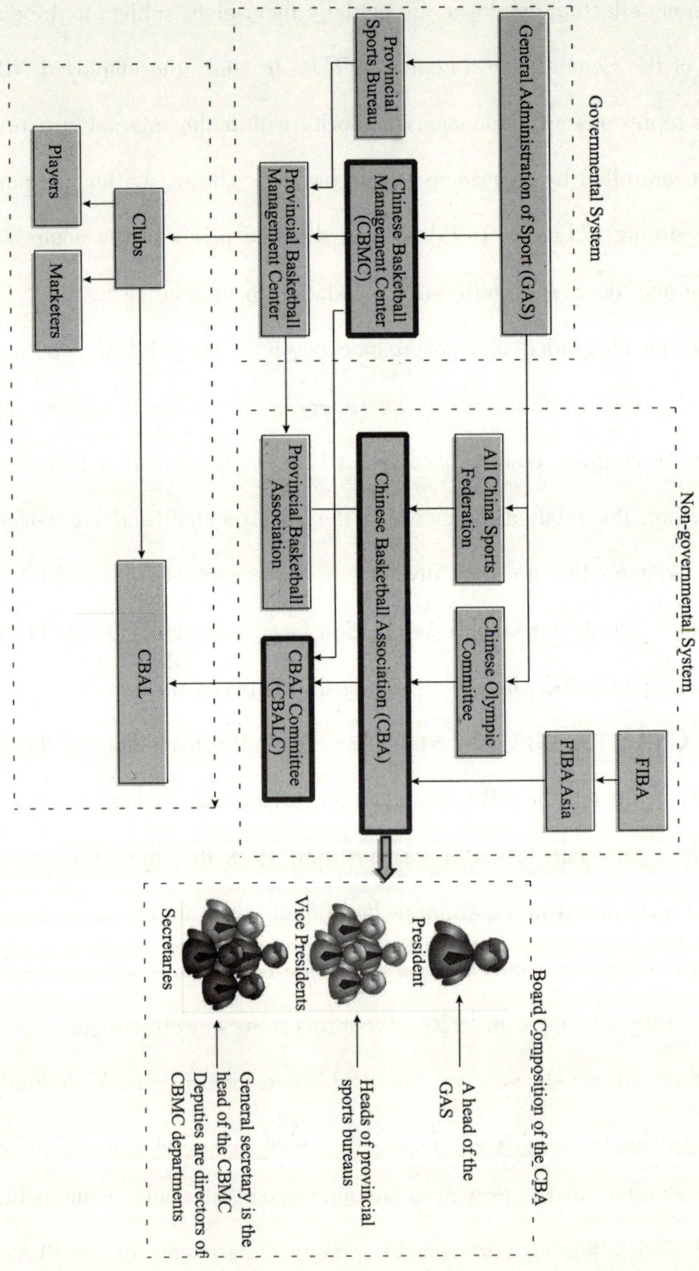

Figure 5-2 Governance Structure and Power Allocation of Chinese Basketball

The national committee is the premier seat of power of the CBA, and is constituted of a standing committee and a group of representatives(normally heads) from lower basketball associations, e. g. provincial basketball associations. In practical operation, the representatives' voices are very weak except for their right to present a proposal during the national committee meeting convened every four years(CBA, 1998b). Routine affairs are overseen by the standing committee, which is composed of a group of governmental officials including a president who is a head of the GAS, vice-presidents who are the heads of provincial sport administrations, the head of the CBMC, a general secretary who is also the head of the CBMC, and vice-secretaries who are the directors of the CBMC departments (CBA, 1998b).

The CBMC. The CBMC, the deputy secretarial office for the CBA, was established on 24 November 1998 as a unit subordinate to the GAS. Therefore, the heads of the CBMC are appointed by the GAS. The CBMC had seven departments under Li's leadership, as shown in Figure 5-3.

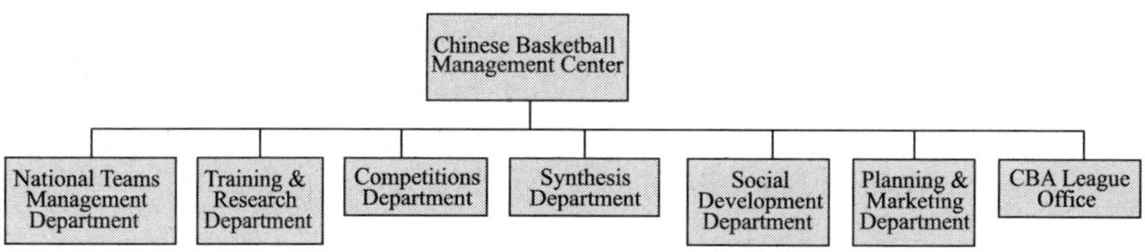

Figure 5-3 Administration Structure of the CBMC(2005—2009)

1. The National Teams Management Department is responsible for building and managing men's and women's national basketball teams at all levels. This is the CBMC's foremost role and includes organizing, instructing, and supervising training, managing international match schedules, the selection of coaches, and providing backroom services and ethics education

for the national teams. The four most influential international basketball events are the basketball competitions in the Olympic Games, the Asian Games, the FIBA World Basketball Championship, and the Asian FIBA's Basketball Championship. The CBMC also organizes the Stanković Continental Cup and some other friendship matches, inviting or visiting other countries every summer. For example, the men's national team played 37 games in the summer of 2007. (CBMC, 2011)

2. The Training and Research Department is responsible for enhancing the performance of Chinese elite basketball, instructing and managing basketball clubs across the country, conducting scientific research on basketball, and the assessment and registration of athletes and coaches (CBMC, 2011).

3. The Competition Department is responsible for scheduling all nationwide basketball competitions, including the National Basketball League (NBL, est. 2005), the Women's Chinese Basketball Association, the women's Yiji (secondary) League, other national and international basketball tournaments and matches in major sports events, as well as the development of referee teams (CBMC, 2011).

4. The Synthesis Department plays a supporting role and deals with issues of regulation across the CBMC, foreign affairs, publicity and media, financing, party affairs, censorship and audit, personnel, labour unions, properties and security (CBMC, 2011).

5. The Social Development Department is responsible for building basketball reserve squads, organizing youth training camps, and managing mass participation, as well as for the registration and management of lower basketball associations (CBMC, 2011).

6. The Planning and Marketing Department is responsible for planning and developing the Chinese basketball industry, marketing basketball competitions relating to the national teams and professional leagues, and managing the properties of the CBAL(CBMC, 2011).

7. The Professional League Office is responsible for all the affairs of the CBAL(CBMC, 2011).

Taking the composition of the CBA and the CBMC into account, it is seen that the CBMC is the true and dominant power in governing Chinese basketball. It should also be noted that the CBMC is under the pressure to meet the interests of the GAS, which is still focused on winning international games. Such a Chinese-style personnel formation is also evident in the broader public sector, known as"One Personnel, Two Boards"(dual portfolio). In other words, the CBA is still under control of Chinese government in spite of its embrace of non-governmental principles in the charters.

The CBALC. The creation of the CBALC in 2005 was a substantial development in the first phase of the NSP. It is comprised of the following stakeholders: 1) representatives from each club(usually the chairperson or the CEO), external experts in law, economics, or financing relating to the basketball industry, and the directors of departments in the CBMC; 2) a vice-president, as well as the president of the CBA and the vice-director of the CBMC; and 3) a president, as well as the president of the CBA and the director of the CBMC(CBA, 2005c). According to the NSP's second-phase plans, this Committee would be reorganized into the CBA Company, a shareholding corporation, as follows: 1) the Company would be administrated by the Board of Governors, and representatives of the CBALC would take over chairs on the board; 2) a non-official CEO(like the NBA's Commissioner) would be hired to oversee the board; 3) the CBMC would only take certain chairs on the board, while its major responsibility would be overseeing the national teams; and 4) fixed stock would be shared by all stakeholders(CBA, 2004b).

Unfortunately, Li's NSP was disbanded by Xin Lancheng, a conservative, who replaced Li as the director of the CBMC after the Beijing Olympics. Xin announced his governing principles as soon as he assumed office in early 2009, which were obviously intended to negate Li's previous reform(Xin, 2009). He contended that: 1) the objectives of the NSP were at odds with the reality of Chinese basketball. The role of local sport administrations and governments are ambiguous while the clubs' power was excessive. Thus, going forward, the CBMC would insist on the government having a leading role in administrating Chinese sports and make good use of the"Juguo Tizhi"in the market economy; 2) the league's membership determination and withdrawal mechanism should be improved. All the clubs would be required to register with local sport administrations and basketball management centres so as to be supervised by local governments; 3) the league should give priority to the training arrangements for national teams and the CBAL season should be cut back. Meanwhile, the per-game on-court time of international players should be shortened to guarantee the cultivation of potential youth players; 4) the ideological building for the clubs and the players should be enhanced; and, 5) media propaganda should be further controlled(Xin, 2009).

As a result, the CBALC and the CBMC's League Office were dismantled. The CBAL is once again administrated by the CBMC's Competition Department, while the CBMC as a whole prioritizes building and training the national teams. This implies that even though some manner of down-to-earth sport reformation is on the cards and remains strongly called for by Chinese sportspeople, the Chinese government will continue to monopolize the governing power in sport to serve national interest after the Beijing Olympics.

5. 4. 2 The Product Market

A product market is a mechanism that allows people to easily buy and sell products(O'Sullivan, 2003: 283). In the production process of professional team sports, the combination of contests between teams, which is normally known as a league, is the product ready to be consumed by sports fans. To emulate the NBA's product marketing model, the NSP abolished the league's promoting and relegating system before the 2004—2005 season began. According to the NSP, the CBAL also started to adopt a closed-membership system and to normalize the membership determination process. Since then, the CBAL has successfully duplicated the NBA model in formatting the league's scheduling, including organizing summer camps and pre-season games, the regular season, all-star games, playoffs, and the finals(CBA, 2004b).

The Summer Camps and Pre-season Games

1. Following the summer break, NBA teams have training camps in late September. After the training camps, a series of pre-season exhibition games are held.

2. The CBA started to organize pre-season games in the 2004—2005 season. However, the CBA does not organize a training camp during the summer. This is because the camp's function in evaluating new players and adjusting the team roster is unnecessary for most CBAL teams due to the fact that player-transferring is still inactive in the CBAL, and the new recruits normally come from within their own squads.

The Regular Season

1. There are two types of scheduling that professional sports leagues normally adopt: a round robin system or an elimination tournament. The NBA regular

season schedules use a round robin system. Currently, during the regular season, each team plays 82 games, 41 home and 41 away.

2. The CBAL regular season is also based on a round robin system. During the regular CBAL season, a team meets all other teams in the league two to three times, half of the time at home and half away. The regular season normally begins in the autumn and ends in spring, with no fixed date circulated. The time span and number of games to a great extent depend on the national teams' arrangements and the ins-and-outs of the different teams. For example, the 2006—2007season saw 50 days off in the league's schedule to allow for the national team's preparations for the Asian Games(CBA, 2006b) ; the 2007—2008 season saw the shortest ever CBAL season because of the preparations needed for the 2008 Beijing Olympics(CBA, 2007b) .

The All-Star Game

1. In February, the regular season in the U. S. is put on pause to celebrate the annual NBA All-Star Game. Fans throughout the U. S. , Canada, and on the internet submit their votes and the players receiving the most votes in each position in each conference are given a starting spot on their conference's All-Star team. Other attractions of the All-Star break include the Rookie Challenge, where the top rookies and second-year players in the NBA play against each other in a 5-on-5 basketball game; the Skills Challenge, where players compete to finish an obstacle course consisting of shooting, passing, and dribbling in the fastest possible time; the Three-Point Contest, where players compete to score the highest number of three-point field goals in a given time; and the NBA Slam Dunk Contest, where players compete to dunk the ball in the most entertaining way according to the judges.

2. In the spring, normally between the regular season and the playoffs, the

CBAL holds an All-Star Game as well. Although this event had been introduced since the first Jiaji League season, in the CBAL it is organized more along the lines of the NBA's All-Star Game. The CBAL does not divide and name the two All-Star teams by conference, but rather by geographical regions(such as south and north), colours(such as red and white), and symbolic animals(such as dragon and tiger). In the Jiaji League, the rosters were decided by the CBA or by journalists. But they are now voted for online by fans. Whoever receives the most votes in each position in each team is given a start, while bench players are appointed by the teams' coaches, who are usually hired from the two leading teams in the regular season. As in the NBA, the player with best performance during the game is rewarded with a Most Valuable Player (MVP). Other attractions like the Rookie Challenge, the Skills Challenge, the Three-Point Contest, and the Slam Dunk Contest are copied from the NBA.

The Playoffs

1. The NBA Playoffs begin in late April, with eight teams in each conference going for the Championship. The three division winners and the team with the next-best record from the conference are given the top four seeds. The next four teams are given the lower four seeds in order of success. The playoffs follow a tournament format. Each team plays an opponent in a best-of-seven series, with the first team to win four games advancing to the next round, while the other team is eliminated from the playoffs. In the next round, the successful team plays against another advancing team from the same conference. All but one team in each conference are eliminated from the playoffs.

2. The CBAL Playoffs begin one week after the regular season ends. In the Jiaji League, teams were divided into three divisions: Division 1(1st-4th), Division 2(5th-8th), and Division 3(9th-others), with each division following an elimination

tournament system to determine the rankings. The best team in Division 1 wins the championship while the two losing teams in Division 3 are relegated to the lower league. Under the NSP, the CBAL adopted an elimination tournament system. The eight best teams qualified for the playoffs. Like in the NBA, higher seeded teams availed of certain advantages. The first seed begins the playoffs playing against the eighth seed, the second seed plays the seventh seed, the third seed plays the sixth seed, and the fourth seed plays the fifth seed, so having a higher seed means a team faces a weaker team in the first round. Similarly, the team in each series with a better record in the regular season has home court advantage in all following rounds. In short, the elimination tournament pattern is the same as in the NBA except for the number of games in each series. The Jiaji League followed a best-of-five in all series. In the CBAL, the final games follow a best-of-seven pattern, whereas all other rounds follow a best-of-five pattern.

The Finals

1. The final playoff round, a best-of-seven series between the victors of both conferences, is known as the NBA Finals, which are held annually in June. The victor in the NBA Finals wins the Larry O'Brien Championship Trophy. Each player and major contributor-including coaches and the general manager-on the winning team receives a championship ring. In addition, the league awards the Bill Russell NBA Finals MVP Award to the best performing player of the series.

2. Similarly, the champion of the CBAL is presented with the Mou Zuoyun Cup[①]. The Finals are usually held in April but if the national teams' arrange-

---

① Mou Zuoyun enjoys high prestige and commands universal respect as a major contributor to the development of basketball in the PRC. The Asian Basketball Confederation awarded him a "Lifetime Achievement Award" in June 1997. The CBA awarded him a "New China Basketball Outstanding Contribution Award".

ments mean cutting short the league, they will be held earlier, in March or February. The best performing player of the series is awarded a CBAL Finals MVP. Other trophies, such as championship rings, T-shirts, and caps are also adapted from the NBA.

5. 4. 3 The Capital Market

A capital market is a market in which business enterprises(companies) and governments can raise long-term funds(O'Sullivan, 2003: 283). The main participants in the capital market for the professional team sports industry are the owners. They invest money to hire players as labour and assemble their teams into a league to collectively produce sport goods for benefits. Compared to the relatively smooth process of emulating the NBA in product market, Li's reformation in the capital market encountered much difficulty.

Ownership of Clubs. There are two types of ownership among the NBA's 30 teams: individual equity and investment syndicate equity. The individual equity ownership model of sports organizations can take one or both of the two following forms. The first form involves a single, independently wealthy owner, such as owners Mark Cuban and Michael Jordan, who can take either a passive or active role in the club's decision making(Rosner & Shropshire, 2011: 3). The second form involves a group of individuals who pool their resources to acquire ownership of the team. League rules usually require that one individual be deemed the majority owner and/or specify that one individual be labelled as the final decision maker(Rosner & Shropshire, 2011: 3). In the NBA, the majority owner's family must have a 15% stake in the team(Rosner & Shropshire, 2011: 3). In an investment syndicate owned sport team, some documents typically outline the rights and responsibilities of each investor(Rosner & Shropshire, 2011: 3). This transparent ownership structure enables NBA clubs to carry out their own business with little governmental intervention.

In contrast, governmental intervention in Chinese professional basketball has effects not only at the state level, but also at the provincial and municipal levels. As discussed earlier in this chapter, the CBAL was based on the structure of the Top-Eight Tournament, which was an annual national basketball competition between army teams and provincial teams. The best eight teams in the 1994 Tournament were eligible to participate in the first season of the Jiaji League. Before the mid-1990s, army teams were more competitive and had an advantage over other teams because the armies prioritized recruiting the best athletes in the country. Thus, the first Jiaji League season saw six army basketball teams competing in a"professional"sports league. However, since the late 1980s, public capital has been allowed and welcomed by the government in sports-related investment, particularly into non-Olympic sports such as football and basketball. Therefore, corporate investment in sport has been permitted and has been taking place since the early 1990s. The provincial basketball teams, who were confronted with heavy financial cutbacks to their government but still expected to achieve better results in the National Games, soon turned to non-governmental corporate investors, who were at the same time looking for an investment market.

Their alignment in the form of joint-venture clubs are, to some extent, resource-efficient for both stakeholders. On one side, the provincial sport administrations are able to preserve their basketball teams without worrying about finance. The corporate investors, on the other side, do not have to invest in facilities for training players, building reserve squads, or in the venues. This corporate model has resulted in the army teams lagging behind the provincial teams. By the end of the 2000—2001 season, the Bayi Army was the only army team that remained in the Jiaji League. The other army teams were either disbanded or merged with professional clubs.

With the implementation of the NSP, all CBAL clubs were required to be corporate-owned. The Bayi Army had to co-build the club with corporate investors. Since then, all clubs have been involved in the open market to a greater or lesser extent. Up until the 2011—2012 season, however, there were still six types of shareholders to be found in CBAL clubs: private enterprise, state-owned enterprise, public company, the army, sports colleges, and sport administration bodies. The property of a club is owned by one shareholder or is a joint venture between two or more shareholders. Table 5-3 shows the ownership of CBAL clubs in the 2011—2012 season.

This joint-venture ownership model has led to an unbalanced power allocation within the clubs. In the case of sport administrations as a shareholder(sports colleges are usually owned by sport administrations) , the power is in reality in the hand of the sport administration, which controls resources, including players, coaches, and venues. As such, corporate investors have difficulty having their demands met during decision-making processes. This tension between shareholders has led to a number of negative situations. For instance, when Qiu Dazong was hired as the head coach of the Jiangsu Nangang Basketball Club in July 2012, Jiangsu Sport Administration refused to provide food for him in the Xianlin Training Base. The reason given by the Jiangsu Sport Administration was that he had been hired by the club, but not by them. As a result of these tensions, it is common to see a corporate investor withdraw partnership before a season starts or even during the season.

Table 5-3 Ownership of CBAL Clubs in the 2011—2012 Season

	Club	Owner(s)	Type of Ownership
1	Guangdong Hongyuan	Hongyuan Group	Private Enterprise
2	Liaoning Panpan	Panpan Group & Liaoning Sport Admin.	Private Enterprise & Government
3	Jiangsu Nangang	Nangang Group & Nanjing Sports College	State-owned Enterprise & SportsCollege
4	Dongguan Xin Shiji	Xin Shiji Real Estate Co.	Private Enterprise
5	Shandong Huangjin	Huangjin Group	State-owned Enterprise
6	Bayi Jinlu	Fubang Group & Bayi Army	Private Enterprise & Army
7	Fujian SBS	SBS Group	Private Enterprise
8	Zhejiang Guangxia	Guangxia Real Estate Co.	Public Company
9	Beijing Shougang	Jinyu Group & Shougang Group & Beijing Sport Admin.	Public Company & Government
10	Zhejiang Chouzhou Yinhang	Chouzhou Commericial Bank & Zhejiang Sports Tech. College	Private Enterprise & Sports College
11	Xinjiang Guanghui	Guanghui Group	Private Enterprise
12	Shanghai Dongfang	Tigershark Investment Co.	Private Enterprise
13	Jinlin Longruncha	Longruncha Group & Jilin Sport Admin.	Private Enterprise
14	Foshan Longshi	Nanhai Nenggxing Group	Private Enterprise
15	Shanxi Fenjiu	Zhongyu Group	Private Enterprise
16	Tianjin Ronggang	Ronggang Group	Private Enterprise
17	Qingdao Shuangxing	Shuangxing Group & Qingdao Sport Admin.	State-owned Enterprise

Source: adapted from CBA(2012).

In addition to these issues, problems can also exist even if the clubs are entirely owned by corporate investors, and they are still unable to manage all their affairs without some intervention from local governments or sport administrations. Thisis particularly evident in releasing and contracting players, which will be discussed in the next section. Some clubs which are in co-operation with state-owned enterprises tend to be heavily dependent on the local government or sport administration. Even for those in co-operation with privately owned corporate investors, they are still dependent upon local governments. A key reason for this is that few CBAL clubs so far have been able to balance their cheque books without receiving awards or allowances from local governments or sport administrations, as one senior staff of a CBAL club, has confirmed:

> In the Jiaji League, each club spent about RMB 2 million(EUR 0. 25 million)①. In the CBAL, the expenditure of each team has gone up to between RMB 6 million(EUR 0. 75 million) and RMB 15 million(EUR 1. 88 million). The award to our champions from the municipal government is vital to balance the club's income and expenses. (Interviewee No. 26)

Therefore, dependence on local governments or sport administrations has greatly weakened the clubs' power in liaising with local governments. Apart from this, with the abolition of the NSP, all clubs are required to register with the appropriate sport administrations in order to be eligible to play in the CBAL. This further weakens the power of non-governmental shareholders.

The Formation of a Capital Market. The ownership model of the NBA franchises allows the investors to operate the clubs in market-oriented ways. By

① Approximately, 1 Chinese Yuan = 0. 125 Euro

utilizing a franchise system and territory monopoly, the NBA's capital market operates as a cartel, which has been defined as "a group of firms that organize together to control production, sales, and wages within a business" (Sage, 1998: 196). This cartel model that the NBA franchises form has ensured profit-maximization for investors. It has made the NBA teams rich entities over the past number of decades.

The CBA Company in the NSP was in reality a similar form of cartel, and looked like a promising way to profit-maximize the league and the clubs. As Li argued:

> Forming a cartel is very important for a (closed-membership) sports league to earn the maximum amount of money. In the U. S., they need tailored laws to protect the existence of the cartel. But here in China, if we set up a CBA Company, plus use our advantages from government support, we will finally make the league a money-making organization. (Li, 2007)

However, with Xin's directorship and his governing principles of "Juguo Tizhi" for international competitions, in addition to provincial or municipal administrations' tendency to prioritize the National Games, it is now difficult for Chinese professional basketball to form a profit-maximized capital market, because issues such as schedules and labour transfers come second to international games and the National Games. Nevertheless, Chinese basketball marketers are still expecting the advent of a government-detached basketball market. Yao Ming stated on The 30th China International Sporting Goods Show 2012:

> At present, each club loses RMB 20 million to 25 million [EUR2. 5 million to 3. 13 million] each season; the more we invest, the more we lose. Deducting the RMB 12 million [EUR 1. 5 million] bonus from the league,

> each team loses about RMB 10 million [EUR 1.25 million] on average. The CBAL is one of the smallest sports leagues in the world. Only 32 games are arranged for each team, 16 of which are home games. As club owners, we wish the amount could increase to 50 games or more. Only in this way can we make money from gate tickets and draw a sufficient number of sponsors. (Yao, 2012)

In the meantime, Yao suggested that a non-governmental organization, something like Li's CBA Company, should be established. He argued:

> At present, governors and investors have not yet formed an incorporation of interest groups. In my opinion, the CBAL should be governed by an independent organization, which should incorporate the power of club owners. (Yao, 2012)

Bao Mingxiao added support for Yao Ming's viewpoint:

> To achieve this, a CBA company could be set up jointly by the CBA, club owners, and other significant investors. The company would hold the sole governance power, the CBA would act as a shareholder, and their profits used to facilitate national team and mass basketball development. Meanwhile, the company would encourage the investment of public capital. It would expand China's basketball agent market and basketball market. It's not difficult to do this. The company should adopt stock system. We could consider employing a CEO as well. (Bao, 2012b)

Zhang Beihai, the manager of the Shanxi Zhongyu Basketball Club, stated: "The sports league should be market-driven, but the CBA is governmental. They should not act as both a policy-maker and a shareholder" (Zhang, 2012a). The

CEO of Infront Sports & Media China (Infront) , Ma Guoli, held a somewhat pessimistic view on Chinese basketball reformation, but he regarded Yao Ming's suggestion as viable: "It seems that the power of the CBA and the CBMC will not be taken over in the near future. But a CBA Company is possible, you see, football has such a company. I think we can also do that. "(Ma, 2012) .

5. 4. 4 The Labour Market

The labour market functions through the interaction between workers and employers (O'Sullivan, 2003: 283) . The quality of workers(the players) is the most significant determinant in the production of professional team sports. High-quality players are crucial for generating fan interest, and the allocation of players can even promote competitive balance between teams in sporting contests. Therefore, roster restocking is a matter of considerable importance and interest to the league, teams, and their fans (Quinn, 2008) . It is generally comprises a player reserve system, player mobility, and a player salary determination process.

The Player Reserve System. In the NBA, the nationwide player reserve system benefits from a large pool of grassroots and collegiate players, as well as a lower league.

1. The Amateur Athletic Union(AAU) , established on 1 October 1888, is one of the largest non-profit volunteer sports organizations in the U. S. . Basketball makes up the biggest portion of the AAU's programme, as close to 50 per cent of its more than 1. 1 million memberships are for basketball(AAU, 2012) . In high schools, basketball talents are trained in both the AAU club and schools with decent facilities, such as indoor arenas and fitness machines, and by experienced coaches, most of whom have previously played for professional basketball clubs or college teams.

2. After graduation from high school, talented young basketball players in the U. S. compete for scholarships offered by member universities of the NCAA. This intercollegiate sport system plays a significant role in keeping sports talent in the U. S. . A large number of rookies in the NBA are drafted from NCAA teams.

3. The NBA Development League, or NBA D-League (NBDL), is the NBA's official minor league basketball organization. Players can be promoted or relegated between the NBA and the NBDL. Many former NBA draftees, waived players, and undrafted players have played in the NBDL. Some of the called-up NBDL players have developed successful NBA careers after they are promoted to the NBA.

Chinese elite basketball players are selected and trained in three systems: the sports school system, the educational system, and the public system(see Figure 5-4).

1. The sports school system, formed in the 1950s, was adapted from the system used in the former Soviet Union. Under this system, young players are trained full-time in state-supported sports schools. Athletes with potential are promoted through a pyramid system from municipal-level sports schools to provincial-level or army teams, and the best are selected for the national teams. The number of players coming from this system has shrunk dramatically since the 1980s. Under the *Olympic Strategy*, a great number of provincial and municipal basketball teams were dismantled due to lack of financial support. It was reported that the count of 75 premier basketball teams and 1, 323 players in the 1980s had fallen to 41 teams and 593 players in 1993(SPCSC, 1993).

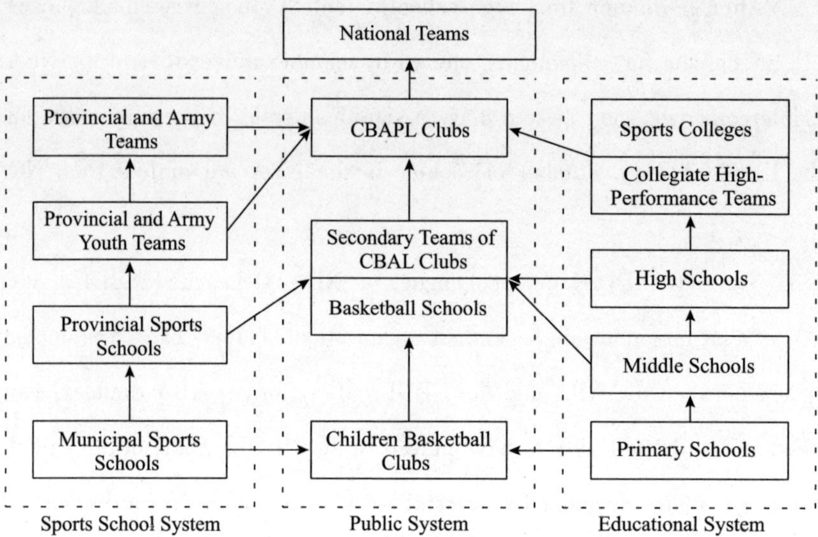

Figure 5-4 The Selection and Training Systems of Chinese Elite Basketball

2. The educational system, which is similar to the reserve system used in the U. S. , seemed to be promising for fostering elite basketball players in late 1990s. This system provides opportunities for primary and secondary school students to be recruited by sports colleges or higher-level teams, namely, the secondary teams of professional clubs and the collegiate high-performance teams. In the educational system, several basketball organizations have been set up to foster basketball reserves, such as the Chinese University Basketball Association(CUBA) , the China High School Basketball League, and the Chinese Collegiate Basketball League. However, so far, few professional players in the CBAL have come directly from the educational system. Up to 2012, there were only a handful of players recruited by CBAL teams. One senior staff in the CBMC has commented that: "China is short of training facilities and professional coaches in the schools and universities. We are unable to follow the American model"(Interviewee No. 7) .

3. As a result, hope has been turning toward the public system. The public

system, in particular the secondary teams of professional basketball clubs, has become the cradle for nurturing most young Chinese basketball talents. In the past, potential players in municipal sports schools tended to be promoted to the provincial teams or army teams, while the talents in high schools went to the college teams. In the past decade, however, the CBA clubs have put great effort into looking for young talents throughout the country to build their reserve teams. With the implementation of the NSP, the CBMC issued a standardized *Membership Regulation* which requires that:

> All clubs are responsible for building basketball squads; each club should set up or co-build at least one secondary team with at least 12 registered players. The clubs should provide at least RMB 500, 000 [EUR 62, 500] for the squad. (CBA, 2004b)

Consequently, the CBAL clubs' expansion of their reserve rosters has led to the emergence in recent years of specialized basketball schools, established with the co-operation of both the NBA and the CBA.

Player Mobility. There are three main ways that an NBA team goes about the annual business of roster assembly. The first way is to acquire new players via the NBA Draft. The NBA Draft is an annual event at which the 30 teams from the NBA can draft players who are eligible and who wish to join the league. It is processed in a reverse-order-of-finish player recruitment system (NBA & NBPA, 2005; Quinn, 2008). The second way an NBA team restocks its roster is by signing "free agents". Free agents are players who are considered under league rules to own the rights to their own services to a greater or lesser degree, and are therefore permitted to form contracts with teams for those services (NBA & NBPA, 2005; Quinn, 2008). The third method NBA teams use to assemble rosters is via inter-team trades and purchases of players whose rights are owned by other teams in the league(NBA & NBPA, 2005; Quinn, 2008) .

In Chinese professional basketball, however, a rigid player register system, which is similar to the reserve clause, is still in use to prevent mobility of players between teams. Under the reserve clause, although both the player's obligation to play for the team as well as the team's obligation to pay the player is terminated, the player is not free to enter another contract with another team. The player is bound to either negotiate a new contract to play another year for the same team, or to ask to be released or traded (NBA & NBPA, 2005; Quinn, 2008) . The reserve clause was first abolished in baseball in 1975, and other major U. S. professional sports including basketball soon followed in the late 1970s. The reserve clause system has, for the most part, been replaced by the free agency system.

According to the *Management Methods Relating to Basketball Player Registration and Mobility* issued by the CBMC:

> Upon the expiration of a contract between a player and a club, the club retains the right to sign an extending contract and register it with an appropriate basketball association for the player. The extension time depends on how many years the player has played for the club. If the player has played for the club for one to three years, the extension time is one year; if the player has played for the club for four to six years, the extension time is two years; if the player has played for the club for seven years or more, the extension time is three years. (CBMC, 2003)

According to this regulation, a player should become a free agent once the extended years are covered. In practice, however, only a very few CBAL players have succeeded in signing a new contract with another club. The major reason for this is that, in the *Statutes of the Chinese Basketball Association*, it also regulates that:

> All players participating in any national basketball competitions, including the CBAL or its youth league, must be registered with the CBA or its subordinates(such as provincial basketball associations). The club a player is playing for is authorized to execute registration with the basketball associations. (CBA, 1998b)

As a result, before signing a new contract with another club, a player should be released not only by the club, but also by the local basketball association. It should be noted, again, that local basketball associations are still under control of local sport administrations or local governments. The aim of local sport administrations or governments, however, is to the greatest extent possible to achieve high levels of performance in the National Games, which are held every four years between provincial districts. It is an important platform for the GAS to recruit athletes into the national teams. The performance that a local sport administration achieves in the National Games is normally directly associated with the financial grant that the sport administration can receive in the next national-game-cycle. It is also a very important assessment of the capabilities of the leaders of local sport administrations. As a result, the clubs, on behalf of the sport administrations, may tend to net and farm players for the sake of National Games rather than the league (Interviewee No. 11). Thus, end-of-contract CBAL players are in reality still considered in terms of the interests of local sport administrations. This power monopoly of clubs and local sport administrations has meant that inter-team trading rarely occurs.

Since inter-team trading is impractical, the CBA started employing a method for temporary inter-team exchange known as the"reverse-pick system" in 2002.

With the reverse-pick system, each club should put four players onto a collective list. Players on this list can then be picked by any club in four rounds. Each round follows a reverse order according to the club's ranking in the previous season. The lowest-ranked club is entitled to make the first pick while the champion team takes last pick. In practical terms, this player mobility system does not function as a useful method of restocking CBAL teams' rosters(CBMC, 2003). The disadvantages of this system are evident: 1) the clubs will not put their top players on the candidate list. Most listed players so far have been inexperienced players or rookies from secondary teams. Thus, they can't elevate performance of the new team in a short time; 2) most teams tend to pick their own players based on the consideration that grooming their own players seems more efficient than getting used to new lower-ranking players. It also avoids the possible loss that might occur when, once an exchanged player is getting mature, he is called back to his home/original club; 3) before the picks begin, the team manager usually informally informs other managers not to pick his players if the club wants to keep those players, which even makes the system difficult to operate(Interviewee No. 26& No. 11). Taking the 2011 pick for example, only three rookie players out of 64 on the list were exchanged with other teams through this system. One senior staff in a CBAL club also stated that:

> Few clubs are willing to trade their players. The pressure to win in the National Games is very high. For some clubs, they prefer to put their redundant young guys on the bench than to help other clubs' roster building. (Interviewee No. 15)

Echoing this position, one professor in a sports college, who is specialised in management of Chinese sports, commented:

> The CBA's transfer system is like a pool of backwater. A player-redistributing system should be adopted to balance the rosters of CBAL teams; only in this way can the league produce better basketball contests. (Interviewee No. 5)

The Player Salary Determination Process. The salary determination process used in the NBA is strictly subject to the Collective Bargaining Agreement. Players have two sources of income. Collectively, players are guaranteed to receive a fixed minimum rate of revenue in salaries and benefits from the league's entire income, which is known as "Basketball Related Income" (BRI). For example, the minimum rate for the 2011—2012 season was set at 51.15% (NBA & NBPA, 2005). Individual salaries are negotiated between the players and the clubs subject to the collective bargaining agreement in effect at the time of negotiations. Players have both minimum and maximum salaries, and both are based on how long the player has been in the league. The minimum salaries are fixed and scaled upward each season. The extent to which teams are able to negotiate with a player is limited by several factors, among which a salary cap is the most functional for each team (NBA & NBPA, 2005). A salary cap is a limit on the amount teams can spend on player contracts. The basic idea behind a salary cap is that a team can only sign a free agent if its total payroll will not exceed the cap (Humphreys & Howard, 2008: 201). The salary cap system is beneficial to professional team sports and it has been widely accepted that there are two main benefits derived from salary caps: the promotion of parity between teams, and cost control.

In the CBAL, however, there are no universal salary determination procedures, nor is there a collective salary for the players. The salaries of individual players vary from club to club and is kept confidential. There is even no normative labour contract between the clubs and the players. Worse still, unlike most other professional sports leagues in the world, where a labour union is usually set up to protect players' rights and to liaise with club managers and the league, no such union has ever been formed to protect CBAL players' rights. The tension between players and clubs on the issue of salaries has been extraordinary. Negative events occur frequently. For instance, when Mengke Bateer left the Beijing Shougang Basketball Club, he first had to retire for one year and then register to another club. Before the 2012—2013 season started, Yang Li and Wu Nan of the Jiangsu Nangang Basketball Club announced their retirement because the club had offered them unacceptable salaries. Some clubs, like the Liaoning Panpan Basketball Club, offer long-term contracts to new players to take advantage of them, such as the"5 +3"contract, which refers to the club maintaining the right to renew the player with a 3-year contract after the expiration of the first 5-year contract. The worst part of this system is that the poorly regulated labour market of the CBAL has resulted in evidently uneven competitive balance in CBAL games. In the history of the league, the Bayi Army Team(Club) dominated the first half, winning 8 championships in 12 seasons, and the Guangdong Hongyuan Basketball Club took over dominance in the other half with 8 championships in 10 seasons. The Shanghai Dongfang Basketball Club and the Beijing Shougang Basketball Club won once each in 2001 and 2012 respectively. No other team has ever won the title. Only 6 teams(clubs) have ever competed in the finals up to the 2012—2013 season.

In terms of the labour market, players in CBAL clubs are the weakest actors in the power hierarchy of Chinese basketball(see Figure 5-1). Their authority is weakened not only by the interests of the state, but also by the provincial and municipal governments' interests. With Li's NSP, an NBA-isomorphic labour market was proposed and temporarily put into practice: 1) in terms of the player reserve system, to set up a Chinese Basketball Development League under the CBAL, which would provide player reserve support for the CBAL; 2) in terms of labour mobility, to initiate a player mobility system and a player draft system; to draft a normative player labour contract for the clubs, which would be supervised by the CBA; and to employ a free agency training camp; and 3) in terms of salary determination, to create a player salary determination system, in which the collective salary of all CBAL players would be set at around 33%. This idealized reformation seemed to be a way to redress the low competitive balance of the CBAL. However, with Li's retirement, it has turned out that such "openness" was only an academic exercise and will never be adopted as long as the stereotypical state-centralized selection and training system under "Juguo Tizhi" retains its hold over Chinese basketball.

5.5 Conclusion

This chapter has presented an overview of grobalization/glocalization processes at work in the governance of basketball in China. McDonaldization, a key process of grobalization, refers to the growing power of a single governance form and its increasing influence throughout the world. The NBA had come to dominate the North American basketball market by the late 1980s. Based on this success, the league then launched global strategies aimed at integrating into world basketball. This is also attributed to the collapse of amateurism and the commercialization of most Olympic sports, as well as FIBA finally accepting professional basketball players in 1989. Since the 1992 Barcelona Olympics, the NBA has dominated world basketball and infused it with commercialism, and expanded its business to various overseas markets, setting up overseas offices and holding overseas games, especially in Europe and Asia. In this way, the phenomenon of McDonaldization in basketball took shape.

McDonaldization in basketball provided a successful governance model, from which Chinese basketball could draw lessons. In 2003, the CBMC gave up the European model and advocated the NSP, which aimed to turn the Jiaji League into an NBA-isomorphic league named the CBAL through the employment of a franchise system. But the vertical-centralized power allocation of Chinese basketball has prevented the NBA's governance model being fully assimilated in the Chinese context. The NSP was terminated in 2009 and the government's dominance over Chinese basketball was secured. As a result, Chinese professional basketball is being de-McDonaldized and glocalized with the infusion of Chinese traits into the CBAL. In terms of governance authority, Li Yuanwei's proposed reformation towards a market-driven governing body was finally swept over in favour of the stereotypically Chinese nationalized governance model, which is characterized by the state government's dual portfolio. The product market succeeded in cloning the NBA's model, but the prioritization of the national teams still negatively impacts on the league's gaming schedules. In the capital market, CBAL clubs are in some respect dependent on provincial and municipal government authorities, which results in the incentives in club-building resting more on the National Games than on the professional league. Thus, the clubs fail to pursue profit maximization. In the labour market, player mobility is stunted since the clubs favour netting and farming their own talents for the sake of success in the National Games. Players' interests are also deserted and unprotected under the "Juguo Tizhi".

Chapter 6. Globalization and the Chinese Basketball Market

6. 1 Introduction

This chapter examines the interplay between the grobalization of the NBA in China and the glocalization of Chinese basketball, focusing on an economic perspective. Capitalism is the key concept of Ritzer's grobalization theory in this realm. Buick and Crump define capitalism as "an economic system based on the generalized production and circulation of commodities-goods and services on sale in a market-and the production and circulation of these commodities is centered around the drive for profit"(Buick & Crump, 1986: 7). The power of capitalism is so radical that, Ritzer argues, no other force has contributed more to globalization (Ritzer, 2007b: 21). Developed from Marx's understanding that "capitalist firms must continue to expand or they will die, and when possibilities for high profits with a given nation decline, capitalistic businesses are forced to seek profits in other nations", he suggests that such capitalistic firms are eventually led to explore and exploit possibilities for profit in more-remote and less-developed regions

(Ritzer, 2007b: 22). The NBA is in the vanguards of these American capitalistic firms.

Meanwhile, Schwarz and Hunter (2012: 3) suggest that for an individual sports firm, marketing is normally undertaken through three domains: 1) marketing of sports, which is the marketing of sports and sports associations such as the Olympics and sports leagues; 2) marketing through sports, which concerns the use of sporting events, sporting teams and individual athletes to promote various products. In this case, the products can, but do not have to, be directly related to sports; 3) grassroots sports marketing, which is the promotion of sports to the public in order to increase participation. It is part of the field of marketing known as social marketing (Schwarz & Hunter, 2012: 3). The following discussion will focus on these domains. The first section delineates the NBA's three marketing domains in China, marketing of the NBA games, marketing through the NBA games and its grassroots marketing. The second section depicts how Chinese basketball has undertaken marketization with emphasis on its adoption of the NBA's marketing strategies under the NSP. The third section addresses the strength and share of the Chinese basketball market held by the NBA and the CBAL by analysing their advantages and disadvantages.

6. 2 Grobalization and the NBA's Chinese Marketplace

In the U. S., the entertainment industry is a significant and fast-growing economic sector of which American professional sports form an important worldwide segment that has been in the forefront of the drive for sports commercialization and globalization. As depicted in Table 5-1 in the last chapter, the NBA's strategies of tapping into Asian markets were carried out at the start of David Stern's global campaign, particularly in Greater China. Since the establishment of its first overseas office in Hong Kong in 1992, Greater China has been a major overseas market for the NBA. To service its exploding popularity in China, the NBA set up a regional office in Beijing in October 2002 and in Shanghai in 2004(Jiang & Zhang, 2010: 77). In January 2008, the NBA China Group was set up to conduct all the NBA's business in Greater China. It attracted an investment of USD 250 million(EUR 187. 5 million) from five giant corporations, including the Walt Disney Company, the Bank of China, Lenovo Group, the Li Ka Shing Foundation and the China Merchants China Investment Management Limited(Jiang & Zhang, 2010: 77). Timothy Chen, former head of Microsoft's China operations and previous chairman and president of Motorola's China unit, spearheaded the office(Jiang & Zhang, 2010: 77). NBA China is now headquartered in Beijing, with branches in Shanghai, Hong Kong and Taipei, currently totaling over 100 staff(Jiang & Zhang, 2010: 77). China, as the fastest-growing economic giant in the world, has taken up a significant portion of the NBA's global business territory and is now the NBA's largest market outside the U. S..

6. 2. 1 Marketing of the NBA Games

NBA Games on Chinese Media. Television has been the most powerful media carrier for the diffusion of sports since the mid-20th century. Selling television broadcasting rights of sport events has become big business with the deals being major revenue sources for professional sports. The NBA received its first television broadcasting contract before the 1953—1954 season with DTN, which carried 13 regular season games at a cost of USD 39, 000(EUR 29, 250) (Sarmento,

1998). After DTN folded in 1954, National Broadcasting Company(NBC) and the NBA forged a contract that kept the league on television for the next seven seasons, from 1954—1955 season to 1961—1962 season. The league was dropped from NBC in 1962, but found a home on ABC, who paid USD 650, 000(EUR 487,500) for the rights annually(Sarmento, 1998). ABC and the NBA renewed the contract in 1964, together with ESPN's involvement in the same year. The new contracts doubled the NBA's income from television broadcasters(Sarmento, 1998). Since then, the figure has gone up rapidly.

With the effort of NBA's overseas offices since the 1990s, the NBA has established an extensive television network globally. Global television coverage of the 1996 NBA Finals between Chicago and Seattle reached a record of 169 countries on six continents in 40 different languages(NBA China, 2011c). The Bulls' 107-90 win in Game 1 at the United Center earned a 16. 8 rating and a 31% share on NBC and was viewed in a record 16, 111, 200 homes(NBA China, 2011c). The league's 2005—2006 season reached a record high of 215 countries and territories through 164 international broadcasters in 43 languages. More than 800 games were distributed internationally and more than 44, 000 hours of programming were delivered to broadcasters around the world(NBA China, 2011c). It is estimated that the overall amount of broadcasting fees received by the NBA increased from USD 188 million(EUR 141 million) in 1990 to USD 660 million (EUR 195 million) in 2002(Andreff & Szymanski, 2006: 6). A recent investigation by SportBusiness. com shows that the NBA's income from global television rights contracts has risen to 9th place among all sports entities in 2012, Table 6-1shows the detail.

In its Chinese market, however, selling broadcasting rights for money appeared to be impractical at the beginning. The NBA's popularity in China is arguably owed to its extensive engagement with Chinese television broadcasters. However, David Stern might never have imagined the NBA's dramatic media exposure in China today, tracing back to 1989, as he had to wait for three hours before he could talk to a Chinese Central Television(CCTV) executive so as to peddle his NBA broadcast contract(NBA China, 2011a). Before that, only some videotapes of the 1985 NBA Finals were shown in 1986, while the 1987 NBA All-Star Games were broadcast with delayed recording. Stern offered CCTV a revenue-sharing deal for broadcasting a game or two each week from 1990, plus the NBA would convey the free-of-charge signal to CCTV(NBA China, 2011a).

Table 6-1 Top 10 Sports Properties by Global TV Income

	Property	Duration	Years	Estimated fee($ bn)
1	NFL	2006 to 2013	8	3. 855
2	Summer Olympics(London)	2012	1	2. 5
3	2010 FIFA World Cup	2010	1	2. 19
4	2014 FIFA World Cup	2014	1	2. 5
5	English Premier League	2007—2008 to 2009—2010	3	1. 641
6	Italian Serie A	2010—2011 to 2015—2016	6	1. 324
7	Winter Olympics(Vancouver)	2010	1	1. 3
8	UEFA Champions League	2009—2010 to 2011—2012	3	1. 228
9	NBA	2008—2009 to 2015—2016	8	1. 03
10	French Ligue 1	2008—2009 to 2011—2012	4	1. 007

2014 World Cup: Deals yet to be concluded in Spain and sub-Saharan Africa.

2010 and 2012 Olympics: Latin America(excluding Brazil), free-to-air rights in sub-Saharan Africa.

Source: adapted from SportBusiness. com(2012).

With the emergence of China's market economy in the mid-1990s, Chinese no longer see sports as merely a national game. Sport spectating is gradually accepted by Chinese as a kind of leisure consumption, which offered the NBA an opportunity to deliver its games readily. In 1994, CCTV broadcast the first game of the NBA Finals live, marking the first time an NBA game had ever been carried live in China(NBA China, 2011b). CCTV also broadcast the other six games of the 1994 NBA Finals. CCTV-5 was established in 1995 as the first sports channel in China. The new nationwide television network signed a long-term contract with the NBA to broadcast NBA's regular games, playoffs, finals and the All-Star games since 1996. At that time, CCTV covered at least 90% of households throughout the country(Jiang & Zhang, 2010: 9 – 14; NBA China, 2011b).

CCTV-5 paved the way for Chinese provincial and municipal TV broadcasters to establish their own sports channels with 42 being set up by 2003(NBA China, 2011c). The NBA's television network has continued expanding in China since then. A combination of nationwide and local broadcasters increased the total of NBA television partners in China to 54 for the 2010—2011 season(NBA China, 2011c), as shown in Figure 6-1. However, CCTV-5 no longer receives a free signal from the NBA with the rapid expansion of China's sports spectating market. Since the 2002—2003 season, CCTV-5 is not only required to share half of its income from advertisements with the NBA, but also to pay for the broadcasting rights(Jiang & Zhang, 2010: 9 – 14; NBA China, 2011b).

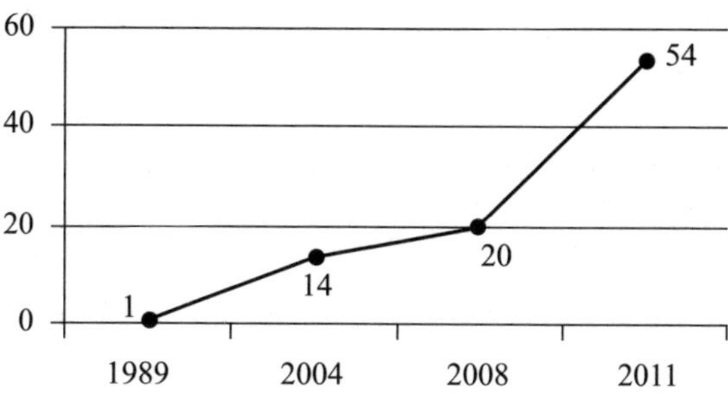

Figure 6-1 Number of Chinese Television Broadcasters Showing NBA Games

Source: adapted from NBA China(2011a; 2011b; 2011c).

Besides TV broadcasts, with the rise of new media technologies, the NBA has been transforming its methods of global diffusion. Internet and mobile phones have become two new media distributors for the NBA's marketing in China since the early 2000s. This is particularly evident since the establishment of NBA. com/China in 2003. Taking the 2004—2005 season for instance, the NBA launched the first-ever NBA Fan Day voting on NBA. com/China on 21 March 2005, enabling NBA fans in China to vote for their favourite game and watch the game according to their own choices and interests. More than 20, 000 fans cast their votes on NBA. com/China from 21 to 23 March with the New Orleans at Houston match-up receiving the most votes at 11,000(NBA China, 2011c). In order to better-serve Chinese fans, NBA. com/China launched Play-By-Play Game Statistics in Simplified Chinese on 25 April, marking the first time that the Network provided a real-time text play-by-play service in a language other than English (NBA China, 2011c). As for mobile service, the NBA signed a multi-year marketing partnership agreement with China Mobile on 7 April 2005, making China Mobile the NBA's official telecommunications service provider in China. China Mobile is authorized to utilize a range of NBA marketing assets to promote its services and distribute NBA wireless content to millions of NBA fans across China(NBA China, 2011c).

By all the above market-expanding strategies, the NBA has established an extensive media network in China.

The Chinese NBA Players. Another step in the NBA's grobalization in China has been to enroll Chinese basketball players. International players have made a great impact on the rosters of NBA teams since the FIBA voted to eliminate the distinction between amateurs and professionals. Before the 1980's, only 8 international basketball players had ever played for NBA teams(Jordan et al. , 2000: 217). Those early international players were mostly from European countries but they were not guaranteed a place in their own teams, so most of them faded out shortly after their arrival in the NBA(Jordan et al. , 2000: 217). This ruling means that international players could play in the NBA without being disqualified from representing their countries in the Olympics, which activated the flow of international players into the NBA throughout the 1990s(Eschker et al. , 2004). However, the migration of international players has accelerated more rapidly in recent years. Before 1995, only 1 or 2 international players were drafted each year. However, the number of international players drafted grew from 3 in 1995 to a record of 14 in the 2002 NBA Draft(Eschker et al. , 2004; NBA China, 2011c). From the 2001 Draft to the 2006 Draft, there were a total of 87 international players selected(Eschker et al. , 2004; NBA China, 2011c). At the end of the 2005—2006 regular season, the NBA featured 82 international players from 38 countries and regions on team rosters, both active and inactive(Eschker et al. , 2004; NBA China, 2011c). Playoffs rosters have a record of 44 international players from 25 countries and regions. The San Antonio Spurs have the most with 7. There were even 12 international players featured in 2006 NBA All-Star events(Eschker et al. , 2004; NBA China, 2011c). This trend shows how NBA teams are expanding the way they are selecting players in the draft. It also reflects NBA's globalization strategy of expanding its global market by accepting international players thereby stimulating its overseas market. Players like Pau Gasol(Spain), Dirk Nowitzki (Germany), Yao Ming(China), Tony Parker(France), Hedo Türkoğlu(Turkey), Nenê(Brazil) and Luol Deng(UK) are changing the landscape of the NBA to include a wide array of players from all over the globe.

The NBA has been dedicated to enrolling Chinese elite basketball players since the late 1980s. The following Table(6-2) shows the list of Chinese basketball players who have been in contact with or picked by NBA teams. From the table, it can be seen that the scouting of Chinese player by the NBA started in 1987. Since then, a total of 6 Chinese players have been selected and scouted to play basketball in the NBA. Song Tao became the first player from China and even Asia drafted by a NBA team when the Atlanta Hawks selected him in the 3rd round of the 1987 NBA Draft. However, he could not go to training camp due to serious knee injuries(NBA China, 2011b). Wang Zhizhi, one of China's most talented basketball players in history, was selected by the Mavericks in the second round of the 1999 NBA Draft with 36th selection overall. He signed with the Mavericks on 4 April 2001 and made history as the first NBA player from China when he played his first NBA game against the Atlanta Hawks on 5 April where he scored six points(NBA China, 2011b). Mengke Bateer became the second player from China to play in the NBA after he joined the Denver Nuggets in February 2002(NBA China, 2011b).

Table 6-2 Chinese Basketball Players Contacted or Picked by NBA Teams

1	1987	Song Tao	Atlanta Hawks
2	1995	Ma Jian	Atlanta Hawks
3	1998	Hu Weidong	Orlando Magic

Continued

4	1999	Wang Zhizhi	Dallas Mavericks
5	2002	Mengke Bateer	Denver Nuggets
6	2002	Yao Ming	Houston Rockets
7	2003	Xue Yuyang	Dallas Mavericks
8	2004	Liu Wei	Sacramento Kings
9	2005	Tang Zheng Dong	Dallas Mavericks
9	2007	Yi Jianlian	Milwaukee Bucks
10	2008	Sun Yue	Los Angeles Lakers

Recruiting international players can not only improve the quality of NBA games, but it is also a powerful approach to grobalize the league. Yao Ming, who was born in Shanghai, started playing for the Shanghai Sharks as a teenager and played on their senior team for five years in the Jiaji League winning a championship in his final year. There is no one who is as big an ambassador as Yao Ming. Thus, the NBA sees its salvation in the 7-foot 6-inch Chinese sensation-and in 1. 3 billion hoops fans(Larmer, 2005a). After negotiating with the CBA and the Sharks to secure his release, Yao was selected by the Houston Rockets as the first overall pick in the 2002 NBA Draft. NBA. com provided comprehensive coverage of the NBA Draft 2002 in Chinese. When Yao Ming finally landed in Houston, a new era of the NBA and Chinese basketball began, as the welcoming slogan of Houston city said: "Be Part of Something Big!"

Above all, Yao's debut in NBA games made the league even more popular in China. According to a research report in January 2011 by HoopChina. com, which was based on polls and online desktop research applications, among the retrieved 51,474 questionnaire samples 37. 8% of the basketball fans said they started watching NBA games because of Yao; while only 9. 5% of them said they would give up watching NBA games if Yao retired; one third of the interviewees showed an interest in the products endorsed by Yao(HoopChina. com, 2011). Another case that shows Chinese NBA players' appeal to Chinese fans is that on 9 November 2007, Yao played against fellow Chinese NBA and Milwaukee Bucks player Yi Jianlian for the first time. The game, which the Rockets won 104 – 88, was broadcast on 19 networks in China, and was watched by over 200 million people in China alone, making it one of the most-watched NBA games in history(Li, 2010).

The NBA China Games. Besides airing their regular games and playoffs on television, digital media and the recruitment of international players, landing overseas games is another important strategy of the NBA to expand its global market. The match between the Phoenix Suns and Utah Jazz at the Tokyo Metropolitan Gymnasium in Japan in 1990 was the first time an NBA regular season game had been played outside North America. It was also a breakthrough for any other major American professional sports teams. The first-ever NBA China Games were announced during the 2004 All-Star Weekend, a conference was specially organized for this announcement beginning with two games to be held in Shanghai and Beijing. David Stern stated on the conference, "The NBA China Games are the logical next step in the NBA's long-term relationship with Chinese basketball and Chinese fans. We have worked closely with the CBA, as well as the sports authorities of Shanghai and Beijing"(NBA, 2011b).

The NBA is also the first American professional sports league to stage games in China. The two games between the Houston Rockets and the Sacramento Kings, as announced at the conference, were played in Beijing and Shanghai on 14 and 17 October 2004. They were organized in conjunction with Beijing Municipal Bureau of Sports and Shanghai Administration of Sports. Original taste was the selling point of the 2004 NBA China Games. To preserve the NBA's original taste, all the stadium facilities were transported from America, including over 200 floorboards, lights, the public address system, even the bathrooms for players. In addition, all the staff, including the cheerleaders, were appointed from the NBA (Yu et al., 2005; NBA, 2011b). With a capacity of 11,500 seats in the Shanghai Stadium and a capacity of 17,500 seats in the Capital Stadium, tickets were sold out a month before the games (Yu et al., 2005; NBA China, 2011c). Ticket prices for the two games ranged between RMB 180 to 3000 (EUR 22.5 to 375), and the VIP lounge cost about RMB 100,000 (EUR 1250) (Yu et al., 2005). Marketing partners for the NBA China Games 2004 included: Anheuser-Busch, Kodak, The Coca-Cola Company, Reebok and The Walt Disney Company, parent company of the NBA's broadcast partners ABC and ESPN (NBA, 2011b). Since then, NBA China Games have been played almost every year. The following table lists the NBA China Games since 2004.

Table 6-3 List of NBA China Games since 2004

Year	Host Cities	Games No.	Visiting Teams
2004	Shanghai, Beijing	2	Houston Rockets, Sacramento Kings
2007	Shanghai, Macao	2	Cleveland Cavaliers, Orlando Magic
2008	Beijing, Guangzhou	2	Golden State Warriors, Milwaukee Bucks
2009	Beijing	2	Denver Nuggets, Indiana Pacers
2010	Beijing, Guangzhou	2	Houston Rockets, New Jersey Nets
2012	Beijing, Shanghai	2	Miami Heat, Los Angeles Clippers

6. 2. 2 Marketing through the NBA

Extensive media exposure of the NBA simultaneously expanded the sponsorship market with a combination of world-class China-based corporations and multinationals. Since the early 2000s, Chinese enterprises have been making good use of NBA's media coverage nationally and internationally for publicity. The sponsors usually pay a certain fee to the NBA and, in turn, receive a license to use the NBA's name, logo, players, team logo and game highlights in their products or advertising. For instance, Yanjing Beer signed a six-year contract worth USD 7 million(EUR 5. 25 million) with Houston Rockets in 2002 to advertise its brand logo in Toyota Center Square(NBA China, 2011c). On 18 January 2005, a new, multi-year, strategic marketing, partnership agreement was announced with Li-Ning Sports. Under the agreement, Li-Ning would feature selected NBA players in its advertising efforts and utilize the league's extensive marketing and media assets in the China market to promote the Li-Ning brand and help market Li-Ning footwear(NBA China, 2011c). This strategy has benefited both Li-Ning and the NBA. Since October 2009, NBA licensed merchandise are sold in 115 Li-Ning shops in 38 cities of 19 provinces(NBA China, 2011c).

The following table shows the marketing partners with NBA China in 2011. Of these 22 marketing partners, 11 are industries, ranging from sports gear to food and drinks. In addition, up to 2011, NBA merchandise was available in 50, 000 retail outlets in China(Bao, 2011b).

Table 6-4 Marketing Partners of NBA China in 2011

Sponsors	Industry Category
Amway Nutrilite	Health Drinks
Tsingtao Beer	Beverage
Mengniu	Food and Milk Industry
Coca Cola	Beverage
China Mobile	Telecommunication
Sina Network	Network Media
Tencent Network	Network Media
Hornitex Industry	Wood Industry
OPPO	Digital Product
Haier	Electrical Appliance
Tsing Hua Tong Fang	Digital Product
Motorola	Digital Product
Adidas	Sports Apparel
Peak	Sports Apparel
Li-Ning	Sports Apparel
Nike	Sports Apparel
Anta Sports	Sports Apparel
Reebok	Sports Apparel
Dr Shoes	Casual Wear
Guirenniao Shoes	Casual Wear
Vancamel	Casual Wear
China Everbright Bank	Financial Industry

Source: adapted from NBA China(2011c).

Therefore, the NBA-logo has been one of the most popular and remunerative symbols in the Chinese sports consumption market. A daily life story told by one of the respondents concisely depicts the NBA's marketing magic:

> In the morning, I take 300 ml Mengniu milk for breakfast, which is endorsed by the NBA. I surf online for news about the NBA and basketball with my Lenovo laptop, also endorsed by the NBA. During the afternoon, I keep eyes on the NBA games, particularly on the Pacers. Getting back from the office, I serve myself a bottle of NBA-endorsed Yanjing Beer, then turn on my high-definition Haier television, also endorsed by the NBA, to watch the playbacks of today's NBA games. Like other NBA fans in China, I love basketball a lot as I play the game with my friends at least twice a week. I am also keen on collecting signed NBA star cards, Pacers' jerseys and Air Jordan sneakers. This hobby costs me about half of my salary every month. When the Indiana Pacers visited Beijing for their China Games in 2009, the front-row ticket cost me two months' salary, but no problem, it is worthwhile, as long as I can see my home team in a short distance, I want to welcome them in Beijing! (Interviewee No. 18)

Moreover, marketing of the NBA games has activated a fast-growing basketball market stretching into wider industrial sectors in China. As for Foreign Direct Investment(FDI) , for instance, the NBA and the Anschutz Entertainment Group (AEG) , one of the leading sports and entertainment presenters in the world, announced plans to design and operate at least 12 arenas of at least 19,000 seats in China in October 2008(NBA China, 2011c) . Huang Jianhua, which is the biggest shareholder of Cleveland Cavaliers with 15% stock, took over China's NBL(est. 2003) and purchased a CBAL Club, the Jilin Tigers, in 2009(Sun et al. , 2010) .

Yao Ming purchased the Shanghai Sharks for about USD 3 million(EUR 2. 25 million) in 2009(Sun et al. , 2010). Their investment has deepened the NBA's market in China.

Besides direct investment, sporting goods manufacturing is another way the NBA has been influencing the Chinese basketball market. As is known to all, China has been the biggest Original Equipment Manufacturer(OEM) and export country over these two decades. The sports industry is no exception, particularly since the mid-1990s. For example, the alignment of Nike, as a major sports goods manufacturer, with the coastal cities where local economies rely heavily on exports, has taken particular advantage of China's low-paid and labour-intensive resources industries. China has been the biggest manufacturer of Nike products for more than two decades(Jiang & Zhang, 2010: 62).

The 21st century began with China's involvement in the WTO, providing transnational companies with many opportunities to enter the Chinese basketball market. Reebok was the earliest global sponsor by virtue of Yao's charisma, putting Yao's signature sneakers into the Chinese market as soon as Yao Ming played his first NBA game(Jiang & Zhang, 2010). In 2003, Reebok and Yao Ming signed a new contract aimed towards the Pan-Asian market. Up to 2006, there were more than 150 Reebok chain stores selling apparel, sneakers and accessories (Jiang & Zhang, 2010: 62). China is also the biggest market for NBA's official basketball sponsor, Spalding. Besides these companies, some other TNCs, particularly in sportswear and drinks such as Adidas and Coca Cola, are also playing a considerable role in the Chinese basketball market(Jiang & Zhang, 2010). As a reverse marketing flow, local sports goods manufacturers in China have, as a result, undergone an evolution from sweatshops to internationalbrands. NBA stars have been gradually accepting and signing endorsements with Chinese sports makers, such as Jason Kidd for Peak Sports and Kevin Garnett for Anta Sports(Jiang & Zhang, 2010).

6. 2. 3 Grassroots Marketing

Grassroots marketing has been a significant strategy of the NBA. One respondent, who was working for the NBA's Beijing Office and NBA China during 2005—2010, noted that:

> Our relationship with a strong network of television and digital media outlets has brought us plenty of sponsors and advertisers. We just need to talk(with the cooperators) on fees, because we have a good brand. But grassroots are very important, we need to keep enlarging the fan groups or consuming groups for our sponsors. So our company hosts hundreds of touring basketball events for fans and conducts community enrichment programs every year. (Interviewee No. 12)

Thus, besides bombarding Chinese television screens, print and cyber space with NBA stars' images, the NBA sponsors and players put every effort into ensuring face-to-face communications between the NBA stars and fans during every summer, usually in the name of promoting basketball. For example, from 25 to 31 August 1997, David Robinson of the San Antonio Spurs and Joe Smith of the Golden State Warriors held basketball clinics with thousands of children in Taipei, Taiwan, Hong Kong and Beijing(NBA China, 2011b). During 10 to 14 August 2001, L. A. Lakers guard Kobe Bryant traveled to Hong Kong and Beijing to promote the sport of basketball. Between 24 to 26 July 2002, Vince Carter was invited by Nike to visit Beijing, Hong Kong and Taipei(NBA China, 2011c). The main objective for this trip was to express Carter's support for Chinese youth basketball. Carter donated a basketball backboard to the CBA and was then featured as a judge for a youth slam-dunk contest at the National Badminton Training Hall. On 3 to 6 August 2005, LeBron James toured Yokohama, Japan, Beijing and Hong Kong on behalf of Nike(NBA China, 2011c).

Additionally, the NBA is promoting Chinese basketball with schools to further expand its fanbase, such as the China Junior NBA, an event the NBA and Amway China undertook in partnership with the China School Sports Federation. The inaugural China Junior NBA took place from 31 August to 18 December 2005. The league was composed of three divisions with 120 schools in 15 cities participating and it was divided into four levels: school level, city level, regional level, and national level. The winning team, coach and chaperone were rewarded with a trip tothe NBA All-Star Game 2006 in Houston(Jiang & Zhang, 2010: 71).

The NBA's presence in China is not only basketball games, but also challenges and entertainment for the youth. For example, NBA Jam Van, the NBA's premier interactive touring program, made its first overseas tour to China in 2005. The Jam Van travelled to 11 Chinese cities, tipping off on 28 July in Shanghai and running through until 2 October in Beijing(NBA China, 2011c). The journey covered 8, 175 kilometers, including three municipalities and six provinces in its quest to bring the NBA experience to fans all over China. The fans can try the newest NBA(electronic) games, as well as enjoy NBA highlights on the Van. They can also participate in many kinds of basketball activities with the NBA stars, such as shooting and ball-handling(NBA China, 2011c). On 16 May 2004, the Playoffs Viewing in Beijing featured more than 250 fans at the Sports City Bar for Game 5 between the Wolves and Kings. The half-time entertainment featured Chinese rapper using"Kings & Wolves"and"NBA China Games"theme in their lyrics to work up the crowd. They were accompanied by playground ballers showcasing flashy ball handling skills(NBA China, 2011c).

To conclude, the NBA's marketplace is fast growing and has deeply reached its potential marketing domains: marketing of the games, marketing through the games and grassroots marketing. The next section will focus on how the Chinese basketball governors react and integrate with the NBA's grobalizing market.

6. 3 Glocalization and the Emergence of an Indigenous Basketball Market

6. 3. 1 The"Marketization"of the Jiaji League(1995—2003)

As discussed in the previous chapter, although the CBA is constituted as a non-beneficial and non-governmental organization, it is clear that the officials from the government are the true power in governing the Jiaji League or CBAL. During the process of marketing the league, government officials are monopolizing the power in the same way. However, the Chinese basketball governors do not market the league by itself, but work with marketing agents. To generate sufficient income to become self-supporting, before the inauguration of the Jiaji League, the CBA signed a commercial contract with International Management Group(IMG) for six years. The contract was worth USD 2. 5 million(EUR 1. 88 million) for the first year and USD 3 million(EUR 2. 25 million) for the remaining years(CBA, 1996). IMG brought the Jiaji League two considerable sponsors soon after signing the contract. During those years, the Jiaji League was sponsored by two large cigarette companies, "555"and Hilton. With their support as the named sponsors of the league and other sponsors(in a small way), such as Nike, Gatorade and Ford, IMG managed to survive. This co-operation model with sports agents provided a certain success when developing China's professional basketball market(CBA, 1996; 1997; 1998a; 1999; 2000; 2001). Li Dunhou, Vice-director of the GAS Finance Department, claimed that:

> We earned more than 3 million(EUR 2. 25 million) per year by selling the commercial rights of the Jiaji League, including the naming rights of the league, promotion rights, and 75% of the advertising rights of the stadiums, to the IMG. (Li, 1999)

After this 6-year contract, the IMG refused to renew the contract with a higher fee as the CBA claimed. The reason for IMG's retreat was that cigarette companies were prohibited from sponsoring sports competitions by the Chinese government after 2001. But most Chinese marketing partners of IMG at that time were cigarette companies. It was difficult for IMG to raise the price to the CBA in a new three-year contract as the IMG itself was in financial crisis(CBA, 2002). Later in that year, Yang Cheng News Group took over from IMG as the marketing agent of the Jiaji League, offering RMB 35 million(EUR 4. 375 million) per year. Ironically, the CBA forgot to sign a formal contract with the Yang Cheng News Group who refused to fulfill their previous oral agreement with the CBA when they began to realize that their commercial rights would be subject to interference from government officials. This caused a crisis over how the 2001—2002 Jiaji League season could start within 45 days with insufficient financial support(Tan, 2008). In order to solve this problem, the CBA had no choice but to run the league at the Zhonglan Sport Development Center, which was owned by the GAS(CBA, 2002; Tan, 2008).

In this period(including the"Initial Season"), television broadcasting of the Jiaji League games was neither beneficial nor popularizing the league to the audiences. In the first three seasons, CCTV broadcast the games without any fees paid to the CBA. For some less-popular clubs, they had to pay a certain amount of money to CCTV for exposure(CBA, 1996; 1997). In the 1997—1998 season, CCTV provided a two-minute advertising interval for the selected clubs(CBA, 1998a). In the 1998—1999 season, Jiangsu Nangang sold their broadcasting rights to Jiangsu TV for RMB 500,000(EUR 62,500). Liaoning Hunters received RMB 150,000(EUR 18,750) by selling the broadcasting rights for the whole season. This figure was equivalent to 2.3% of the total revenues that all the CBAL clubs generated in the season(CBA, 1999). In the 1999—2000 season, Zhongguang Network, which was owned by China Sports Publications Corporation under the GAS, started to market the broadcasting rights of Jiaji League games collectively. Zhongguang Network changed its name to Huaao Xingkong Network in early 2000(CBA, 2000). In 2001, Huaao Xingkong Network reached a contract with CCTV-5, who would pay RMB 2.8 million(EUR 0.35 million) for 60 games in the coming season. This marked the first broadcasting contract for the Jiaji League. 23 provincial or municipal television broadcasters also signed a contract with Huaao Xingkong Network in that season. In addition, Huaao Xingkong Network produced the *Lanqiu Fengyun(Basketball Time)*, a 30-minute basketball program about the Jiaji League, for the broadcasters. However, revenue from selling the league's broadcasting rights was far from sufficient to support the league's expenditure(CBA, 2001; 2002).

In short, the major ways in which the Jiaji League could generate income were by selling commercial rights to sports agents or selling the league's naming rights themselves in the Jiaji League period, as shown in Table 6-5. The league's income and expenditure managed to stay balanced in the last two seasons with the support of Motorola(CBA, 2002; 2003). But the withdrawal of Motorola pushed the league into financial difficulty again. Before the 2003—2004 season, a Taiwan company promised to offer RMB 20 million(EUR 2. 5 million) for the league's naming rights. But it withdrew one day before the media conference to launch the new name was to take place. Fortunately, China Unicom agreed to take over the contract. But that season was still in deficit, with the league losing RMB 15 million(EUR 1. 875 million) (CBA, 2004a). Thus, the Jiaji League basketball marketization program was humbled.

Table 6-5 Naming Rights Sponsors for the Jiaji League(1995—2003)

Season	League Name
1995—1996	555 China Men's Basketball Jiaji League
1996—1997	Hilton China Men's Basketball Jiaji League
1997—1998	Hilton China Men's Basketball Jiaji League
1998—1999	Hilton China Men's Basketball Jiaji League
1999—2000	Hilton China Men's Basketball Jiaji League
2000—2001	Hilton China Men's Basketball Jiaji League
2001—2002	Motorola China Men's Basketball Jiaji League
2002—2003	Motorola China Men's Basketball Jiaji League
2003—2004	China Unicom China Men's Basketball Jiaji League

Source: adapted from the Jiaji League's schedule from 1995 to 2003.

6. 3. 2 The Rise of the CBAL Market with the NSP since 2004

Intensifying marketization of the CBAL was one major task identified by Li Yuanwei in his NSP. The central concept of the NSP in relation to marketization was to amplify "competing basketball" into "entertaining basketball" and "money-spinning basketball"(CBA, 2004b), which was inspired by the branding operation of the NBA, as Li recalled:

> The first time I watched a NBA game was in 2000 in Miami. I was shocked by what I saw in the stadium: fans were queuing to buy hot dogs, drinks and merchandises; it was like a weekend party rather than a sports competition; dancing performance by cheerleaders heat the game up; sponsors were doing all kinds of commercial promotions on the court; the cameras captured Hollywood stars and well-known persons from time to time; when the home team lost the game, the fans were still enjoying their party, not being depressed or resentful as [would] normally happen in Chinese sports contests. Since then, a concept of branding the games, serving fans, serving media, serving sponsors' is impressed in my mind. I wish I could bring such basketball games and culture to Chinese basketball fans. (Li, 2007)

Therefore, with the implementation of the NSP, the CBMC advocated the key marketing strategy named "One Focus and Three Services", which was to focus on branding the league and serving the fans, serving the media and serving the sponsors(CBA, 2004b). Although branding is a fundamental marketing strategy in sports business, it was something untouched in Chinese professional basketball when Li decided to do so, because most Chinese sports officials had no experience in sports marketing. Li said:

> To be honest, I didn't have much knowledge about branding. I had been working on teaching and doing research in universities and institutes before joining the CBMC. My previous years in the CBMC concentrated either on athletic training or competition management. I hardly had any knowledge about economics and marketing. (Li, 2007)

He went on to state:

> However, I decided to emphasize the importance of branding the league after the research report released by, and [at] the suggestion of, the Shanghai Qianrui Sports Business Consultancy Corporation. And I finally found out why the CBAL lagged so far behind the NBA in terms of sponsor marketing in China. For a long time, we have tried our best to target and build relationships with Chinese giant marketers, such as China Mobile, Lenovo Group, Air China and Mengniu Group. But they were so eager to sponsor the NBA, [that they deserted] the CBAL. The cause of this is the disparity of brand value between the two leagues. That is why I emphasized branding the league in the NSP so much. (Li, 2007)

Marketing of the CBAL Games. As a result, to better brand the league, the 2004—2005 season witnessed a set of changes in the league's schedule to increase the number of CBAL games: (This is also discussed in Chapter 5) the promotion and relegation system was abolished; the league was divided into two conferences; the number of games for each team was increased to three each week. The total number of CBAL games was increased to 317 from 155 in the previous season(CBA, 2005b). More importantly, the CBMC picked the Shili Media from tens of candidates as the branding agent in 2004. Since then, with the help of Shili Media, the CBAL has adopted a series of branding strategies. The first strategy was to re-image the league which innovatively integrates traditional Chinese cultural elements into the games(CBA, 2005b). (This will also be discussed in the next chapter.) For example, the logo of the CBAL was changed from a common basketball image to the "Face of Basketball", which infused a traditional Chinese face from the Beijing Opera into a basketball image. In the 2004—2005 season, a slogan of "My Team, My Game and My CBA!" was put forward(CBA, 2005b). The slogan was changed to "Your Turn on the Court!" in the 2005—2006 season(CBA, 2006a) and was changed again to "Emperors in Flames of War!" in the 2006—2007 season(CBA, 2007a) and "Force of Three Swords!" in the 2007—2008 season(CBA, 2008).

Therefore, the opening game of the 2004—2005 season demonstrated a new face of Chinese professional basketball. Before the game started, the "basketball babies"(cheerleaders), which was made up of a team of young and beautiful girls hired from professional dancing studios in Beijing and Shanghai, performed and danced on the basketball court. Under the neon lights, a huge octagonal lantern support was upraised. With the gorgeous fireworks flaming from the floor, the lantern support was cracked and a huge basketball signing "CBA" turned up with rock music to the 6000 spectators. Then a group of young men in traditional Chinese Tai Chi costume jumped to the court and started to play street basketball with Tai Chi strikes. They were followed by a dancing lion playing with a basketball around the court(CCTV-5, 2011-11-14).

Regarding "serve the media", the NSP made great efforts to improve the relationship between the CBMC and media workers(CBA, 2004b). Li Yuanwei acknowledges the power of the media in sports marketing and the importance of transparency to achieve good governance, he said:

> In my opinion, we should treat media workers sincerely, respect them

and support them. We should not stand high above them as governmental officials. Only by behaving in this way can we achieve the most efficient cooperation. (Li, 2007)

He enumerated two lessons he had learnt from his predecessor, Xin Lancheng. The first one occurred at a press conference. Liang Xiyi, a renowned journalist from Xinhua News, asked Xin, "Can the CBMC provide better service to the media?"Xin answered, "You are working for your career, I am working for my career, so why do I need to serve you?"(Li, 2007). The second happened at a buffet lunch during the Shanghai Basketball Routine Meeting in 1999. One young newspaper reporter asked Xin, "Mr. Xin, I heard that you don't like newspaper reporters..."Xin glared at the young men and answered directly, "Yes, you are right! "(Li, 2007). Learning from this, the NSP formulated that: from 2004, the CBMC 1) appoints one media spokesman to share information on the league with media workers; 2) holds a media salon on the first Monday night of each month; 3) holds regular media conferences; and, 4) arranges open days for the national teams' training activities(CBA, 2004b).

Notwithstanding, income attracted from selling broadcasting right is still minor. It is still hindered by the monopolistic broadcasting system in China. There is only one nationwide sports broadcaster, CCTV-5, which holds the sole authority to decide which or whether CBAL games are put on, and tends to reduce the broadcasting fee. Ma Guoli, CEO of Infront, commented:

Some low-profile CBAL clubs have to pay extra money to CCTV-5 for exposure. It is abnormal for a developing sports industry. In many countries, selling television broadcasting is a major source of income. But in China, this immense market is locked away. The monopoly position of CCTV-5 should be broken in order to expand China's sports broadcasting market. (Ma, 2012)

Marketing through the CBAL Game. To attract more sponsors for the league, the CBMC created a new mode of sponsorship. The league naming rights were cancelled to be replaced by four types of sponsors: the chief sponsor, the sneakers and apparel sponsor, marketing partners and general authorized suppliers (CBA, 2004b). As for the chief sponsor, the CBMC and Infront came up with a seven-year contract in 2005. According to the contract, Zhonglan & Infront Company, which is jointly owned by the CBA and Infront, is set up as the marketing agent of the CBAL. Infront had a 49% shareholding and the CBA held the remaining 51%. Infront provided USD 6.5 million (EUR 0.81 million) each year for the expenditure of running the league, while all the commercial rights, including those from the venues of all clubs, were operated by Infront. At the end of each season, the CBA shared 85% of the total income with Infront taking the remaining 15%. Additionally, Infront had priority to renew a five-year contract after the expiration of this contract in 2012 (CBA, 2006a).

Soon after its establishment, Zhonglan & Infront contributed to fostering the CBAL market. First, Zhonglan & Infront merged with the Basketball Company, which was holding the rights to run the official CBA website and the real-time statistics of the CBAL games. Second, in 2006, Zhonglan & Infront renewed the contract with Leisu Sports Supplying Company, which had been producing CBA-authorized merchandise since 2001. According to the contract, Leisu would give up its own brand and was authorized as the only factory to produce and sell authorized CBA merchandise. The CBA would receive a commission on a portion of Leisu's revenue (CBA, 2006a; 2007a).

Third, and significantly, as for the sneakers and apparel sponsor, Zhonglan &

Infront and Anta Sports have achieved a win-win alignment since 2004. In the past, sneakers and apparel providers were categorized as general authorized suppliers. Except for the first two seasons when they were collectively supplied by the league, the clubs had to seek out suppliers on their own. For some strong teams, such as the Bayi Army Basketball Club, Gungdong Hongyuan Basketball Club, Jiangsu Nangang Basketball Club and Liaoning Panpan Basketball Club, sports gear suppliers were eager to provide gear for their players. But for those weak teams, few suppliers were willing to sponsor them. Thus, Zhonglan & Infront attempted to obtain a sneakers and apparel sponsor for the CBAL(CBA, 2005b; 2006a; 2007a). Li said:

> It is a good way to generate more income for the league [through appointing a sneakers and apparel sponsor], and we are happy to provide this good service for the clubs. (Li, 2007).

However, most giant sports suppliers showed little interest in sponsoring the CBAL. Li recalled:

> At first, we wished to cooperate with a giant sports suppliers, Nike, Adidas or Li Ning, one of those three. But they were not willing to enter the sponsorship with us, because they didn't consider investing in the CBAL would benefit them. I understand them anyway. The CBAL was not popular enough to draw their interest. I didn't lose heart, but it made me more determined to brand our league. (Li, 2007)

Before the 2004—2005 season tipped off, Zhonglan & Infront signed a three-year contract appointing Anta as the "CBAL Authorized Sneakers and Apparel Sponsor"(CBA, 2005b). Anta was a less well-known sports manufacturer and supplier at that time. It was an OEM for Nike, Adidas and Converse before it started to promote its own brand in the late 1990s(Jiang & Zhang, 2010: 458 – 467). On signing the contract, Anta worked with the Sports and Exercise Research Center under the GAS to design sneakers that fit Asian feet. They also hired top designers throughout the world to design basketball footwear and jerseys for CBAL players(Jiang & Zhang, 2010: 458 – 467). The co-operation of Anta and CBA was a very successful case of sports sponsorship. When Anta started to sponsor the CBAL in 2004, its annual turnover was RMB 310 million(EUR 38. 75 million), which jumped to RMB 670 million(EUR 83. 75 million) in the next year. In 2006, it nearly doubled again to RMB 1. 25 billion(EUR 156. 25 million) and the figure kept increasing to RMB 2. 98 billion(EUR 372. 5 million) in 2007 (Jiang & Zhang, 2010: 458 – 467). Anta and the CBA renewed the contract for another five years in 2007. The annual turnover of Anta jumped to RMB 4. 63 billion(EUR 578. 75 million) in 2008 and RMB 5. 87 billion(EUR 733. 75 million) in 2009(Jiang & Zhang, 2010: 458 – 467). Ding Zhizhong, CEO of Anta commented, "The CBAL is different today, Anta is different, too. Both the CBAL and Anta are rising in value. We advanced side by side these years, and we have achieved win-win co-operation"(Jiang & Zhang, 2010: 466).

On the whole, with the branding strategies and the effort of Zhonglan &Infront, the CBAL's sponsor marketing has kept growing since 2004. As depicted in the following figure, the total number of CBAL's sponsors increased from 7 to 23 within the 9 seasons from 2004 to 2013.

Grassroots Marketing. Grassroots marketing was part of the "serving the fans" strategy which Li Yuanwei also directed towards the construction of a Chinese basketball culture. Besides the basketball events for fans and mass participants (which will be discussed in the next chapter), the CBA has also conducted commu-

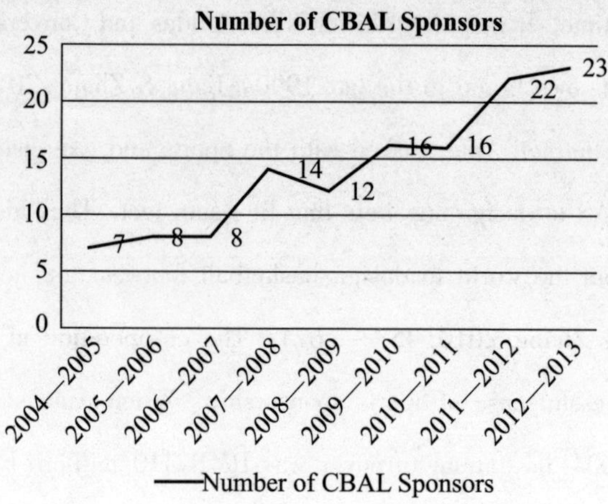

Figure 6-2 Number of Sponsors of the CBAL

Source: adapted from CBA(2004a; 2005b; 2006a; 2007a; 2008; 2009; 2010; 2011b; 2012).

nity enrichment programs since 2004. In 2005, the CBA and the "China Youth Development Fund" jointly launched a welfare project named "Growing-up Together with CBA" (CBA, 2005b). At the beginning, the Fund encountered financial difficulty. The budget of the CBMC had been running out for the reason that hiring media and public relationship consultancy companies had taken up most of the budget. But for Li Yuanwei, "this project is significant for the CBA to build up a healthy image [within] society. It is also the social responsibility of basketball practitioners" (Li, 2007). Therefore, the CBMC decided to make use of the first sum of money that Yao Ming handed in to the CBMC for permitting him to play in the NBA, which was USD 160,000 (EUR 20,000). The CBMC also encouraged clubs and sponsors to contribute to the fund. It was successful. They raised more than RMB 10 million (EUR 1.25 million) in a couple of months (CBA, 2006a; 2007a; Li, 2007). With the fund, 6 "hope schools", 50 "hope libraries" and 280 "hope playgrounds" were built in poor provinces such as Xinjiang, Xizang, Guangxi, Yunnan, Hunan etc. within four years beginning in 2006 (CBA, 2006a; 2007a; Li, 2007).

However, with the closure of the NSP in late 2009 and the return of Xin

Lancheng's"elite-sports-prioritized"governing principle, these grassroots basketball campaigns were replaced by a"Further Building Chinese Basketball Reserve Pool Project" in 2010, which aims to help building the elite basketball reserve pool rather than developing Chinese mass basketball(Xin, 2009; 2010).

In general, the CBAL's market gradually emerged under the NSP and keeps expanding even after the closure of the NSP in 2009. The following section will take a look at the current strength and weakness of the NBA's market and the CBAL's market.

6. 4 McDonald's or Shanghai Food?

6. 4. 1 Current Degree of the NBA's Market Growth

As a pioneer of new global capitalists, the NBA is among those American-made cultural exports which were successfully and continually output to the world after the Cold War. In today's China, the NBA's market is far more influential than that of the CBAL. It is reported that the NBA's total revenues from broad-casting rights, branded product sales, and sponsorships in China were roughly USD 50 million(EUR 37. 5 million) to USD 70 million(EUR 52. 5 million) during 2005 to 2009, compared to approximately USD 15 million(EUR 11. 25 million) for the CBAL(Bao, 2011b). Nevertheless, the NBA's revenue in China is tiny compared with the USD 4 billion(EUR 3billion) or so the league earns each year in the U. S. "We are just scratching the surface in China, "one staff of NBA China said(Interviewee No. 13).

For the NBA, doing business in China might not be as easy as they expected. There are some disadvantages that the NBA finds hard to overcome: 1) few Chinese players are capable enough to be recruited by NBA teams; 2) there is less governmental support in China; 3) what the NBA can localize in China is a commercial brand, not a tangible league. When talking about the Chinese players' capability to be recruited by NBA teams, the first point is evident by noting the impact of the Chinese players on the NBA's popularity in China. The statistics below from HoopChina. com show that at least 58. 7% of basketball fans(2003—2010) and 56. 6% of sports fans(2003—2010) started following the NBA games after Yao became a player in the NBA(HoopChina. com, 2011). The survey also found that the NBA's fans base was steadily expanding until 2007, then the number of new fans decreased by over a half between 2007 and 2010, due to Yao's injury in early 2009.

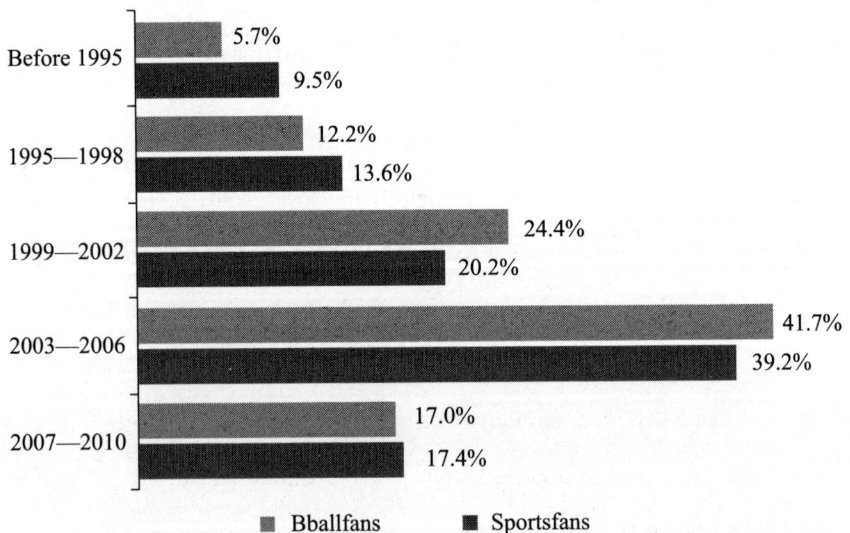

Figure 6-3 Yao Ming's Impact on the NBA's Fan Base in China

Source: adapted fromHoopChina. com(2011).

Figure 6-4 further shows the different percentages of the NBA's online traffic which was brought by Yao in different periods from September 2009 to December 2010. It can be concluded that through the entire 2009—2010 season, the NBA's online exposure dropped steadily because of Yao's injury. A sudden dramatic increase occurred when Yao came back to the court at the beginning of 2010. But it started to drop again after another injury to Yao.

On the contrary, CCTV-5 tended to broadcast more CBAL games than NBA games in reaction to Yao's retirement in 2011 and Yi Jianlian's return to Guangdong Hongyuan Basketball Club in 2012. Therefore, the NBA has to hard-sell Jeremy Lin, a Taiwanese descendant. But it seems that the Chinese fans are not interested, indeed, none of the respondents-basketball-playing supporters or basketball-consuming supporters-felt that the NBA's promotion of Jeremy Lin would affect their interest in NBA games.

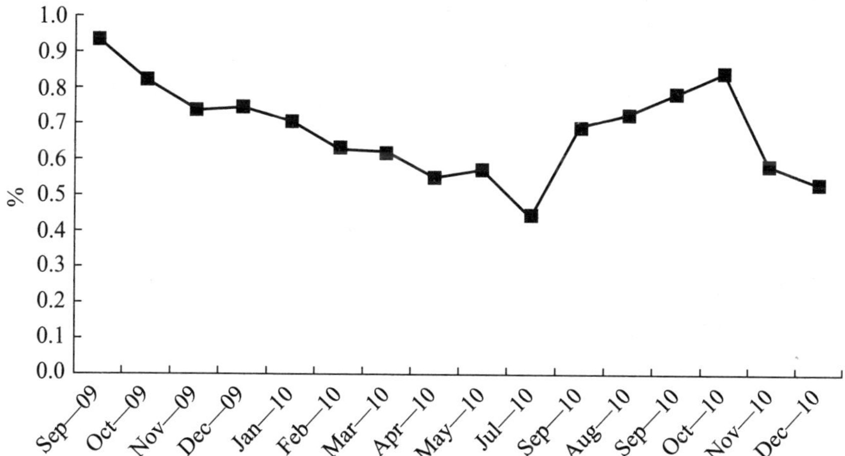

Figure 6-4 Yao Ming's Impact on the NBA's Online Exposure in China

Source: adapted from HoopChina. com(2011).

The second disadvantage of the NBA-lack of governmental support-is also evident. And there are also some lessons the NBA needs to learn about doing business in China, as illustrated in the following two stories told by Li Yuanwei:

> For example, during the 2008 NBA China Games, David Stern wished to pay a visit to a state leader who was in charge of sport policy in the State Council. The secretary office serving this leader agreed to Stern's request, but required him to do some necessary paperwork first. However, after the NBA finished and submitted all the required documents, his application was rejected because the NBA's proposal didn't fulfill the minimum requirement for being received by this state leader, which was regulated by the central government. This irritated Stern and he took the earliest flight back to America. (Li, 2011)
>
> …
>
> To give another example, the NBA was stopped from selling all the tickets for the 2008 NBA China Games by the Beijing Public Security Bureau for the reason of"hindered security". The NBA's arrangement of holding a celebration between Chinese fans and NBA players on the court was stopped again for the same reason… Security is one reason, however, the more important reason was that the NBA didn't even tip its hat to the Beijing Municipal Government(which leads the Security Bureau) before the organization of the 2008 NBA China Games. (Li, 2011)

The NBA's lack of governmental support overlaps with its third disadvantage-failing to establish itself within China. Resulting from the two aforementioned disadvantages, the NBA understands the significance of"localizing"their own games in the Chinese market. However, both of the NBA's two strategies for establishing itself, which were to bid to become the commercial agent of China's national teams, Team China, in 2006, and to set up a professional basketball league in China in 2008, were rejected by the CBA. In regard to the bidding to become commercial agent, Infront and the NBA were the most two promising bidders. On the side of Infront, which was the commercial agent of the CBAL, it was their eagerness to win the bid so as to maximize their benefits in cooperating with other sponsors(CBA, 2007a; Li, 2011) . On the other side, the NBA had mapped the Chinese market out as their core target in their global plan. Thus the NBA offered a high bid of USD 10 million(EUR 7. 5 million) in sponsor fees to the CBA(CBA, 2007a; Li, 2011) . Li Yuanwei stated that the CBA had been close to doing a deal with the NBA, but had finally picked Infront as they could not get over their doubts about the insecurity that the NBA might arouse in the Chinese basketball market. He stated:

> Imagine, if the NBA takes control of Team China and the CBAL one day in terms of commercial operation, the CBA and Chinese basketball will be vassals of the NBA. We can't accept such consequences. But [the] possibility is potentially out there. Since the implementation of the "reform and opening-up" policy, a lot of local brands want to exchange technology and money with their market through co-operation with international brands, but some of them lose their market whereas little technology has been gained, some even disappear from the market after the so-called co-operation. It is an alert for Chinese basketball. (Li, 2011)

As for setting up a China-based basketball league, the NBA's proposal was strongly rejected by the CBA. In April 2008, the NBA hired McKinsey & Company Inc. at a cost of USD 1 million(EUR 0. 75 million) to project the NBA China league(Li, 2011) . According to the proposal, the league would copy the NBA's operation model and would recruit players and enroll clubs from other Asian countries. Current CBAL clubs would have priority to join the league with an entrance fee of USD 50 million(EUR 37. 5 million). The naming rights would be in the hands of the CBA(Li, 2011). The NBA and the CBA would each hold a half-share. But for the CBA, this project was totally not making sense, as Li stated:

> This project was definitely with an American logic, and it was totally impractical in the land of China. Imagine, if the new league was formed, then how to deal with the CBAL? And the NBL(est. 2005), or other marketing partners? Also, it was impossible for the CBAL clubs to join the league. I don't think there are any CBAL clubs that could afford that money. Even if they have that money, it would be at a likely risk for them to lose money. (Li, 2011)

6. 4. 2 Current Degree of the CBAL's Market Growth

On the contrary, the CBAL admittedly remains quasi-professionalized, as discussed in the previous chapter. Moreover, this league can hardly compare to the NBA in terms of product quality and commercial operations. However, despite the NSP being somewhat a duplication of the NBA, it has successfully pushed the CBAL market further. As Li argued:

> Although I don't regard the CBAL as a veritable professional sports league, it is undoubtedly the best sports league in China. Learning from the NBA is our magic weapon. In other words, our strategy of"Nalai Zhuyi"from the NBA has propelled the CBAL to the No. 1 professional sports league upon the football league within only a couple of years(Li, 2011).

Table 6-6 summarizes the contribution of the NSP to the Chinese basketball market which is compiled from the CBA's annual report from 2004 to 2009.

Table 6-6 Summary of the CBAL's Marketing Report

2004—2005 season source:

• An audience of more than 1. 23 million attended the CBAL games, which is double last season's; the ticket price for the first-row seats went up to RMB 3, 500(EUR 437. 5), which was the highest in league history.

• Audiences totaling more than 2. 24 million have followed the entire season, which is 6 times higher than last season.

• According to the report of CCTV-5, TV rating for the Finals was 2. 3% (each point stands for 10 million people) and 2. 8% in the 4th quarter; all the five final games were broadcast worldwide by NBA TV and Asia-wide by ESPN.

2005—2006 season source:

• The season lasted for 5 months, 308 games were played in 44 rounds by 15 teams in the regular season, plus 19 playoff games and 5 final games, in total, 332 games were played in the entire season, which made a historical high.

• The number of domestic television broadcasters increased to 19 from 13 in the previous season; a total number of 214 million views were recorded by CCTV-5; ESPN and NBA TV broadcast all the playoff games with 145 million views recorded.

• 6 clubs have claimedto be making a profit, comparing to 3 in the previous season; 8 clubs have claimed higher income was generated from admission tickets than last season.

• The league has got rid of financial difficulty; the total value of the CBA's properties in 2006 had risen by 387. 98% compared to 2004; revenue generated from marketing the national teams in 2006 was more than 10 times that of 2002; total revenue generated by the CBAL in 2006 was about 10 times that of 2003 or 2004.

2008—2009 season source:

• The season lasted for 6 months, 450 games were played by 18 teams in the entire season, which again reached a historical high; the new regulation on international player recruitment has greatly improved the quality of CBAL games.

Continued

2008—2009 season source:

• 1. 69 million seats were sold, with an average audience of 3, 566 per game.

• According to CSM Media, 383 print media have reported on the CBAL; a total number of 14, 113 articles were released, 89% of the contents of these articles were positive; this media exposure has generated RMB 136 million(EUR 17 million) compared to the previous season's RMB 32 million RMB(EUR 4 million).

• 20 domestic television broadcasters showed CBAL games for a total of 4, 190 hours, compared to 2, 162 hours inthe previous season; this television exposure generated an estimated advertising value of RMB 723 million RMB(EUR 90. 38 million).

• The branding strategy for the CBAL has been successful, the value of the CBAL was estimated at USD 240 million(EUR 180 million) to USD 370 million(EUR 277. 5 million) in 2009.

Furthermore, although the demise of the NSP in 2009 has slowed down the marketization of Chinese basketball, there are still some advantages for the CBAL in coping with the NBA's mighty business expansion in China. Above all, as a reverse global labour flow, the CBAL is benefiting from increasing arrivals of high-quality international players, particularly from the NBA. The CBAL is now a major destination for out-of-contract NBA players, which has greatly improved the quality of CBAL games. International players have been playing a significant role in the roster of many CBAL teams since the league began. In the first season, Zhejiang Team imported the first ever international player in Chinese basketball history, Mikhail Safin. This Uzbekistan player helped the Zhejiang Team, a newly promoted team from the Yiji League, to gain qualification to play in the Jiaji League with a ranking of 6^{th}(Chen, 2007; Shi, 2009). Since then, all CBAL clubs except the Bayi Army have imported a great number of international players in their roster. In the late 1990s, on average, less than 20 international players in each season were hired by CBAL teams, which increased to double figures from the 2000s due to the CBA allowing substitutions of international players during a season(Chen, 2007; Shi, 2009). The quality of those international players has also improved a lot during the past decade. At the beginning of the league, most international players were from Eastern Europe or from the U. S. who were not qualified to play in the NBA. But in recent years, most of the international players in the CBAL have experience of playing in NBA teams. More and more NBA players, and coaches, are being hired by CBAL clubs, even star players such as former first-pick player Steve Francis and Kenyon Martin, as well as former NBA MVP Tracy McGrady. Stephen Marbury, in particular, has been playing in the CBAL since 2009 and has recently brought the Beijing Ducks a heroic championship title over the Guangdong Hongyuan Basketball Club. To express their high appreciation, 1. 02 million basketball fans signed to build a bronze statue of Marbury in front of the Wu Ke Song Stadium Square, in 2012.

Moreover, there are some inherent advantages for the CBAL in consolidating its market. First, it holds a geographical advantage in comparing to the NBA. The CBAL games are played during prime time, which suits all kinds of Chinese audiences. Most NBA games are shown in the morning(Beijing time) when most audiences are not available to watch these games through either television or the internet. Second, a great number of NBA supporters in China are in fact following Chinese players. When these Chinese players stop playing in the NBA, such followers are likely to turn their eyes back to the CBAL. Apart from the case of Yao Ming, discussed previously, there has been another case with the recent return of Yi Jianlian for the 2012—2013 season. With Yi rejoining the Guangdong Hongyuan Basketball Club, the number of CBAL games broadcast by CCTV-5 has increased to 7, more than twice last year's number(CBA, 2013). Before that, only one game was live on Wednesday, Friday and Sunday respectively. Since the

2012-2013 season, Tuesday, Wednesday, Friday and Sunday have one game live, plus three games broadcast during the week (CBA, 2013). Third, the CBAL games will never be eliminated or replaced by the NBA's presence, since they are local games from within China which could help preserve local and Chinese supporters. Beneath the conspicuous nationalism in Chinese sport from a global or international perspective, there is also existing a force of "sport regionalism" (Hua, 2004) which is stimulating the formation of a CBAL fans community. From the interviews with basketball supporters, it is found that it has been almost uniform that the CBAL followers tend to support their local clubs, which are usually former provincial teams. This phenomenon is a remnant from the pre-professional era.

Therefore, the indigenous basketball market does not shrink but keeps expanding in the post-NSP seasons. During the 2011—2012 season, the attendance rate achieved 77.82%; CCTV-5 broadcast 51 games live and 67 recorded, 23 local television broadcasters transmitted 1614 games and the Finals achieved a television rating of 1.83%, which was higher than the NBA and was top to all sports programs broadcast throughout the year. All these figures are historical highs (CBA, 2012). The brand value of the CBAL also keeps rising. In 2004, Anta offered only RMB 10 million (EUR 1.25 million) to be the chief sponsor. But in 2010, when Nike signed to sponsor only the basketballs in the games, it cost RMB 20 million (EUR 2.5 million) (CBA, 2012). In 2012, Li-Ning signed to be the chief CBAL sponsor, paying RMB 2 billion (EUR 250 million) for a five-year contract (CBA, 2012). These figures all reflect that the CBAL market is potential and attracting various marketers to put investment into.

In sum, the grobalization/glocalization interplay between the NBA and the CBAL has been expanding the Chinese basketball market. As Li Yuanwei commented:

> I tot ally agree that the NBA has contributed greatly to expanding the capacity of the Chinese basketball market and the development of basketball in China. They have also provided us with a great deal of resources and experience in professionalizing Chinese basketball. The market for basketball here in China is big enough to accommodate both the NBA and the CBAL. So I see the NBA's presence in China is an opportunity for both of us to make a big cake, rather than a threat of invading Chinese basketball market. (Li, 2007)

He further echoed his words to David Stern when he rejected the NBA's proposal for building a NBA-like professional basketball league in China, "McDonald's is popular in Shanghai, but it doesn't affect the business of Shanghai food"(Li, 2011).

6.5 Conclusion

This chapter has presented an overview of the grobalization/glocalization processes at work in the Chinese basketball market. Capitalism is the driving force behind these processes. In relation to the NBA's grobalization, it was shown that China has become its biggest overseas market. The NBA's business in China is pervasive throughout the three marketing domains. First, the NBA's strong network of television and digital media outlets have cultivated a developed sports show market in China. To take full advantage of demand in this market, the NBA began holding NBA China Games for Chinese consumers in 2004. Second, the NBA's global expansion has activated a sponsorship market that attracts a combination of world-class Chinese corporations and multinationals, incorporating China's sporting resources into the on-going global economic flows. Third, the NBA has motivated the development of Chinese grassroots basketball with a variety of promotional campaigns that are run by their sponsors. As for the glocalization of Chinese basketball, the CBAL, under the NSP, learned from the NBA's marketing principles to transform the Jiaji League's competition-oriented basketball into basketball for entertainment and profit. Therefore, a local basketball market has been gradually taking shape under the CBAL in contrast to the low degree of marketization of the Jiaji League. With regard to market share, the NBA has certain disadvantages despite the strength of its position in China. These include the participation of few Chinese NBA players, a lack of governmental support, and the failure to create a tangible league. The market for the CBAL is expanding, despite the low-quality competitions, owing to certain inherent advantages: the arrival of high-level international players and the return of Chinese NBA players, prime time broadcasting hours, and its ability to appeal to the local tastes of regional followers.

Chapter 7. Globalization and Chinese Basketball Culture

7. 1 Introduction

This chapter examines the interplay between the grobalization of the NBA in China and the glocalization of Chinese basketball focusing on a sociocultural perspective. Americanization is the key concept of Ritzer's grobalization theory in this realm, which is defined as "the export of products, images, technologies, practices, and behavior that are closely associated with America and Americans"(Ritzer, 2011: 50) . Americanization is inclusive of forms of American cultural, institutional, political and economic imperialism(Ritzer, 2007b: 28) , but ultimately points to the American dominance in global consumption(Ritzer, 2011: 50) . Economic grobalization of the NBA in China is highly intertwined with Americanization. During this process, Americanization exports American values and, consequently, transplanted the Americanized consumer culture into Chinese basketball. In this regard, the first section of this chapter offers a view on how the NBA has deconstructed the mainstream Chinese basketball culture and reconstructed it in an American way, stressing the ultimate formation of a consumer culture within Chinese basketball. With regards to glocalization, the later sections concern the reaction with Chinese basketball and how cultural hybrids are created in coping with the NBA culture. In doing so, the second section looks at the nation's response with the NSP. The third section moves on to the response from Chinese basketball grassroots.

7. 2 Grobalization and the NBA's De/reconstruction of Chinese Basketball Culture

7. 2. 1 The Basketball Diplomacy

Before the NBA implemented global strategies in the mid-1980s, some NBA teams had been making global appearances, referred to as"goodwill trips"by the league, for over a decade. The most notable trip had occurred in 1979 when the Washington Bullets traveled to China. Those goodwill games were often considered"little more than exhibitions put on by what were then the best basketball players in the world"(Kirchberg, 2007: 202). However, to some degree, the Bullets' exhibitions in China had political connotations.

In the early 1970s, the Ping Pong Diplomacy encouraged political dialogue between China and the U. S. , as well as opening the door for Chinese sports. In 1979, China witnessed the implementation of the"reform and opening-up"policy, commencing with the establishment of a Sino-U. S. diplomatic relationship, between two countries with entirely different social ideologies and political regimes.

Thereafter, the two governments undertook a great number of official or non-governmental bilateral visits to each other in order to enhance state relationships (Ding, 2004: 5 – 7).

Sport built a bridge for them again. On 29 January 1979, Deng Xiaoping, then vice prime minister of the PRC, was invited by the U. S. government to watch a basketball exhibition by Harlem Globetrotters① during his state visit to the USA (Ding, 2004: 5 – 7). Before the event took place, President Carter regarded Deng's visit a vital event in his political career. Therefore, he took charge of the reception three weeks before Deng's arrival and addressed the Chinese people through Chinese broadcasters, stressing the significance of the new relationships between China and the USA (Ding, 2004: 5-7). At that time, "Zuo" (left, conservative) ideas took hold in Chinese politics. Chinese people could hardly accept such western-style basketball performances with "hot basketball girls" and "hippie show". However, Deng was so excited by the exhibition that he was laughing, clapping and cheering (Ding, 2004: 5-7), which demonstrated his acceptance of western culture and, to some extent, his dismissiveness of the "Zuo" ideas.

Deng's positive response to the Harlem Globetrotters' performance emboldened the U. S. government greatly. It was in this context that the NBA landed in China. In return for Deng's visit to the U. S., on 9 April of the same year, an American basketball team comprised of NBA stars was sent to China and later competed with Chinese basketball teams in Beijing and Shanghai (Xinhua News, 1979; Ding, 2004: 5-7). The Washington Bullets, led by Wes Unseld and Head Coach Dick Motta, visited China in August and played two exhibition games against the Chinese national basketball team and the Bayi Army team. These bilat-

① The Harlem Globetrotters are an exhibition basketball team that combines athleticism, theater and comedy.

eral friendship tours in sport, together with the ever-improving Sino-U. S. relationship, were the cause of China and the USA boycotting the 1980 Moscow Olympic Games(Xinhua News, 1979; Ding, 2004: 5-7). In the summer of 1985, as part of the cultural and educational agreements between China and the U. S., the Chinese national basketball team arrived in New York to begin a month of training and practice against NBA teams, including the New York Knicks, New Jersey Nets, Indiana Pacers, Chicago Bulls, Washington Bullets and Cleveland Cavaliers. Known as the NBA China Friendship Tour, the Chinese team trained with Boston Celtics assistant coach Ed Badger while getting special instruction from NBA legends Red Auerbach and Pete Newell(NBA China, 2011a).

Even though those initial interactivities between the NBA and China are regarded as political events. They had, on the one hand, facilitated America's approach to the new China through basketball; while, on the other hand, fulfilling the necessity for China to learn more about western culture in the early post-reform era. Furthermore, the introduction of the NBA brought Chinese people not only fancy individual basketball skills and game strategies, but also the innovation of a sports industry. At that time, Chinese people were viewing sport at elite level as a tool for building national pride, while mass sports were undertaken with the slogan of "Youyi Diyi, Bisai Di' er!" (Friendship First, Matches Second!). Sport had little association with commercialism. Even the top Chinese basketball players were provided with unadorned domestic-produced sports gear, such as "Meihua" white knit vests and "Huili" cloth shoes. The American players, however, had showed their socialist rivals fashionable apparels and sneakers which were sponsored by transnational sports companies, such as Converse, Adidas and Nike. One of my respondents, a professor argues:

Those early interactive visits in association with the NBA are the groundwork for their aggressive marketing in China today. They changed the ideas of many Chinese towards sports at that time. That is, sports can be involved into business. (Interviewee No. 4)

7. 2. 2 From Political Assumption to Mass Leisure: the NBA and the Changing Idea of Chinese Sports Spectatorship

Before the NBA games were signaled to China, sports had been shown on television occasionally since the 1960s. CCTV and other Chinese television stations had produced their own exclusive sport programs for decades, blendingthe political assumptions and ideas of China into the media they produced and broadcast(McCune, 2011). For instance, the CCTV's broadcasts of the 1984 Olympic Games marked the first time a sports program was beamed live into Chinese households. When CCTV spotlighted the moment Xu Haifeng won the first Olympics gold medal in Chinese history, the whole country was alive with patriotic fervor. During the 1980s, television programs about Chinese women volleyball teams were frequently broadcast by CCTV to disseminate nationalism and patriotism(Chen, 2007; McCune, 2011).

Therefore, when CCTV presented NBA games to its Chinese audience in the early 1990s, it appeared to be an unprecedented openness to western media culture. Despite the NBA games being broadcast on the basis of the popularity of basketball in China, David Stern's product featured something entirely new: the games being shown featured no Chinese athletes and were being played in a country half-way around the world. McCune(2011) argues:

Where Chinese sports broadcasts had previously focused almost exclusively on Chinese national teams and athletes, contextualizing their actions with the logic and ideology of the PRC, the NBA represented a media discourse without nationalist Chinese overtones.

Besides NBA games, peripheral television content about the league's teams and players, which were manufactured by NBA Entertainment, also attracted interest in China. NBA Entertainment is a company which manages the NBA's, Women's National Basketball Association's(WNBA), and NBDL's television, film, internet, publishing, photos, consumer products, marketing partnerships, media properties, and event relationships in the U. S. and internationally. The company was founded in 1982 and is based in Secaucus, New Jersey and operates as a subsidiary of NBA Properties(NBA, 2011a). On 27 October 1990, NBA Entertainment launched the weekly half-hour *Inside Stuff*, which contained spectacular NBA game recaps and highlights, playbacks and player interviews(NBA China, 2011b). *Inside Stuff* was upgraded on 21 October 1991, when NBA Entertainment announced the promotion of the second weekly half-hour, *NBA Action,* on NBA television nationally and internationally(NBA China, 2011b). This TV series covers the history of major NBA events, characters and games, as well as NBA stars' daily lives and community activities. In November 1995, the NBA launched a TV show called *NBA Dei Di*(NBA Zone) with Asia Television Limited(ATV)① in Hong Kong. It marked the debut of the first NBA co-produced show in Asia(NBA China, 2011b). Print publication has also seen another transformation of Chinese leisure entertainment with the NBA. In May 1999, *NBA Shi Kong*(NBA Space & Time), a Chinese version of *Hoop* magazine, debuted in China. It marked NBA's first publishing licensed agreement in Asia(NBA China, 2011b). Since then,

① ATV is a very popular television broadcaster in the Cantonese district of China, although it's based in Hong Kong.

newspapers and magazines tailored for the NBA have mushroomed and remained hot sellers, such as *Lanqiu Xianfeng Bao* (Basketball Vanguards), *Koulan* (SLAM), *MVP*, and *Lanqiu* (Basketball).

It was through accepting this entirely-new American media culture that the first generation of sports fans emerged in China. Zhao Yu, a famous Chinese writer, recalled:

> In pre-reform China, it was not easy for us to get a book, let alone getting to know what basketball is in the outside world. But I often "dunk" in my dreams. I start running from the half court line, dribble, take off, fly...fly over the free-throw zone, then I slam the basketball into the rim with my strongest force... I believe such a dunk has ever come into the dreams of millions of Chinese youth. A decade later, the great Michael Jordan, does the real dunks on the television, the same as that in my dream...I think, for millions of Chinese youth, they obtain their identities on American culture through the game of basketball. (Zhao, 2011: 2)

One of the respondents has also noted the transformation of Chinese sport spectatorship with the power of NBA's media culture since the early 1990s. He stated that:

> I remember the first time I watched NBA games through CCTV's videotapes was in 1993. The NBA games are so different [from the Chinese basketball games], they are so fantastic. You see, the players in the NBA are very tall and strong, they can dunk very easily. They handle the ball so well. And they are playing very fast. I also follow the Shanghai Team, this is because they play for my hometown. But I became crazy on NBA games since then even though the players are not Chinese. (Interviewee No. 29)

This reveals the emergence of NBA basketball fandom in China. Another respondent added to the trend with his memory of middle school, he stated:

> I started to keep my eyes on NBA games from 1992 when the Dream Team swept all other teams and won the gold medal. Since then I began to follow the NBA games broadcast on ATV. In fact, at that time, many of my classmates started watching NBA games. I was in my middle school then. We exchanged our VCDs of NBA Games. During [our] spare time, NBA games and stars became our hot topics. (Interviewee No. 35)

The emergence of NBA basketball fandom has, on the one hand, detached the"nationalist overtones"(McCune, 2011) from Chinese sport spectatorship, on the other hand, it has increased the grassroots of Chinese basketball participants, as one of the respondents noted:

> At the beginning, I liked watching the Olympic Games, World Cups or other international competitions with China's participations. My family would sit together to cheer for China's teams when the big games were on, particularly with those sports [where] we might win medals, such as diving, ping pong and weightlifting. But after watching the NBA games, I, um... just wanted to play basketball...I wanted to learn to shoot, to dribble..."(Interviewee No. 44)

This feature of Chinese basketball fans is distinct from football fans who were first attracted by European football. Although football still remains popular on the media, it has not led to mass participation. Since the early 1990s, basketball has gradually overtaken football to become the most popular participation sport in China. This can be reflected by the words from one respondent:

> Playing football was the first choice for the boys before the NBA came in. We liked the Japanese football stars very much, such as Kazuyoshi Miura. *Soukou no Strain* (a series of Japanese football-themed animation) was also very popular with us. But it all changed in my first middle school year(1995) when CCTV started to broadcast NBA games and highlights. Believe it or not, almost all of us started to play basketball. Only a very few kept playing football. (Interviewee No. 36)

It is also worthy of note that another force resonating with NBA basketball to drive Chinese youth to the basketball court was the Japanese anime series *Slam Dunk*. This was adapted from a basketball-themed manga series written by Takehiko Inoue(a Japanese cartoonist) from the end of 1990 to the middle of 1996. It is about a basketball team from Shōhoku High School with a story and characters largely adapted from NBA basketball. The central character of *Slam Dunk* is Hanamichi Sakuragi, a redheaded and fiery juvenile delinquent who joined the Shōhoku High School basketball team because of his crush on Haruko, the younger sister of the captain. The story depicts Sakuragi's growth from a violent, self-centered ruffian ignorant about basketball into a team player almost able to control his huge passions and raw talent in order to help the hitherto losing team in its quest for the Japanese high school championship(Jefferson, 2003).

Therefore, resulting from the extensive diffusion of the NBA's media culture and the emerging basketball fandom, spectating basketball has been transformed into a significant mode of entertainment in the leisure time of Chinese people since the turn of the new century. It can be seen from the increasing exposure of basketball, the NBA in particular, on CCTV-5. Since the 2005—2006 season, CCTV-5 has co-produced *NBA Time*, a 90-minute NBA highlights program, which airs every Friday during prime time(NBA China, 2011c). Hosted by local basketball commentators and experts, the show recaps a week of NBA excitement and action, news and local NBA events such as the NBA Jam Van, Junior NBA China and off-court news and player tours. This program was later turned into a program called *Basketball Park*. Most recently, CCTV-5 launched another program, *NBA Frontline*, on 21 February 2013 which is broadcast on Thursday 7: 30pm weekly. With its theme song, *Start Right Away*, the program also holds a slogan to promote NBA culture:

> You may often watch NBA games, but they are not the frontline [of the NBA]; you may be enchanted by block-shoots, dunks and clutch-shoots, but they are not the cream [of the NBA]; you may be fascinated by the active NBA superstars, but the historical figures [of the NBA] are more respectable. (CCTV-5, 2013-2-21)

Beside exposure on television, online content relating to the NBA is usually placed on the top sports volumes of most Chinese web portals. Moreover, with the spreading of NBA basketball culture, basketball players in China have become more and more popular and well-known. According to the *2012 CSM Media Report*①, among the top 15 popular sport stars in China, basketball has the most with five, including: Yao Ming (1st), Michael Jordan (5th), Kobe Bryant (6th), Allen Iverson (10th) and Yi Jianlian (15th), all of them are (or were) NBA stars (CSM, 2012). The following section will take a closer look at Chinese NBA fandom through a case study of the fans' community of the Indiana Pacers.

① CSM Media Research is a joint venture between CVSC-TNS Research (CTR), a subsidiary company of CCTV, and the Kantar Media. It operates the world's largest TV & radio audience measurement panel network.

7. 2. 3 Sports Cults, Collective Identities, and the Chinese NBA Fan Community: A Case Study of the ChinaPacers

Turning sports spectators into fans is only the beginning of the NBA's effort to reformulate China's basketball culture. Over the past two decades, NBA stars and teams have achieved a strong deeply-embedded identity with Chinese basketball fans community, which has formed through their collective memories as a form of nostalgia.

Michael Jordan is beyond all questions the most influential transnational sporting ambassador raising the NBA to a cosmopolitan league. The globally-phenomenal fever of Jordan has been well documented by academia. For example, to examine the interconnections and disjunctures that distinguish the complex relationship betweenthe global media and meaning within the context of contemporary transnational sporting culture, Andrew et al. (1996), using the term "Jordanscapes", have explored the relationship between globally-mediated cultural products, and the cultural contingencies of three markedly distinct localized contexts: New Zealand, Poland and Britain. Relating to the Chinese context, LaFeber (2002: 15) has observed Jordan's popularity:

> It's not supervised for them(remote Tibetans) knowing Michael Jordan. He was the most famous athlete and one of the most recognizable people in the world. Jordan and his "Red Oxen," as his team was known in much of Asia, had gained renown fortheir basketball championships.

Jordan is such a popular sport star in China that he was once named the third most well-known figure in Chinese history, paralleling with Premier Zhou Enlai(LaFeber, 2002: 13). However, when Jordan finally retired in 2003, Chinese

NBA fans turned their eyes on other superstars, such as Kobe Bryant and LeBron James, and certainly Yao Ming. This also echoed the research result of Kaplan and Langdon's(2012) survey of Chinese fandom for American professional sports, Chinese fans are more likely to follow their favourite professional sports team because of an individual athlete.

Distinctly, for some NBA fans, their loyalty to a star may extend to the team. The Indiana Pacers began playing in 1967 as a member of the ABA and was acquired by the NBA in the merger of 1976. The team is located in Indiana's capital city, Indianapolis. It is a city far less known to Chinese than other cities like New York, Los Angeles or Chicago. In Indianapolis, the Pacers are also less favoured by natives than the annual Indianapolis 500, the Brickyard 400, the Indiana Fever in the WNBA and Men's and Women's NCAA Basketball Tournaments. Compared to other NBA teams, such as the Chicago Bulls, Los Angeles Lakers, Miami Heat and Boston Celtics, Indiana Pacers is minor. But for their Chinese fans, the Pacers are truly big.

ChinaPacers. com, home of the largest fans community of Indiana Pacers in China, was founded by Holick Lee(Interviewee No. 16) and Howard Lee(Interviewee No. 17), two brothers, on 20 July 2000. They have written more than 2, 500 daily reports in their spare time, and the website achieved two million visits in early 2013. This website, together with a QQ① group and a message board, are the major online' hang-outs' for the Chinese Pacers fans to follow Pacers' games and to share their memories of following the Pacers. They organize a gathering each year and fans of the team come from all parts of China. Some of them may take a train spending more than 30 hours on the journey. At the party, the fans play 3 on 3 or

① QQ is one of the most popular instant messaging softwares among Chinese younger generation developed by Tencent Holdings Limited.

5 on 5 games in their Pacers-logo apparel and sneakers endorsed by Pacers' players, as is shown in Picture 7-1. The ChinaPacers have just finished their nationwide get-together in Shanghai on 30 April 2013. About 30 fans from all over the country participated in the event. While the boys are playing basketball, the girls have another way to show their love. For example, they will draw portraits for the Pacers. In the 2008 gathering they made a cake with a Reggie Miller image on it to celebrate his birthday, which is shown in Picture 7-2.

Their tribal doctrine came from Reggie Miller, one of the NBA's best shooters of all-time, who attracted his Chinese fan base mainly during the second half of the 1990s when the Indiana Pacers and the Chicago Bulls were battling in a heated series for the Eastern Conference Finals. Jordan was at the height of his career while Miller was renowned as"being the enemy"or"the brave underdog"of the unbeatable airman. Holick Lee noted that,

Picture 7-1 A Group Photo of the Members of the ChinaPacers Community

Source: photo taken by Holick Lee on 30 April 2013.

While Jordan and his famous shoes generated a large group of followers, true basketball fans had a stronger appreciation for fundamental basketball, hard work and a never-give-up determination epitomized by"Miller Time"①,

① It refers to Miller's greatest clutch-shot moments in the NBA games.

Picture 7-2 A Cake with Miller's Image Made by the ChinaPacers Community

Source: photo taken by the author on 4 October 2008.

and so the story of Pacers fans in China began. (Interviewee No. 16)

Therefore, the classical clutch-shots of "Miller Time" are the most touching nostalgic events during the gathering. The idea of reproducing a video series about Miller's greatest moment in the games firstly came up during their gathering in 2007. Now they have re-enacted three videos entitled "Great Pacers Moment Recreation", which includes: 1) Miller's eight points in 8.9 seconds which led the Pacers to a 107-105 victory in Game 1 of the 1995 Eastern Conference Semifinals against the Knicks; 2) Miller's game-winning 3-pointer after he shoved Michael Jordan in the 1998 Eastern Conference Finals; 3) Reggie's 3-pointer that he banked in at New Jersey in the first round of the 2002 playoffs. But the most touching moment for them was Reggie's last game in the 2005 playoffs.

Nowadays, despite the fact that most of the Pacers games are broadcast online, the fans still cherish the game thread on the message board, where they share so many memories. Holick Lee noted,

> From Reggie banking in the 40-footer in New Jersey, to the record-breaking 61-win season; from the Auburn Hills episode to the trade of Ron Artest; from Danny Granger being selected No. 17 to receiving the Most Improved Player trophy in Conseco Fieldhouse, the fans experienced more than 900 game-mornings, nine NBA Drafts, all kinds of offseason player movements, and even the demolition of Market Square Arena. (Interviewee No. 16)

Through ChinaPacers. com, the fans shared their joys and tears, they become close friends, and two fans even got married. One of the respondents(Interviewee No. 19), from Shanghai, got to know another respondent in this study(Interviewee No. 20), a girl from Xi' an, on the ChinaPacers. com in 2002. They chatted about the Pacers online and fell in love with each other. They lived in two cities separated by 1,000 kilometers but shared the same faith. In 2008, they were married in Shanghai and became China's first Pacers Couple.

Although Miller is not on the court any longer, the ChinaPacers' loyalty and commitment to the Indiana Pacers doesn't change. One respondent, a Pacers fan from Gansu, noted that the Pacers are in their blood when he said:

> The Pacers have weaved into the fabric of my everyday life. My value perceiving the world has been changed because of Miller. I would choose loyalty over wealth and I believe nothing can replace hard work. I have been in love with this team for 17 years and I will love them as always. (Interviewee No. 21)

Spending half a year's salary to watch a basketball game, many fans regard it as insane. However, for the fans who have been following them long enough, they will understand. One respondent (Interviewee No. 18), a 27-year-old (in 2011) Chinese Pacers fan, took a 20-hour flight from Beijing to Indianapolis in 2011 to realize his 17-year-long dream, to watch a NBA game of the Indiana Pacers. On the interview with Fox Sports during the game, he confessed to millions in the worldwide audience:

> [I follow the Pacers] mostly because of Reggie Miller, you know, everybody loves Jordan, but I don't want to follow everybody, I love the feeling of being' enemy', so I love Reggie since 1994 till now... It's some kind of faith, it supports me to move on, Reggie, if you are watching this, I have some words for you, you have so many fans in China, they are diehard fans. We love you from our hearts. We love being the enemy with you Reggie... Reggie, thank you, you are my idol, you are my power of going on... (Fox Sport, 2011)

7.2.4 Individualistic Liberalization: the NBA and Chinese Subcultures and Consumption

Basketball is a team sport that appropriately accommodates traditional Chinese culture in which collectivism is highly cherished. As a result, from the Soviet-model playing style since the early 1950s to the "Xiao, Kuai, Ling" (small, fast, agile) playing style since the early 1980s, teamwork and chemistry are emphasized both in offense and defense in Chinese elite and mass basketball. However, attributed to the NBA's trends of being dominated by individual superstars, individualism has become a pervasive concept in Chinese basketball nowadays.

The creation of these"selves"in Chinese basketball is closely related to the NBA's global media exposure and promotion market. In an earlier paper, Andrew Morris(2002) has observed that:

> The old debate over the team versus the individual, as much a part of modern sports history in China as it is anywhere else, has been rendered almost moot by the relentless worldwide NBA marketing of stars like Michael Jordan, Penny Hardaway, Shaquille O'Neal, and Kobe Bryant.

He further points out two important expressions of this spirit in basketball discourse. One is the most thrilling and individualistic staples of the modern game, the slam dunk, which, he argues, is a site where fans' desires converge with the basketball bureaucracy's marketing quest(Morris, 2002). Another important site for his discussion of the individualist element is in the person of erstwhile NBA star Denis Rodman who is known to all for his negative characteristics but is imaged by the media and advertisers as a reflection of selfhood(Morris, 2002). Additionally, the result of a survey that Morris conducted by mail in 1999 has demonstrated some of the"selves"across basketball participants in China-that the game is"my choice"or that it"shows my skills". Many respondents' parents support their interest in basketball because it is "my interest" or "my ideal" or "my life's goal". Others explained that through basketball they could"show my own individual style" or simply"make more and more people know who I am"(Morris, 2002).

Over the past decade, however, these"selves"have been amplified by Chinese basketball-playing enthusiasts following Morris's(2002) observation. Above all, in addition to the slam dunk that most basketball participants are unable to finish, other handsome individual scoring skills are tending to be the favourites, such as crossovers, cut-ins and in-your-face shots. Even at the elite level, individualistic plays are also increasingly impacting Chinese basketball. The recruitment of Chen Jianghua into the national team in 2006, who is known for his individual skills and for this reason is nicknamed the "Chinese Allen Iverson", serves as a good case.

A more evident sign of the infusion of individualism into Chinese basketball-in-play is the emergence of streetball. Streetball is a variation of basketball, typically played on outdoor courts and featuring a significantly less-formal structure and more relaxed attitude towards the game's rules. As such, its format is more conducive to allowing players to publicly showcase their own individual skills. Streetball was introduced to Guangzhou from Hong Kong in the early 1990s(Chen & Wu, 2006). The first large-scale 3 on 3 streetball competition was organized in Guangzhou by the Yangcheng Evening News Group. About 300 teams showed their skills. In 1999, Guangzhou witnessed another mega streetball event with 1, 590 teams participating(Chen & Wu, 2006). The Chinese Streetball Association (CSA) was established in 2002 when more than 50, 000 streetball enthusiasts registered with the CSA(Chen & Wu, 2006). Since then, streetball has become popular throughout China. Moreover, this basketball style has seen more and more homogenized with American streetball. American streetballers, such as Hot Source, are becoming a well-known name among Chinese youth.

As in Morris's(2002) early observation, playing basketball is still illustrating "the centrality of the sport to the lives and identities of so many Chinese youths". Their worship of basketball and NBA stars is still a significant element for their new imagination of personal identity. NBA fans like the ChinaPacers have demonstrated their worship of NBA stars through their common-shared fandom. But in another way, the charismatic power of NBA stars is also shaping the personalities of many Chinese through basketball-in-play. One respondent, a fan of Allen Iverson, told the author his hard road to be recognized on the court:

> I can't remember the first time I touched [a] basketball. But I won't forget one moment in my 6th year of primary school. Before a basketball match against our next-door class, the head teacher was choosing her starters and I raised my hand, but she just said loudly to the crowd: "those who are not tall enough will not be counted!" I was a small guy in the class. I felt very bad at her words but I didn't want to be looked down upon. Since then, I practised very hard. I practised dribbling the ball with a plastic basketball barefoot at noon and in the sun. After class or sometime at nights, I took my ball out, went to the playground to practise again. It wasn't all about fun, but about winning and self-respect. When I felt tired, the mottoes of Allen Iverson, "Only the Strong Survive!" and "Fear No One!" reminded me to keep on moving. (Interviewee No. 36)

If the recognition of Dennis Rodman identifiesa certain degree of ideological emancipation of the Chinese since the middle 1990s (Morris, 2002), then the warm welcome for Allen Iverson since the late 1990s has reinforced the ideas of democracy in Chinese society, at least in the sporting sphere. "Being different" might be considered as somewhat rebellious and against the interpersonal harmony of the traditional Chinese world-view, but Iverson is really different. Born into a poor family in Hampton, Virginia to his single 15-year-old mother, Iverson struggled on the basketball court and was finally selected first overall by the Philadelphia 76ers in the 1996 NBA Draft. Listed at just six feet tall, Iverson became the shortest first overall pick ever in a league normally dominated by big men and in a basketball world where Jordan was regarded as the God of the NBA or even of basketball, Iverson claimed on entering the NBA, "I never really dreamed of being like Mike... but I damn sure wanted to be like Allen Iverson". But this small man does impress the basketball world with an honorable NBA career, including:

1 NBA MVP Award(2001), 11 NBA All-Star Awards(2000—2010), and 4 NBA Scoring Champion Awards(1999, 2001—2002, 2005).

The mottoes of Iverson, "Only the Strong Survive!" and "Fear No One!" certainly imaged his life story and triumphant NBA career. On the other hand, they are driving the youth to be different or to be cool as in the imagination of Iverson, their Afro-American hero. In China, such difference and coolness conveyed by NBA's black stars like Iverson has also set fire to the transformation of Chinese basketball culture into a pop culture in conjunction with the growth of streetball. Whenever Iverson appeared on the basketball court or media, his distinctive personal appearance was instantly recognized with baggy pants, oversized shirts, tattoos, cornrows, and custom-made diamond necklace. Today, baggy pants and oversized jerseys, instead of the short, tight and narrow-edged basketball apparel, are the most popular gears seen on Chinese basketball courts. Off the court, baggy pants, oversized shirts, tattoos, cornrows, and custom-made diamond necklaces have become essentials for Chinese youth to produce what they call "street culture", in which western rock and hip-hop music and dressing-emulation from pop stars are usually blended. Further, Iverson's mottoes are virtually two promotional slogans of Reebok, which elevates Iverson from a role model to a global commercial spokesman to peddle sports goods to the youth. Thus, "Only the Strong Survive!" is marked on the sole of The Answer IV, a pair of Iverson-signed sneakers made by Reebok which was released in 2001.

While Iverson's mottoes are metaphors for individualism and difference, two mainstream globalized corporate symbols, Nike's Swoosh and Jordan's Jump Man, have accelerated the collective intensification of cultural industrialization. One of the most recognizable brand names in the world, Nike's corporate slogan—"Just Do It"—has become a maxim in both public and private life, and the Swoosh logo is ubiquitous globally(Miller et al., 2001: 56). Additionally, Nike features stars who allegedly play for idealistic reasons rather than crass commercial motives("I Love This Game!"), and "desire" emulation ("Be Like Mike!"; "I am Tiger Woods!") (Miller et al., 2001: 57). The alignment of Nike and Jordan is the most powerful global commercial force ever, as LaFeber(2002: 15) argues:

> Jordan was especially famous for he was the superhuman who flew through the air in television advertisements as he endlessly and effortlessly dunked basketballs and, simultaneously, sold Nike sneakers.

Since the mid-1990s, post-reform China has been experiencing a consumer revolution. Economic transition has contributed to a massively growing advertising industry and much of the apparently novelty-seeking materialism of the younger generation is cultivated by advertising and marketing(Tsang, 2010: 151). As a result, these advertising campaigns of sports TNCs have turned Chinese youth, to a greater or lesser degree, from basketball-playing fans into basketball-consuming fans. In highlighting the popularity of Jordan and the win-win situation between NBA stars and the TNCs in China, Morris(2002) commented,

> Nike, author of this seamless Jordan mythology and modern sporting goods marketing as we know it, is such a unanimous choice among these basketball players/fans that its Swoosh, not the PRC's five gold stars, has perhaps become the most enduringlyhegemonic symbol in China today.

Morris' (2002) observation in the late 1990s is also telling the fact of those years:

> [15 years ago], Chinese youth in far-off towns and villages dreamed of a comfortable pair of Nikes, even though they knew that these things are simply not for them.

Even in the urban areas, buying a pair of Nike sneakers was once unaffordable for many Chinese youths. One of the respondents, who was born and grew up in Foshan City, Guangdong Province, said:

> I am not kidding. Having a pair of Huili shoes was one of my dreams in primary school years. When I entered middle school [1993], most boys in my class wore Huili. But I couldn't afford RMB 32 [EUR 4] for them. Before the third year [1995], I wore the cheaper cloth sports shoes which cost me about RMB 8 [EUR 1]. Then I had a pair of fake Huili for RMB 15 [EUR 1. 88]. (Interviewee No. 27)

But this is no longer the case in China today. In the past, there were only a few Nike shops in the urban area of a city, but now Nike shops and their factory shops are easy to find in most high streets in China, as in western countries. They are now also opening their franchises in some townships of coastal cities, as well as online shops, such as Taobao. com, T-Mall. com and jd. com.

While this corporatized sport consumption has, to some extent, demonstrated the modern lifestyle of Chinese people, it can seem more like a postmodern obsession born of the rhetoric of cultural globalization. A high degree of consumerism has been cultivated in the Chinese basketball-consuming cohort, particularly the sneaker lovers. Some of them are buying sneakers to live out their teenage desires. For example, after graduated from Sun Yat-Sen University in 2005, the aforementioned respondent is now a senior manager in an import and export company in Guangzhou, earning more than RMB 20,000 (EUR 2,500) a month. To "buy his memories", he spends a considerable sum of money in buying sneakers each year. He now has a full set of Air Jordans (see Picture 7-3), from Air Jordan I to Air Jordan XXVIII, which cost him about RMB 100,000 (EUR 12,500). He said:

My colleagues spend money on high-end digital products for hobbies, such as digital single-lens reflex cameras [DSLR] and intelligent mobile phones. But I prefer collecting basketball shoes. Actually I don't know how much money I have spent on sneakers. For playing basketball, two pairs a year are enough. But most sneakers I bought will be sealed in a plastic bag then stored in a customized wardrobe. I take them out and recall my past time through these sneakers from time to time. That is why I place a pair of Huili shoes next to an original pair of Air Jordan I [very rare and valuable]. (Interviewee No. 27)

Picture 7-3 The Nike Air Jordans Collection of One Respondent in This Study

Source: photo taken by the author on 22 July 2012.

Whereas some of them are newly seduced by the marketing magic of corporate advertisers and NBA stars, as one of the respondents said:

My first sneakers were The Kobe 2K5. I remember there were several

> colorways released, black and white, gray and white, red and white, the Lakers [yellow and purple], black and white and blue, white and red and grey. But I finally picked the atlas-designed ones, because there is a map of Los Angeles on the shoe vamp. LA is my dream city. When I look at those shoes, I want to know what time it is now in LA and if Kobe has begun his morning training… On the 2005 All-Star Games, Kobe wore a pair of stockings and he wrapped the leg-tube to the upper of The 2K5. I learnt that and kept dressing in this way for quite a while … The 2K5 started my sneakers' life. Then I bought The Kobe 1, the first signed sneakers of Kobe. The ones I bought were the all-star colorway ones, but Kobe appeared on the All-Star Games with another colorway ones, the white and red and blue. Then I decided to get these sneakers … The Kobc 2 were firstly on Kobe's feet in the Christmas Game of 2006 … Since then, I have bought about 30 pairs of Nike sneakers …(Interviewee No. 40)

Even though local sports-goods makers are growing, Chinese NBA/basketball fans still prefer foreign brands. One of the respondents, a veteran sneakers collector, commented with a critical view:

> Endorsed by Dwyane Wade, many fans suspect whether the Wade Zhidao can compare [with] Nike's Foamposite. They feel RMB 1, 300 [EUR 162. 5] is too expensive to buy a pair of Li Ning sneakers, but it's fine to buy a pair of [the] same grade sneakers from Nike. That they prefer [a] foreign brand is quite true. For local brands, even though you sign the best NBA stars, you are still a Chinese brand, born to be inferior. Even Nike take the Zoom off [from the sole], they still buy them at a high cost. In contrast, you see Under Armour is the flavor now. They are fresh and set up in 1996,

but only because they are American. (Interviewee No. 45)

However, for most young Chinese sneakers lovers, buying sneakers is only a way to get closer to, or to look like, their NBA heroes who are far away in America. They have little interest in supporting homemade basketball goods, as one of the respondents stated:

> When I received The Kobe 4, Kobe 5 and Kobe 6, I realized Nike is crafty. They claim high technologies are injected. But what I see is lesser and thinner leather but more and more plastics used. Worse, the carbon board is less supportive than before. However, the price [of Nike sneakers] is going up steadily ... Anyway, buying Kobe's sneakers, just like a hobby, becomes a habit. I know Nike is tricky, but I just can't stop spending money on them. I love Kobe so much. (Interviewee No. 38)

Therefore, it's revealed that the NBA's grobalization has reformatted Chinese basketball culture with the infusion of an Americanized way of spectating, participating and consuming sports. The following two sections take on the reaction of Chinese basketball.

7.3 A Resistant Voice from Above: The Nation's Culturalization of Chinese Basketball

When Chinese basketball culture seemed to be jeopardized by the convergent power from the NBA and similar global commercial agents, there emerges a force from the nation that aims to triumph over the "destabilizing and unsettlingly diverse desires and loyalties that the Chinese youth are manufacturing, redefining, and selling from the NBA culture"(Morris, 2002). This is specifically set off by a series of conferences and forums led by the CBA.

7. 3. 1 The First Chinese Basketball Culture Forum

Since Li Yuanwei assumed office in the CBMC in 2003, he has been seeking the way out, which is to constructan indigenous basketball culture. At the 2005 CBAL Club Owners Summit on 26 April, Li pointed out that promoting basketball culture is a significant task to secure the reformation of Chinese professional basketball and would be one key point in the CBMC's workbook for the coming years (Li, 2005b). During the meeting, he also announced his main work schemes during his tenure, which included preparation for the Beijing Olympics, reformation of the CBAL's governance structure, promotion of grassroots basketball, and the building of basketball culture. Then he stressed that basketball culture should play a role as the groundwork for the other three projects(Li, 2005b).

However, there was neither a previous definition of basketball culture nor a consensus from basketball practitioners or academic scholars. So the only thing the CBMC could do straight away was to advocate some requirements for the clubs in the newly-regulated membership determination process: each club must organize at least one open day for fans; during the season, each club must conduct at least two public activities with the CBALC, and during the off-season, each club must conduct at least two training camps for their fans(Li, 2005b).

Meanwhile, the CBMC called for a nationwide debate on how to develop Chinese basketball culture. Thus, the CBCF was born, which was jointly organized by the CBMC, the Sport Culture Development Center of the GAS and Soochow University. On 9 December 2005, the first forum was attended by over 100 Chinese basketball practitioners and academic scholars. The topic for the forum was "Building Basketball Culture, Forging Harmonious Basketball". Li Yuanwei highlighted again the significance of building Chinese basketball culture:

> Basketball has been introduced into China for more than a century. During this century, basketball has been widely popularized to the world including China. From a type of physical activity, it has evolved into a new cultural carrier which concentrates political, economic, and sociocultural functions throughout the world. Therefore, it's been imperative for us to re-understand basketball... Following the trend of world basketball, to construct our own culture is significant for Chinese basketball. Only by doing this can we strengthen the development of Chinese basketball. It's foundational and strategic... It's a difficult but lofty and epoch-making task for every basketball practitioner in China ... We will miss the best opportunity to develop Chinese basketball if we don't advocate building Chinese basketball culture at this moment. (Li, 2005a)

Li went on to point out that Chinese basketball culture was facing two major challenges, including the impacts of sports grobalization:

> One is the achievement and spiritual outlook of the national teams in the Beijing Olympics, which is the expectation of our government and the Chinese nation. The other is to fight back [against] the global professional sports giants, such as the NBA, American professional baseball, F1 and European football, to regain our own sports market. We need to draw back not only the sports consumers, but also sports sponsors. (Li, 2005a)

To achieve this, Li stressed that China must emancipate its ideology and remap the blueprint to develop Chinese basketball. Therefore, it was necessary to get rid of the idea of the prioritization of elitism so as to forge the culture of basketball and ultimately construct a harmonious basketball culture(Li, 2005a).

During this forum, a definition of Chinese basketball culture was finally given, which refers to the institutionalization of the ideas and behaviors of basketball spectators and participants, and the incorporation of the understandings, techniques, traditions, and institutions of basketball. It aims to come up with a common view on the values of basketball and achieve socialization and education for individuals. It includes the conceptual and behavioral culture of basketball participants, the' soft' culture in ideology and' hard' culture in material. Thus, Chinese basketball culture includes five cultural elements: competition, entertainment, spectating, historical and sports goods(CBA, 2005a).

In addition, during the round table discussion, the CBMC proposed to issue an outline of Chinese basketball culture and to create a facilitating committee. They also came up with the following proposals: 1) to launch the national team culture building in coordination with the preparation for the Beijing Olympics; 2) to launch the professional league culture in coordination with the reformation of the CBAL, which included two aspects: sports competition culture and fan culture; 3) to launch the building of a Basketball Hall of Fame in order to promote the historical culture of Chinese basketball and 4) to launch a further-education project for all basketball practitioners to professionalize their service (CBA, 2005a).

7.3.2 The Second Chinese Basketball Culture Forum

Two years later, the 2nd CBCF was held on 26 and 27 December 2007. In the view of Prof. Wang Jiahong, convener of the forum, national character is one significant aspect of basketball culture which deserves deeper investigation. So he entitled the forum"Globalization and the National Character of Chinese Basketball Culture"(Wang, 2007), more than 100 practitioners and academic scholars attended the forum, tens of papers were received and they were published in a special issue after the forum. Prof. Lu Yuanzhen echoed Wang's vision, he stated:

> Chinese basketball is merging with world basketball at a fast pace, we must make a contribution to world basketball and make our voice vibrate to the world. This is the internal driving force for us to promote Chinese basketball culture. (Lu, 2007)

During the forum, a draft of the *Outline of Building Chinese Basketball Culture* was made public by the CBMC. The *Outline* aims to map out the ways of building a basketball culture with Chinese characteristics(CBA, 2007c). It embraces the ideas of "basketball is life", which means basketball is a lifestyle and improves life quality. It follows President Hu Jintao's slogan of"human-centered, applying the' Kexue Fazhanguan' (Scientific Outlook on Development) to build a Chinese-characteristic harmonious society"and the strategic deployment of"enhancing the socialist-characteristic cultural development"at the 17th National People's Congress in 2007. It is also the guideline for Chinese basketball practitioners of all kinds throughout the country. In detail, the *Outline* aims to accomplish the government's mission in the Beijing Olympics and to consolidate the social and market foundation for Chinese basketball(CBA, 2007c). Apart from these stereotypical political appeals, the *Outline* represents a breakthrough by taking western values into account when it states:

> Western basketball culture which is characterized by competitiveness, passion, individualism, aggressiveness, and teamwork is a necessary and ben-

eficial complement. (CBA, 2007c)

In the *Outline*, the general principles point out the significance of building Chinese basketball, its definition and its objectives. Following on, five cultural sections are identified which are adapted from the proposals during the round table discussion of the 1st Basketball Culture Forum: 1) building a basketball team culture, 2) building a professional league culture, 3) building a basketball fan culture, 4) building a mass basketball culture, and, 5) building a historical basketball culture. The Chinese Basketball Culture Promotion Committee was set up by the CBMC several months later, which is responsible for the organization and management of the implementation of the *Outline*(CBA, 2007c).

Regarding the building of basketball team culture, collectivism, nationalism, collaboration, hard work and courage are highlighted. It points out that national basketball teams are the highest representatives in the building of a basketball team culture. They are responsible for demonstrating the new image of Chinese sports internationally and earning its reputation nationally(CBA, 2007c). Thus, their mission is to pursue high performance so as to promote the prestige of the nation. "Bayi Ethos", a spirit acquiring most tenacious training and competitive effort developed by the Bayi Army Team, should be assimilated by Chinese national basketball teams at all levels(CBA, 2007c). Further, the *Outline* also identifies the relationship between the team and an individual player, which notes that "collective interest outweighs individual interest" (CBA, 2007c). Therefore, an "individual player's career should contribute to the development of the team, while the team should benefit an individual player's career with long-term support" (CBA, 2007c). For the national team players, "they should have a foresight on the development of Chinese basketball, they should play for the country's interest, and they should be hard-working in training and competing to earn credit for the country"(CBA, 2007c).

For the building of a professional league culture, the *Outline* aims to promote the CBAL brand. To achieve this, the CBMC would follow the concepts of competing basketball, entertaining basketball and moneyspinning basketball, which means to foster elite athletes for the country, to create fun for fans, and to create a fortune for sponsors(CBA, 2007c). More practically, the CBMC would implement more strategies to serve the fans, media and sponsors. Thus, (also see Chapter 6) the slogan of the CBAL was changed to"My Team, My Game, My CBA! "A public welfare project named' The CBA and My Growth' was launched. The logos of the CBA were changed, the champion's cup was named the Mou Zuoyun Cup and championship rings were awarded. Moreover, the CBMC would conduct professional education for players, coaches, referees, and all staff related to the CBAL (CBA, 2007c).

For the building of a basketball fan culture, the Outline aims to construct a temperate spectating atmosphere. On the one hand, fans should mind their behavior when watching the CBAL games. On the other hand, the clubs should offer more affordable tickets and conduct more open days for their fans. For the building of a mass basketball culture, the *Outline* aims to expand the social basketball foundation to foster a reserve pool of players. The CBMC would keep conducting grassroots basketball activities throughout the country(CBA, 2007c). Before that, the first Chinese Basketball Open, the"He Long Cup", was inaugurated on 24 December 2005 at Beijing 8th High School(CBA, 2006a). The 2007 tournament saw more than 3,000 amateur basketball teams competing in nearly 40,000 games in 165 cities of 25 provinces(CBA, 2008). Juan Antonio Samaranch, the former president of the IOC, was invited as the honorary consultant. For the building of a historical basketball culture, the *Outline* aims to keep records and the heritage of

Chinese basketball history(CBA, 2007c). In 2005, the CBMC drafted a scheme and paid a visit to the NBA Hall of Fame and the American Basketball College to learn how they run(CBA, 2006a). On 24 September 2007, the CBMC, sponsored by China Worldteam Investment Holding Group who ran a basketball-themed website named TBBA. com, launched an online museum to showcase the historical heritage of Chinese basketball. The CBMC is also planning to build a Hall of Fame for Chinese basketball in the near future, as suggested in the *Outline*(CBA, 2008).

The CBCRC, the first and only research center in China, was set up by the School of Sports Studies of Soochow University during this forum. Scholars at the center have made great achievements in the research into Chinese basketball culture. Besides the forums, they have published a number of papers in national and international journals and a series of books. To trace back the trajectory of basketball, they have also established research links with Springfield College in the U. S.. More importantly, they have compiled a great amount of research data for basketball culture researchers.

7. 3. 3 The Third Chinese Basketball Culture Forum

On 4 December 2011, the 3rd CBCF was convened, again at Soochow University. A number of important figures from Chinese basketball took part in the forum including: Li Yuanwei, vice-president of the CBA and former director of the CBMC; Yao Songpin, vice-president of the CBA and former principal of Shanghai Sports College; Liang Xiaolong, deputy director of the Politics and Law Department of the GAS; Bao Mingxiao, director of the Sport Social Science Research Center of the GAS; Yao Ming, owner of the Shanghai Dongfang Basketball Club; and Xu Jicheng, assistant director of the sport department of Xinhua News and a senior journalist. In response to the ideas of "basketball is life" advocated in the *Outline*, this forum was entitled "Let Basketball Return to Daily Life" (CBA, 2011a). For Yao Ming,

> The concept of "Let Basketball Return to Daily Life" refers to Chinese people should love basketball and play basketball, but should not involve social benefits and national or individual honor. Basketball should not be only a sport, but also an approach to educate the youth and a lifestyle for all Chinese. (Yao, 2011)

For Li Yuanwei, basketball should be centered on lives, thus, mass basketball should be stressed. Echoing Li, Yao Songping called for both governmental and non-governmental support to achieve this(CBA, 2011a). The forum ended with a round table discussion on "The Function and Future of Basketball Culture under Globalization". To emphasize the role Chinese nationalism should play in fighting the NBA's penetration in China, Prof. Wang Jiahong argued:

> The world is witnessing rapid development and adaption to globalization. Local culture plays a significant role for individual nation states to survive in this process. Thus, preserving Chinese culture and enhancing China's soft power is an important task for us. This task requires us to strengthen our cultural consciousness and confidence and to promote our own national cultural character. Basketball is the creature ofthe civilization of human beings and a common language of the world, which also embodies the soft power of individual nation states. Therefore, constructing our indigenous basketball culture is significant to enhancing and balancing the discourse between Chinese basketball and global basketball, and to preserve the nationality of Chinese culture and the heterogeneity of global basketball culture. (Wang, 2011)

In Wang's opinion:

> During 16-year's professionalization, Chinese basketball has successfully drawn the lesson from western professional leagues in terms of league operation, marketing, resource allocation and governance models. In this process, Chinese basketball has infused a lot of Chinese elements to enhance national consciousness to avoid homogenization. (Wang, 2011)

However, Wang pointed out that there are still some important research fields to be explored: conflict and integration between regnant basketball and Chinese national basketball cultures; the transformation of Chinese sport development and the response of basketball culture; the branding of Chinese professional basketball; the promotion of basketball culture in the context of China's cultural reformation; a theoretical framework for China's characteristic basketball culture; the moral building of basketball teams; the engagement of basketball theories and practice; the development of the function of basketball culture; and the development of a cultural industry in basketball(Interviewee No. 1).

In short, under the NSP and Li Yuanwei's governing principles, basketball officials in the CBA and professors in Chinese colleges have been busy seeking ways out and infusing political and national assumptions to prevent Chinese basketball culture from being homogenized by the NBA culture. Unfortunately and ironically, before we can evaluate their contribution, the flag for the culturalization of Chinese basketball has been put down with the disbanding of the NSP in 2009. Although the CBCFs survive and continue to be held every two to four years, their substantial role in basketball reformation has returned to ordinary academic seminars, as is revealed in the 3rd CBCF.

7.4 A Resistant Voice from Below: the Grassroots' Ethos and the Glocalization of Chinese Basketball Culture

Ideology emerges, changes and diminishes in the spatial-temporal course, whereas culture accommodates, accumulates and evolves through this continuum, as Prof. Lu noted on the 3rd CBCF:

> Culture and ideology interrelate to a great degree, but they are different [concepts]. Ideology is epochal, utilitarian and hierarchical, but [the concept of] culture is much broader throughout time and space. Only if ideology is interwoven with culture and follows the principles of culture can ideology hold sway the discourse. The culture of basketball is no exception. (Lu, 2011).

On the contrary of the festinate top-to-down culturalization strategy from the nation, the Chinese people are casually playing the game of basketball with their well-established traditions and soaring enthusiasm in every corner of the country. This persistence of Chinese basketball's grassroots and the game ethos they have cultivated is, in a down-to-earth way, defining, shaping and glocalizing the indigenous basketball culture, and, is resisting the NBA's cultural grobalization.

7.4.1 Basketball and Its Chinese Citizenship

Distinct from other successful globalized American cultural commodities in China, such as rock music, Hollywood films, jeans and fast food, the NBA's proliferation embraces a more solid cornerstone-a century's popularization of Chinese basketball. Tens of sports were introduced to modern China by westerners, few of which have taken root with the Chinese. Some lasted only for a few years, like baseball in the 1940s, bowling in the 1980s; some are favoured only by a small population, like boxing and diving; while some occur only in particular locations, like equestrianism and skiing; some fail to boom without massive participation, like gymnastics and track-and-field; some seem hard to keep growing, like swimming and volleyball; some may need more observation to comment on, like tennis, outdoor sports and X-games(Lu, 2008). Table tennis, badminton and basketball are the three major imported sports in China today. Table tennis has been the "nation's game"for decades whilst badminton is the first choice in the leisure time of Chinese, particularly in urban areas.

Basketball, however, has become a"national pastime"since its introduction by the Tianjin YMCA in late 1895, when the old China was experiencing the ideological trend of the"Westernization Movement". Hong and Mangan(2002) argue that the diffusion and acceptance of sports in modern Asia was propelled by imperialism and nationalism. Basketball was no exception, as Polumbaum(2002) has also put it, "the introduction of basketball overseas was a logical extension of new conceptions of the relationship of body and soul emerging in Protestantism in the mid-1800s and subsequently enshrined in YMCA's philosophy". Dr. Willard Lyon, who was an American missionary, organized a basketball exhibition to celebrate the establishment of a YMCA medical school four years after the game was invented, marking the inauguration of Chinese basketball(Li et al., 1991: 3). The YMCA's contribution to the initial development of sports, including basketball in modern China, was significant. Basketball was one of the major physical activities in the YMCAs and missionary schools. For example, in 1908, Shanghai YMCA was established and a PE department was set up providing handball, volleyball and basketball courses(Li et al., 1991: 7). The first national game was organized by the YMCA and basketball was selected as a formal competition. The YMCA even appointed a Chinese national basketball team which participated in the first Far Eastern Championship Games in 1913 in Manila(Li et al., 1991: 7).

Chinese nationalism sprang up with the outbreak of the May Fourth Movement in 1919. The Rights Back and Anti-Christian Movement afterwards greatly weakened the power of the YMCAs and missionary schools in modern Chinese sport. However, the consequence was that this conflict between tradition and modernity did not slow down the pace of the promotion of western sports. Modern sport became a major part of modern Chinese culture, although no substantial replacement of traditional sport was simultaneously witnessed(Hong & Hua, 2002). Thus, basketball survived and further diffused throughout the country. Furthermore, China began to participate in basketball competitions on the international stage to support its national identity. Chinese basketball was dominant in Asia during the 1930s. During the 1936 Olympic Games, China joined the IABF and participated in the first ever Olympic basketball competition. Four Chinese basketball referees, including Dong Shouyi, were recruited by the International Basketball Referee Association(Li et al., 1991: 13). Even during the Anti-Japan and Civil Wars from 1937-1949, basketball was highly regarded by the Nanjing National Government and CCP as a military and leisure necessity. Mao Zedong personally played basketball and helped to judge the Huichang Wenwuba Soldier's

Basketball Games. Other significant revolutionaries, such as Zhou Enlai, Zhu De and Helong, were basketball enthusiasts(Li et al. , 1991: 17) .

Survival of a transplanted sport is subject to a great deal of scrutiny by local traditions. According to Lu(2008) , basketball was welcomed and loved by the Chinese who attributed at least three advantages to it. From a physical anthropological perspective, playing basketball requires a lot of crossing, jumping and coulé movements which suit the physical characteristics of modern peoples(Lu, 2008) . Philosophically speaking, playing basketball encourages an individual to stand out on the basis of teamwork, which suits the Chinese traditional philosophy of"He Er Bu Tong"(particularity is accepted but harmony is the premise) (Lu, 2008) . Last but not least, basketball is easy to play, young or old, male or female, individually or by team, every person can shoot alone or make teams with others, indoor or outdoor, in a stadium, on a playground or even on dirt(Lu, 2008) . As a result, even though new China accepted that basketball had been introduced by the hated and hegemonic American imperialists, this did not damage the game's appeal. Until the soccer boom of the 1980s and 1990s, basketball was clearly the most popular sport at elite and popular levels(Morris, 2002) .

In the PRC, the government's use of sports for political purposes has not hindered the proliferation of grassroots' basketball which continues the game's century-long saga in China. Since the early 2000s, the rise of Yao Ming and the diffusion of the NBA have increased the popularity of basketball in China still further. When Chinese youth seek a sporting diversion, basketball comes first. In contrast, football's popularity is falling with the frustrating lack of achievement of the national teams in international competitions. Worse still, football also requires a much bigger pitch to play on, and land is a scarce commodity and getting hugely profitable over the past decade(The Economist, 2011) . On 16 May 2005, Li

Yuanwei proclaimed at the Chinese Sports Round Table during the Global Fortune Forum, "Basketball has become the first sport in China! "He provided five arguments: basketball has the most participants, stadiums, media coverage, potential market and international influence among Chinese sports(Li, 2005c) . He argued:

> Although the Chinese national basketball teams failed to win any medals in the Athens Olympics, some of their matches drew more attention from audiences than most sports, even more than the traditional 'gold-medal' teams. The enrollment of basketball star Yao Ming to the NBA, which was fostered by the CBAL, is the biggest export deal to America. His influence has transcended sport and nation-state borders. He is now a symbol of social spirit. In a recent survey on elite overseas Chinese, Yao Ming has surpassed Zhao Xiaolan [Elaine Lan Chao] and Li Xiaolong [Bruce Lee] to be the first role model of overseas Chinese. (Li, 2005c)

He went on to highlight the prosperity of Chinese grassroots basketball:

> Basketball is the favourite sport of Chinese youth under 18. According to the survey of GAS this year, there are 430, 000 outdoor basketball courts throughout the country, which takes up 60% of all outdoor sports playgrounds. Basketball courts have been built almost in every university, high school, middle school, primary school, and recently-built housing estate. On these courts, basketball competitions are organized every day. For example, the 2005 Kentucky Chinese Youth 3 on 3 Tournament saw more than 13, 200 teams of more than 65, 000 young people competing in 262 cities. In China, there are two nationwide intercollegiate basketball leagues, the CUBA and the Chinese University Basketball Super League(CUBSL) . More than 700 universities participated in the CUBA last season. (Li, 2005c)

7.4.2 The People's Game and the Shaping of an Indigenous Chinese Basketball Culture: Dongguan's Basketball Experience

This section provides a case of basketball in Dongguan to demonstrate the basketball ecology at the grassroots level. Dongguan is a prefecture-level city in the Pearl River Delta in Guangdong Province, with Guangzhou, the provincial capital city, to the north, Huizhou to the northeast, Shenzhen to the south and the Pearl River to the west. Dongguan is only 87 km away from Hong Kong and 89 km from Macau by waterway, so foreign trade has been an important economic sector of Dongguan besides agriculture since modern times (Dongguan Municipal Government, 2011a). Also for this reason, historians of Dongguan reckon that basketball was introduced to Dongguan from Hong Kong (Dongguan Municipal Government, 2011b: 2). The climate of Dongguan is humid subtropical. The average temperature is 22.8°C throughout the year and the average rainfall is 1,756.8mm (Dongguan Municipal Government, 2011a). In this warm city, people can play basketball throughout the year, several months more than those living in the North or outside Guangdong. Therefore, basketball has been the most popular sport in Dongguan, despite the city also being named "Track-and-Field Hometown", "Swimming Hometown" and "Weightlifting Hometown" by the GAS.

It is recorded that basketball was introduced into Dongguan's middle schools in 1912, and soon boomed among the populace. Dongguan Middle School and Mingsheng Middle School had the two best basketball teams in Dongguan. Youxiong Team of Dongguan Middle School won the champion of Cantonese Yiji (youth level) Basketball Tournament in 1935 (Dongguan Municipal Government, 2011b: 2). In the late 1930s, a number of amateur sports clubs emerged in Dongguan.

For example, Xunlei Basketball Team was set up in 1937 and began to barnstorm all over Dongguan(Zhao, 2011: 68). During the Anti-Japan War, the annual municipal-wide basketball tournament was still held. In 1940, Dongguan Middle School Team took refuge in Hong Kong, but they did not miss the tournament and won the championship, which is a widely-recounted folktale in Dongguan(Zhao, 2011: 68).

As soon as the war ended, some basketball teams in Dongguan were sponsored by local businessmen to play exhibition games with outbound teams from Hong Kong and Macau. In 1947, Huaqing Team was set up in urban Dongguan, which it was to dominate for a decade. They located in a home court near the police station and ran a membership club system. The club's expenditure for away games was also covered by the members. This is the embryo of Chinese professional sports clubs(Zhao, 2011: 68). Since then, a number of high-level basketball teams have been created in Dongguan's urban, suburban and military districts, such as Qiaoxin Sports Club, Yuan Shanbei Xunlei Team, Guancheng Chamber Team, Shilong Liuxing Team, Dongguan Middle School Team, and Mingsheng Middle School Team. For night games, organizers usually used three big kerosene lamps to light-up the courts. Local basketball stars soon sprung up with Liu Wennv of Huaqing Team, for example, earning his fame with a clutch-shot in the game against Liuxing Team and being recognized as Dongguan's "George Mikan".

With the outbreak of the Famine and Cultural Revolution in the 1960s, basketball became less popular throughout China. Since the early 1970s, Dongguan basketball recovered gradually(Dongguan Municipal Government, 2011b: 2). In 1976, a lamp-lit basketball playground worthy of RMB 600, 000(EUR 75, 000) was built near the People's Park in Guancheng Town(Dongguan Municipal Government, 2011b: 10). In the post-reform period, basketball is again widely-played in Dongguan. Dongguan Basketball Association was set up in 1982. The first Municipal Basketball Tournament was held in 1984, 1,056 athletes from 88 teams competed in 243 matches, with more than 100,000 spectators (Dongguan Municipal Government, 2011b: 2). Changping Men's Farmers' Basketball Team, representing Guangdong Province, won the championship in the first Fengshou Cup National Farmers' Basketball Tournaments in 1984.

China's market economy has turned Dongguan into an important industrial city since the early 1990s, where FDI is actively sought for and relied on. With the arrival of teenage Chinese from agricultural areas in the West China and Middle China to work in the manufacturing and assembly factories, Dongguan is now the 8th most populous city in China (including Hong Kong and Macau) and 21st in the world (Dongguan Municipal Government, 2011a). Dongguan had 6,949,800 inhabitants at the end of 2008, among which there were 1,748,700 local residents and 5,201,100 permanent migrants from other parts of the country (Dongguan Municipal Government, 2011a). In this rapidly-urbanizing city, basketball plays a significant role in the building of urban culture which can be seen from the following aspects.

First, Dongguan inherits the city's tradition of setting up basketball teams and clubs and organizing basketball competitions at all levels. Following these basketball teams and clubs and their games greatly enriches the leisure entertainment of the citizens. It has the first Chinese privately-owned professional basketball club, the Guangdong Hongyuan Basketball Club. The Hongyuan Club has a history of performing well in the CBAL, winning 8 champions in 9 years from 2004 to 2013. The club's youth team is also dominant. By August 2011, they had won 15 championships in the two most prestigious national youth leagues in China, including a six-peat and five-peat. Now there are five professional clubs besides Hongyuan

Club in Dongguan: Dongguan Xin Shiji Basketball Club, the women's team of Guangdong Province, Changan Baining Basketball Club, Hong Kong Xin Li Bao Basketball Club. These clubs have generated a constant community of basketball fans in the city and from other parts of the country. Basketball stars from these clubs, like Yi Jianlian, Zhu Fangyu, Du Feng, Wang Shipeng, Chen Jianghua, even international player Jason Dixon, are household names in Dongguan. Different from the NBA followers, the basketball fans in Dongguan have a large portion of enthusiasts from the older generation. For example, one of the respondents, who was 58 years old(in 2012), has held a season ticket of the Hongyuan since 1998. To watch the games, he has to drive one and a half hours to the stadium. But during all these years, he has missed no more than 10 games. Since 2009, he has had his little companion to Hongyuan's games, which is his grandson(Interviewee No. 42).

Since 2003, the Dongguan Basketball Tournament which was reorganized from the municipal sports meeting has been a popular event in the city. It starts in early June and ends in late July(see Picture 7-4). The 32 teams from each town and urban area rosters include most top amateurs from throughout the country, which includes retired CBAL players and youth team players of CBAL clubs. Almost every game plays to a full house. The final games are usually broadcast by the Dongguan TV and Guangdong TV and obtain extensive local media exposure. Those games are played in Dongguan Stadium which is also the home court of the Guangdong Hongyuan Basketball Club, which has a capacity of 5, 000 people (Dongguan Municipal Government, 2011b: 8). The final games usually draw more attention than the CBAL games in Dongguan. Below the municipal level, there are also lower level basketball tournaments, such as in Nancheng Urban Area, Dalang Town, and Zhongtang Town(Dongguan Municipal Government, 2011b: 2). In every city, there is a hero. Zhang Guanhao, a native-born amateur who is named"Basketball King of Dongguan", is such a hero of Dongguan. Zhang stands only 1. 85m, but making a slam dunk is easy for him. Without any professional training, his self-trained skills and flexibility make him a splendid scorer. After leading Nancheng Town to three consecutive championships, Zhang became a household name in Dongguan. As the captain of the college team in Dongguan Institution of Science and Technology, Zhang is a very popular figure on campus (He, 2012-4-7). One of the respondents expressed the pleasure of following local basketball stars:

> Different from the professional players, local stars are much closer. To follow the professional players, many fans buy jerseys or other merchandise to get closer to their heroes. Following the local stars, we cheer for them on the court. Off the court, we are friends. We can go out and drink together. (Interviewee No. 46)

Picture 7-4 A Match in the 2012 Dongguan Basketball Tournament

Source: photo taken by the author on 24 July 2012.

Second, participating in basketball is an important component in the leisure and social life of the"Dongguaner"and the"New Dongguaner". In March 2004, Dongguan was named"Basketball City"by the GAS. In 2010, there were 2, 314 basketball courts in public areas, 1, 044 in schools and more than 10, 000 in governmental and industrial sites(Dongguan Municipal Government, 2011b: 3). Every village or community has its own floodlit courts, which means about 100 people can share 1 basketball court. To make Dongguan a basketball-themed cultural city, the Dongguan Basketball Association, jointly with Dongguan Sport Administration, is building a basketball-themed culture park, which includes a large-sized basketball playground, a basketball museum and a basketball hall of fame(He, 2012-4-7).

In Dongguan, basketball is more than a game, it is a lifestyle. Joining in basketball is a good way to promote identity, affiliation and cohesion within communities. According to Cao's(2010) survey in Dongguan on behalf of the GAS, 97. 2% of his respondents said playing basketball helped them to extend their social network; 95. 9% said they were willing to take playing basketball or watching basketball games as their family activities; 51. 4% said basketball was their favourite spectator sport; and 81. 2% had personally attended a basketball game(Cao, 2010). One of the respondents emphasized the significance of basketball in his social life and business in Dongguan. He said:

> I began to run a logistics company in 2006. Believe it or not, at least half of my clients play basketball, so I often organize basketball games to keep in touch with these existing clients. It also helps our company to extend the business network through basketball. (Interviewee No. 27)

Another respondent, a 19 year-old high school student from Liaoning Province, shared his experience of achieving social inclusion through basketball as a New Dongguaner. He stated:

> My parents settled down in Dongguan in the early 1990s. I see Dongguan as my second hometown. This is because of my basketball complex. I have loved basketball since childhood because I was born into a basketball family. My grandfather was a specialized-training basketball player and my elder brother is a professional player, my aunt was a former national team member and a teammate of Zheng Haixia... Local players are flexible but small. I am tall so I can be a good complement to them. I have got into the heart of the city. In Dongguan, there are many matches between secondary schools. So I can make a lot of friends through basketball. We know each other on the court, but normally we will become friends in our lives. Some of us are natives, some are not, but no one cares where others come from. My teammates treat me as a native. For myself, I feel I was born in Dongguan (Interviewee No. 31).

Third, playing basketball is merging into the socialization of Dongguan's younger generation. Stepping into the Changping Secondary School, a banner read "Play Basketball, Release Youth and Passion!" was a visitors' first sight. On the basketball courts, a large crowd of school students was playing 3 on 3. In each of the half-courts, there were 10 to 15 students sharing their youth and passion with a basketball. No different from any basketball court in China, these students are in their American-style gear such as baggy pants, and have handsome individual playing styles. However, many of them are playing for a basketball dream. "I want to become a member of the school team," said one respondent (Interviewee No. 34). Another respondent also shared his self-designed basketball career:

> I am now a starter of our school team. I hope to be enrolled in a good CUBA university, like Guangdong University of Technology or South China University of Technology. Then, if only I could join Hongyuan... if not, I will return to Changping and play for our town [in the Dongguan Basketball Tournament]. (Interviewee No. 33)

The career design of this respondent reflects the intention of many of his classmates in middle schools or high schools. In Dongguan's school, basketball-specialized students are often favoured by good schools and universities with automatic admission. Therefore, the annual Dongguan Secondary School Basketball Tournament is a major event in the city's schools. For instance, the 2009 Tournament lasted almost a month and ended in Changping Secondary School. With 97 teams participating in 372 games, the tournament was divided into 5 conferences and open to non-permanent residents. The final game, Guangming High School versus the Fourth High School, achieved high scores of 73-75(He, 2012-4-7).

In summary, basketball in Dongguan, which has spanned a century-long course of glocalization, has illustrated the definition of indigenous Chinese basketball culture. Admittedly, NBA culture is influential, as all of the interviewees acknowledged, that they follow the NBA to a greater or lesser degree. But in China, there is a grassroots' basketball ecology, as in Dongguan, which is embedded with local norms. For a large group of China's grassroots basketball players, basketball is just a game, for individuals, for families and for their social lives, which is untouched by the NBA's commercial penetration. As Prof. Wang Jiahong argued:

> It's impossible for the NBA's homogenization[of Chinese basketball culture] to take place, as we can expect the advent of Dongguanization in Chinese basketball culture. (Interviewee No. 1)

Prof. Zheng Shangwu added to this argument and further accounted for the hybridization of basketball culture in China between the NBA's grobalization and the glocalization of Chinese basketball. He noted:

> The NBA stars are flying in the sky with their Nike shoes; we are running on the ground for fun. There are no conflicts. (Interviewee No. 4)

7. 5 Conclusion

This chapter has examined the grobalization/glocalization processes in Chinese basketball culture. Americanization is the major facet of the NBA's cultural grobalization. Over the past two decades, the NBA's cultural diffusion in China has cosmopolitanized Chinese mainstream sport tastes and values. First, the NBA's media culture has transformed the concept of sport spectatorship in China from political assumption to a mass leisure activity. This proliferation of sport ideology has led to the emergence of fandom and the formation of collective identities involving NBA stars and teams. The individualism espoused by the NBA is challenging both basketball-in-play and basketball-in-consumption in China. It has ultimately led to the formation of Americanized ways of basketball consumption, especially among the Chinese youth. Glocalization of Chinese basketball is seen, on the one hand, in the nation's endeavours to construct a harmonious Chinese basketball culture to resist the NBA's cultural homogenization. This project was suspended with the cancellation of the NSP in 2009. On the other hand, the Chinese basketball grassroots and the game ethos they have cultivated is also defining and shaping the indigenous Chinese basketball culture.

Chapter 8. Conclusion

8. 1 Research Findings

The aim of this study is to explore the process of globalization in basketball, focusing on the Chinese context, through an examination of its multiple manifestations in the political, economic, and cultural dimensions. Ritzer's (2003, 2007b) grobalization/glocalization theory is applied to achieve this research aim. In light of Ritzer's conceptualization, the globalization process of basketball in China is found to be dichotomized as the result of a contextual and competing interplay between the penetration of the NBA and the consequential negotiation from Chinese basketball. The grobalization and penetration of the NBA in China encompasses the universalization of its governance model in the political and institutional dimension, its expansion of the market in the economic dimension, and its diffusion of cultural forms in the cultural dimension; the glocalization and negotiation of Chinese basketball encompasses its corresponding embracement, adaption, or resistance towards grobalization. Accordingly, the research questions were set out. A qualitative methodological approach was taken, and a combination of two data collection methods, semi-structured interviews and documents, as well as two types of data analysis, thematic analysis and narrative analysis, were adopted to answer these research questions. This section presents the research findings relating to governance, the market, and culture in relation to globalization and basketball in China.

In respect to globalization and the governance of Chinese basketball, there is a conflicting grobalization/glocalization process at work. McDonaldization is the key process of grobalization in the political and institutional realm, and refers to the growing power of a single governance form and its increasing influence throughout the world(Ritzer, 1998: VII; 2010). This study has enhanced the concept of McDonaldization with a case of basketball which has been engendered by the NBA's grobal power.

As noted by Ritzer, McDonaldization has expanded globally because of the economic needs and imperialistic ambitions of the corporation(Ritzer, 2007b: 24). Evidence for this argument was found in the integration of the NBA with international world basketball. Between the 1940s and 1980s, the NBA dominated the North American basketball market. In order to expand its market overseas, the NBA instituted a global strategy in the late 1980s. The McDonald's tournaments in co-operation with FIBA were the NBA's first step in integrating with world basketball. With the collapse of amateurism and the commercialization of most Olympic sports, FIBA finally accepted professional basketball players in 1989. This led to the debut of the Dream Team, which was comprised of superstars from the NBA, in the 1992 Barcelona Olympic Games. The spectacular performance of the Dream Team and the powerful commercial force enveloping them reconstructed the order of the basketball world from stereo to mono and started the move away from diversity towards conformity. Soon after the Barcelona Games, the NBA began to aggressively extend its business beyond the U. S. borders by setting up overseas offices and holding games all over the world.

As a result of all these developments, the NBA's governance model became the paradigm of professional basketball around the world. It also provided a useful archetype for Chinese basketball. In 1994, Chinese basketball began its move toward professionalization and marketization with a view to achieving internationalization. This development was made possible by the further implementation of the market economy, as well as under the pressure of the *Olympic Strategy* in Chinese sport and FIBA's acceptance of professional players. Between 1994 and 2003, the Jiaji League followed the European model with a traditional promotion/relegation system. However, the league encountered financial difficulties. To pursue profit-maximization, the CBMC put forward the NSP in late 2003, a project which aimed to facilitate the adoption of the NBA's governance model with a franchised system. The league changed its name to the CBAL. This local response from Chinese basketball lends support to Ritzer's assertion that the global expansion of McDonaldization is also due to "the fact that businesses and other organizations around the world seek to emulate it and its success, and because it becomes a valued global model" (Ritzer, 2007b: 24). It also reflects the rationalization of sport bureaucracy in China.

To examine the glocalization of Chinese basketball, a comparison of the governance models of the NBA and the CBAL was conducted following Borland's (2006) taxonomy of the stakeholders and infrastructure of a professional sport league, including governing authority, product market, capital market, and labour market. It was found that political nationalism plays a deterministic role in mediating grobalization and producing glocalization (Ritzer, 2007b: 21). In Chinese basketball, the governing powers still prioritize national interest. The vertical-centralized power allocation in Chinese basketball has meant that the NBA's governance model cannot be fully adopted in the Chinese context, since doing so would necessarily imply an erosion of the dominant power of Chinese government. First, in terms of governance authority, the NSP had attempted to set up a market-oriented governing body to detach Chinese basketball from government involvement. It proposed turning the CBALC into the CBA Company. This company would follow the composition of the NBA's board, which has a board of governors and a commissioner. But this plan was ultimately rejected in favour of the stereotypical nationalized governance model, which became part of the government's dualportfoliоin 2009. Second, the product market succeeded in cloning the NBA's model, but the prioritization of the national teams still hampers the league's gaming schedules. Third, in the capital market, CBAL clubs are more or less dependent on provincial and municipal government authorities, specifically in terms of registration and financial support, which results in the supremacy of the National Games over the league. Thus, the clubs have failed to form a profit-maximizing capital market such as that operated by the NBA, where individual equity and investment syndicate equity are the major ownership models and a cartel is formed to ensure owners' monopoly over profits. Fourth, in the labour market, player mobility in Chinese basketball is constrained under a reserve-clause-like registration and transferring system, while the clubs favour netting and farming their own talents for participation in the National Games over engaging in inter-team trading for the benefit of the league. Moreover, the players' interests are unprotected under the"Juguo Tizhi"since they are the lowest actors in the power hierarchy of Chinese basketball. Therefore, there are no salary determination procedures and no collective salary for the players, and individual salaries are not disclosed. There exists no labour union for Chinese basketball players to liaise with the clubs and the league on their behalf.

With regard to globalization and Chinese basketball market, it is demonstrated that this market has been expanding, thanks both to the grobalization of the NBA's business and the glocalization of Chinese local basketball market. Capitalism is the driving force behind this interaction(Ritzer, 2007b: 22). The primary objective behind the NBA's global strategies is to find overseas markets for consumption of its product. Since the early stages of its global strategy, the NBA's major overseas markets have included Asian countries and territories, especially Greater China. After more than two decades of expansion, the NBA's business in China is pervasive throughout the three domains of its market. First, with respect to the promotion of NBA games, the NBA's strong network of television and digital media outlets has cultivated a developed sports show market in China. It has also benefited from the rise of Chinese basketball players, particularly Yao Ming, in the NBA, which has occurred in tandem with the growth in China's sports spectating market. Consequently, the NBA began holding NBA China Games in 2004 to further nurture demand in its Chinese consumer base. Second, the NBA's global expansion has activated a sponsorship market, which draws sponsors from a combination of world-class Chinese corporations and multinationals, thus incorporating China's sporting resources into the on-going global economic flows. Third, the NBA has prompted the development of Chinese grassroots basketball, with a variety of promotional campaigns being held by sponsors.

It was shown that the marketing strategies of the CBAL under the NSP led to the growth of the local basketball market in China, a fact which demonstrates the glocalization of NBA strategies and the adoption of certain forms of capitalistic operations for profit. In the Jiaji League period, Chinese professional basketball was run with an emphasis on winning/performance, but the league was not properly marketized. The limited ways that the league could generate income were selling commercial rights to sports agents or selling the league's naming rights by themselves. In contrast, under the NSP, the CBAL learned from the NBA's marketing principles to transform their predecessors' competition-focused basketball into basketball for entertainment and profit. A key marketing strategy named"One Focus and Three Services"was proposed. It focused on branding the league and serving the interests of the fans, the media, and the sponsors, as in the NBA. Since then, a local basketball market has been rising gradually.

Both the NBA's grobalization and Chinese basketball's glocalization are fighting for market share and each has its own advantages and disadvantages. Despite the fact that the NBA's Chinese market has taken up the largest portion of its overseas territory and remains much more successful financially than the CBAL, there are some disadvantages to the NBA: very few Chinese players are skilled enough to be recruited by NBA teams; there is now less governmental support available to basketball in China; and what the NBA can localize in China is a commercial brand, not a tangible sports league. Conversely, although the CBAL is only quasi-professionalized with inferior product quality and fewer commercial operations than the NBA, the local basketball market continues to expand, both in terms of the marketing of CBAL games and marketing through CBAL games, despite of the abolition of the NSP in 2009. This has made a number of contributions to Chinese basketball, including the participation of more high-level international players, particularly from the NBA, and the return of Chinese players to China(in particular Yao Ming's return after his retirement), which has drawn Chinese audience from the NBA back to the CBAL. The CBAL also has a geographical advantage in that its games are broadcast live during prime time while NBA games are shown in the morning. It must also be acknowledged that the CBAL games retain a"local taste"for Chinese followers, especially for the regional fan communities.

As for globalization and Chinese basketball culture, a result of cultural hybridization was addressed. In mapping out this hybridizing Chinese basketball culture, Americanization was identified as the major facet of the NBA's cultural grobalization. Ritzer defines Americanization as"the export of products, images, technologies, practices, and behavior that are closely associated with America and Americans"(Ritzer, 2011: 50). He further argues that consumer culture is at the heart of grobalization(Ritzer, 2007b: 174). Before the NBA implemented its global strategies in the local market, American basketball set about establishing a mutual relationship with China. The most notable events included Deng Xiaoping's visit to America to watch a basketball exhibition by the Harlem Globetrotters, the Washington Bullets' visit to China in 1979, and the NBA-China Friendship Tour in 1985. These events not only enhanced the Sino-U. S. relationship through sports, but also introduced to China the concept of sport commercialism. Since the early 1990s, the NBA's cultural diffusion in China has inextricably cosmopolitanized Chinese mainstream sport tastes and values with its hegemonic commercial force. First, the large-scale diffusion of the NBA's media culture has proliferated the concept of sport spectatorship in China, which has moved away from political assumption to become a form of mass leisure. It has also stimulated the emergence of a new breed of Chinese sport fans, who now follow not only national sporting heroes but also foreign sport stars. Second, this proliferation of sport ideology has led to the emergence in China of fandom and the cultivation of collective identities involving NBA stars and teams. It has broken down the geopolitical constraints in the traditional Chinese sport complex, which emphasizes domestic regionalism, and replaced it with a de-spatialized transnational sports culture. Third, the dissemination of individualism from the NBA to Chinese basketball culture is apparent. As for basketball in play, individualism is challenging the traditional playing styles of Chinese basketball, both at the elite and mass levels. It has also resulted in the growth in Chinese streetball and Chinese youths' emulating the personalities and appearances of individual NBA superstars. With the influence of sports TNC's advertising rhetoric, sport consumption has become part of the modern lifestyle to which many Chinese now aspire.

Grobalization rarely penetrates localities without tension and resistance(Ritzer, 2003; Shor & Galily, 2012). In China, cultural nationalism is a rising force in constructing the glocality of Chinese basketball culture, motivated by the nation-state from above and the basketball grassroots from below. To guide the long-term development of Chinese basketball and to resist the NBA's cultural predominance, the NSP sought to construct a local Chinese basketball culture in line with the nation's desire to construct a harmonious society. CBCFs have been convened for basketball officials, practitioners, and academics to carry out this project. During the first forum, entitled "Building Basketball Culture, Forging Harmonious Basketball" and held in 2005, an official definition of Chinese basketball culture was given, which consisted of five elements: competition culture, entertainment culture, spectating culture, historical culture, and sports goods culture. During the second forum entitled "Globalization and the National Character of Chinese Basketball Culture" in 2007, the *Outline of Building Chinese Basketball Culture* was produced. It aimed to map out the ways of building a basketball culture with Chinese characteristics. This outline had five focal points: the building of a basketball team culture, the building of a professional league culture, the building of a basketball fan culture, the building of a mass basketball culture, and the building of a historical basketball culture. A number of corresponding strategies with emphasis on grassroots basketball were carried out and the CBCRC was set up in

Soochow University before the NSP was aborted in 2009. In 2011, the third forum was held. Entitled"Let Basketball Return to Daily Life", the forum appealed for the development of grassroots basketball in order to consolidate the substruction of a Chinese basketball system and to enhance the national character of Chinese basketball culture.

The force of the resistance from grassroot Chinese basketball to the NBA's hegemonic influence was noted. I argued that, beneath the nation's superficial culturalization project, grassroots basketball and the game ethos they have cultivated over the past century are unambiguously defining and shaping the indigenous Chinese basketball culture. Basketball was introduced to China by the YMCA along with tens of other western sports. The imperialist bloodline of basketball has had little impact on its evolution in China. It has become the national sporting pastime and the first sport to have been played in every corner of the country. In the urbanizing post-reform China, as shown in the case of Dongguan, basketball is significant in the building of local culture. First, setting up local basketball teams and clubs and organizing basketball competitions at all levels is customary in many Chinese cities. Following these basketball teams and clubs and their games greatly enriches the leisure activities of the citizens. Second, participating in basketball is an important component of the leisure and social lives of many Chinese. Third, basketball is merging into the socialization of the younger Chinese generation. Thus, Chinese basketball culture is on the one hand being reconstructed by the commercialism brought by the NBA, and on the other hand it being preserved and transformed via the indigenous norms emerging alongside China's societal development.

In summary, this study has contributed to the body of knowledge in the fields of sport studies and globalization studies with its panorama of a multifaceted and multidimensional basketball globalization in China. In the political and institutional dimension, it has demonstrated a scenario of dilemma in relation to the globalization of the governance of Chinese basketball. When the localization of the NBA's capitalist setting encounters the state power of China's socialist regime, Chinese political nationalism has tended to provoke a firm entrenchment to protect the government's sovereignty. This conflict has meant that the NBA's governance model cannot be fully assimilated and universalized in the Chinese context. In the economic dimension, the study has revealed that the worldwide spread of capitalism has resulted in the expansion of the Chinese basketball market. The NBA's growing business in China has not overwhelmed the local market. In actuality, Chinese basketball has successfully achieved further commodification and benefited from the adaption of the NBA's marketing strategies. In the sociocultural dimension, this study has evinced the creolization of Chinese basketball culture under globalization. The NBA's cultural diffusion in China has to some extent cosmopolitanized and consumerized Chinese basketball culture in an American way. Chinese cultural nationalism, however, has reacted to this, from the nation-state above and the basketball grassroots below, to resist the NBA's cultural influence.

8. 2 Contribution to Theory

Globalization is an on-going process throughout the contemporary world, but there has yet to be any grand finale across individual nation states. Therefore, researchers are inevitably faced with theoretical issues in exploring the process of globalization. Three theoretical schools, the hyper-globalists, the sceptics, and the transformationalists, are competing and provoking debates on the conceptualization of globalization. In sport studies, a growing number of theoretical and empirical studies have applied the conceptualization of glocalization since it was put forward by Robertson in the 1990s. In recent years, Ritzer(2003, 2007b) has proposed to complement the idea of glocalization with the concept of"grobalization". Thereafter, debate on whether grobalization is a necessary companion to glocalization has been flowing.

In this regard, the aforementioned research findings in relation to the NBA's penetration in China have provided sufficient evidence to argue that taking Ritzer's(2003, 2007b) grobalization into account is necessary and useful. On the one hand, this study has illustrated the utility of grobalization theory, which emphasizes the "imperialistic ambitions of nations, corporations, organizations, and other entities and their desire and need to impose themselves on various geographic areas"(Ritzer, 2003). On the other hand, it has exemplified that grobalization/glocalization can be applied not only to examinations in cultural realm, but also to multiple dimensions, political, economic, and cultural. In addition, the study has shown that the conceptualization of grobalization/glocalization is suitable for delineating the transformation, or dilemma, of globalization. Thus, I argue that it can be used to explore globalization and Asian sport or sport globalization in Asian countries in particular.

8. 3 Research Limitations and Recommendations

In conducting this study, I came across one major difficulty: how to simultaneously incorporate both"history"and"fact"into one account. Rosenau(2007) has observed that the primary weakness of current globalization theories is the failure to link micro-interaction among individual actors and macro-interactions among states and organizations. Ritzer's grobalization/glocalization has been extremely helpful in constructing a solid conceptual foundation for multidimensionally examining the trajectory of globalization. Thus, I set out to accomplish a comprehensive exploration of a multidimensional basketball globalization in this historically-oriented study. However, I found that Ritzer's conceptualization is not indicative enough for further in-depth analysis of each dimension. With hindsight, therefore, I recommend that researchers who apply grobalization/glocalization theory in future studies select one dimension for the basis of their research. Cetina(2007) reminds us that globalization studies are macro-historical in scope and micro-sociological in character so it is also important that future research take into account the necessity of cross-disciplinary knowledge in order to build a firmer theoretical framework.

Appendices

Interview Schedule A

Place: Suzhou, Jiangsu Province, China

Dates: 26 November 2011 to 7 December 2011

No.	Date	Interviewees
1	26 November 2011	Professor in Soochow University
2	27 November 2011	Professor in Soochow University
3	28 November 2011	Professor in Shanghai Sport University
4	30 November 2011	Professor in Zhaoqing University
5	3 December 2011	Professor in Beijing Sport University
6	3 December 2011	Professor in the Capital Institute of Physical Education
7	3 December 2011	Senior Staff Member in the CBMC
8	3 December 2011	Senior Staff Member in the Sports Culture Development Center-of the GAS
9	5 December 2011	Former Senior Staff Member in the CBMC
10	5 December 2011	Senior Staff Member in the Jiangsu Nangang Basketball Club
11	7 December 2011	Senior Staff Member in the Dongguan Xin Shiji Basketball Club

Interview Schedule B

Place: Beijing, China

Date: 23 December 2011 to 4 January 2012

No.	Date	Interviewees	
12	23 December 2011	Former Staff Member in NBA China Company	
13	24 December 2011	Staff Member in NBA China Company	
14	24 December 2011	Staff Member in NBA China Company	
15	29 December 2011	Senior Staff Member in the Bejing Shougang Basketball Club	
		Members of the ChinaPacers Community	
		Age	**Occupation**
16	1 January 2012	33	Journalist
17	1 January 2012	32	Entrepreneur
18	2 January 2012	29	Government Official
19	2 January 2012	29	Real Estate Agent
20	2 January 2012	27	Office Worker
21	2 January 2012	31	Government Official
22	3 January 2012	30	College Lecturer
23	4 January 2012	30	Entrepreneur

Interview Schedule C

Place: Dongguan, Guangdong Province, China

Date: 17 July 2012 to 28 July 2012

No.	Date	Interviewees	
24	17 July 2012	Senior Staff Member in the Dongguan Sports Administration	
25	18 July 2012	Senior Staff Member in the Dongguan Basketball Association	
26	21 July 2012	Senior Staff Member in the Guangdong Hongyuan Basketball Club	
		Basketball Participants	
		Age	Occupation
27	22 July 2012	34	Entrepreneur
28	23 July 2012	44	High School Teacher
29	23 July 2012	30	High School Teacher
30	24 July 2012	18	High School Student
31	24 July 2012	19	High School Student
32	24 July 2012	17	High School Student
33	24 July 2012	18	High School Student
34	24 July 2012	16	High School Student
35	24 July 2012	36	Office Worker
36	24 July 2012	27	Government Official

Continued

		Basketball Participants	
		Age	Occupation
37	25 July 2012	22	College Student
38	25 July 2012	19	College Student
39	25 July 2012	22	College Student
40	25 July 2012	23	College Student
41	25 July 2012	23	College Student
42	26 July 2012	58	Retired Cadre
43	26 July 2012	47	Writer
44	26 July 2012	34	Government Official
45	27 July 2012	35	Government Official
46	27 July 2012	39	Doctor
47	27 July 2012	41	Bank Official
48	28 July 2012	45	Office Worker

Bibliography

A. & C. Black Publishers. (2006) *Dictionary of Sport And Exercise Science,* London: A. & C. Black Publishers.

AAU. (2012) *About AAU Boys Basketball.* Available at: http://www. aauboy-sbasketball. org/(accessed: 2012-3-4).

ACSF. (1952) *General Statutes of the All-China Sports Federation.* Available at: http://www. sport. org. cn/zt/09tyjz/speech/2009-05-21/248878. html (accessed: 2012-5-21).

Alcoff, L. (1998) *Epistemology: The Big Questions,* Hoboken, New Jersey: John Wiley & Sons.

Allison, L. (2005) *The Global Politics of Sport: The Role of Global Institutions in Sport,* London and New York: Routledge.

Allison, L. & Monnington, T. (2002) "Sport, Prestige and International Relations". *Government and Opposition* 37(01).

Amara, M. & Henry, I. (2004) "Between Globalization and Local' Modernity': The Diffusion and Modernization of Football in Algeria". *Soccer & Society* 05(01).

Amara, M. , Henry, I. , Liang, J. & Uchiumi, K. (2005) "The Governance of Professional Soccer: Five Case Studies-Algeria, China, England, France and Japan". *European Journal of Sport Science* 05(04).

Andreff, W. (2008) "Globalization of the Sports Economy". *Rivista Di Diritto ed Economia Dello Sport* 04(03).

Andreff, W. & Szymanski, S. (2006) *Handbook on the Economics of Sport*, Cheltenham, U. K. & Northampton, Massachusetts: Edward Elgar.

Andrews, D. L., Carrington, B., Jackson, S. J. & Mazur, Z. (1996) "Jordanscapes: A Preliminary Analysis of the Global Popular". *Sociology of Sport Journal* 13(04).

Andrews, D. L. & Ritzer, G. (2007) The Grobal in the Sporting Glocal. *Global Networks* 07(02).

Arnaud, P. & Riordan, J. (2002) *Sport and International Politics: Impact of Facism and Communism on Sport*, London and New York: Routledge.

Ashe, A. (1993) *A Hard Road To Glory: A History of The African American Athlete: Basketball*, New York: Harper Collins.

Ba, K. (2005) "The Rise of Sports Industry in Modern China: A Perspective from a Baseball Giant". *Sports Culture Guide*(01).

Bairner, A. (2001) *Sport, Nationalism, and Globalization: European and North American Perspectives*, New York: State University of New York Press.

Bao, H. (2012a) "Challenges and Opportunities of Chinese Leisure Sports under the Trend of Sport Globalization". *Journal of Guangzhou Sport University*.

Bao, M. (2011a) "Professionalization Enhances the Development of Chinese Sport". *Journal of Nanjing Institute of Physical Education(Social Science)*(05).

Bao, M. (2011b) Speech on the 3rd Chinese Basketball Culture Forum. Chinese Basketball Culture Research Center: Digital Database(Internal Document).

Bao, M. (2012b) Speech on the 30th China International Sporting Goods Show 2012. Chinese Basketball Culture Research Center: Digital Database(Internal Document).

Batchelor, B. (2005) *Basketball in America: From the Playgrounds to Jordan's Game and Beyond*, Philadelphia, Pennsylvania: Haworth Press.

Bjarkman, P. C. (1992) *The History of the NBA*, New York: Random House Value Pub.

Borland, J. (2006) "The Production of Professional Team Sports". In Andreff, W. and Szymanski, S. (eds) *Handbook on the Economics of Sport*. Northampton: Edward Elgar Publishing.

Boyle, R. & Haynes, R. (2009) *Power Play: Sport, the Media and Popular Culture*, Edinburgh: Edinburgh University Press.

Breuer, C. , Pawlowski, T. , Hovemann, A. & Jin, R. (2009) "An Analysis on the Competive Balance of the UEFA Champions League". *China Sport Science* (04).

Bryman, A. (2004) *Social Research Methods*, Oxford: Oxford University Press.

Budd, A. & Levermore, R. (2004) *Sport and International Relations: An Emerging Relationship*, London and New York: Routledge.

Buick, A. & Crump, J. R. (1986) *State Capitalism: The Wages System Under New Management*, London: Macmillan Publishers.

Busch, A. (2000) "Unpacking the Globalization Debate: Approaches, Evidence and Data". In Hay, C. and Marsh, D. (eds) *Demystifying Globalization*. Basingstoke: Palgrave Macmillan, 21-48.

Cao, S. (2008) *The History of Sport in China (1993—2005)*, Beijing: People's Sport Press.

Cao, Y. (2010) *Sports Culture in the Construction of a Harmonious Society: A Case of Dongguan Basketball Culture*. Beijing: General Administration of Sports.

CBA. (1996) Financial Statistics of the 1995—1996 Season 555 China

Men's Basketball Jiaji League. Beijing: Chinese Basketball Association (Internal Document).

CBA. (1997) Financial Statistics of the 1996—1997 Season Hilton China Men's Basketball Jaiji League. Beijing: Chinese Basketball Association (Internal Document).

CBA. (1998a) Financial Statistics of the 1997—1998 Season Hilton China Men's Basketball Jiaji League. Beijing: Chinese Basketball Association (Internal Document).

CBA. (1998b) Statutes of the Chinese Basketball Association. Beijing: Chinese Basketball Association.

CBA. (1999) Financial Statistics of the 1998—1999 Season Hilton China Men's Basketball Jiaji League. Beijing: Chinese Basketball Association (Internal Document).

CBA. (2000) Financial Statistics of the 1999—2000 Season Hilton China Men's Basketball Jiaji League. Beijing: Chinese Basketball Association (Internal Document).

CBA. (2001) Financial Statistics of the 2000—2001 Season Hilton China Men's Basketball Jiaji League. Beijing: Chinese Basketball Association (Internal Document).

CBA. (2002) Financial Statistics of the 2001—2002 Season Motorola China Men's Basketball Jiaji League. Beijing: Chinese Basketball Association (Internal Document).

CBA. (2003) Financial Statistics of the 2002—2003 Season Motorola China Men's Basketball Jiaji League. Beijing: Chinese Basketball Association (Internal Document).

CBA. (2004a) Annual Report of the 2003—2004 CBAL Season. Beijing:

Chinese Basketball Association(Internal Document).

CBA. (2004b) North Star Project: The Ten Years' Reform of Chinese Professional Basketball(2005—2014). Beijing: Chinese Basketball Association(Internal Document).

CBA. (2005a) The 1st Chinese Basketball Culture Forum. Chinese Basketball Culture Research Center: Digital Database(Internal Document).

CBA. (2005b) Annual Report of the 2004—2005 CBAL Season. Beijing: Chinese Basketball Association(Internal Document).

CBA. (2005c) Statutes of the Chinese Basketball Association League Committee. Beijing: Chinese Basketball Association.

CBA. (2006a) Annual Report of the 2005—2006 CBAL Season. Beijing: Chinese Basketball Association(Internal Document).

CBA. (2006b) The Full Schedule of the 2006—2007 CBAL Season. Beijing: Chinese Basketball Association.

CBA. (2007a) Annual Report of the 2006—2007 CBAL Season. Beijing: Chinese Basketball Association(Internal Document).

CBA. (2007b) The Full Schedule of the 2007—2008 CBAL Season. Beijing: Chinese Basketball Association.

CBA. (2007c) Outline of Building Chinese Basketball Culture. Beijing: Chinese Basketball Association(Internal Document).

CBA. (2008) Annual Report of the 2007—2008 CBAL Season. Beijing: Chinese Basketball Association(Internal Document).

CBA. (2009) Annual Report of the 2008—2009 CBAL Season. Beijing: Chinese Basketball Association(Internal Document).

CBA. (2010) Annual Report of the 2009—2010 CBAL Season. Beijing: Chinese Basketball Association(Internal Document).

CBA. (2011a) The 3rd Chinese Basketball Culture Forum. Chinese Basketball Culture Research Center: Digital Database(Internal Document).

CBA. (2011b) Annual Report of the 2010—2011 CBAL Season. Beijing: Chinese Basketball Association(Internal Document).

CBA. (2012) Annual Report of the 2011—2012 CBAL Season. Beijing: Chinese Basketball Association(Internal Document).

CBA. (2013) Annual Report of the 2012—2013 CBAL Season. Beijing: Chinese Basketball Association(Internal Document).

CBMC. (2003) Management Methods Relating to Basketball Player's Registration and Mobility. Beijing: Chinese Basketball Management Center.

CBMC. (2011) *The Chinese Basketball Management Center*. Available at: http://www. sport. gov. cn/n16/n33193/n33223/n34901/index. html(accessed: 2011-7-8).

CCTV-5. (2011-11-14) Inauguration of the 2004—2005 CBAL Season. Television Programme: China Central Television

CCTV-5. (2013-2-21) NBA Frontline. Television Programme: China Central Television

Cetina, K. K. (2007) "Microglobalization". In Rossi, I. (ed) *Frontiers of Globalization Research*. New York: Springer.

Chen, F. & Chen, G. (2004) "Television Broadcasting of the Formula One". *Sports Culture Guide*(09).

Chen, J. & Wu, C. (2006) "Origins of Streetball and Its Diffusion in China". *Sports Culture Guide*(06).

Chen, L. , Shi, B. & Zhang, X. (2009) "A Study on the Chinization of Yoga". *China Sport Science*(07).

Chen, X. (1991) "Baseball in Modern China". *Journal of Chengdu Sport U-*

niversity(03).

Chen, X. (2005) "A Study on the Consumption Demand of the F1 Chinese Grand Prix and Its Influence on Economics of Surranding Areas". *Journal of Wuhan Institute of Physical Education*(08).

Chen, X. (2007) "Basketball Culture and Market". *School of Sport Studies.* Doctor: Soochow University.

Chen, X. & Tan, X. (2003) "An Analysis on the Possibility of Marketizing Chinese Baseball". *Journal of Guangzhou Physical Education Institute*(04).

Cho, Y. (2009) "The Glocalization of U. S. Sports in South Korea". *Sociology of Sport Journal* 26(02).

Coakley, J. (2003) *Sports in Society: Issues and Controversies,* New York: McGraw-Hill Financial.

Cochrane, A. & Pain, K. (2000) "A Globalizing Society?"In Held, D. (ed) *A Globalising World?: Culture, Economics, Politics.* London and New York: Routledge.

CSM. (2012) CSM Sports Media Research 2012. Beijing: CSM Media Research.

Cui, L. (2005) "To Construct a New Type of Culture for Chinese Traditional Sports: A Study on the Development of Chinese Traditional Sports under Sport Globalization". *Sports Culture Guide*(03).

Cunningham, C. (2009) *American Hoops: U. S. Men's Olympic Basketball from Berlin to Beijing,* Lincoln: University of Nebraska Press.

Da, P. (2001) "The Diffusion of Rock Climbing in China". *Sports Culture Guide*(01).

Deng, X. (2007) "The Issues of Sport Globalization". *Journal of Physical Education*(05).

Denzin, N. K. (1978) *The Research Act*, New York: McGraw-Hill Financial.

Denzin, N. K. & Lincoln, Y. S. (2005) *The Sage Handbook of Qualitative Research*, Thousand Oaks, California: Sage Publications.

Ding, J. & Wang, G. (2006) "An Analysis on the NBA's Globalization". *Sports Culture Guide*(04).

Ding, X. (2004) *Deng Xiaoping and the Men of the World*, Beijing: China Youth Press.

Dongguan Municipal Government. (2011a) *About Dongguan*. Available at: http://www.dg.gov.cn/zjdg/(accessed: 2011-7-8).

Dongguan Municipal Government. (2011b) *A Chorography of Dongguan Basketball*, Beijing: Zhonghua Book Company.

Dunning, E. (2002) *Fighting Fans: Football Hooliganism as a World Phenomenon*, Dublin: University College Dublin Press.

El-Ojeili, C. & Hayden, P. (2006) *Critical Theories of Globalization: An Introduction*, Basingstoke, England: Palgrave Macmillan.

Eschker, E., Perez, S. J. & Siegler, M. V. (2004) "The NBA and the Influx of International Basketball Players". *Applied Economics* 36(10).

Fan, P. (2006) "A Study on the Dispute Resolution Mechanism in International Sport". *Graduate School.* Master thesis: China University of Political Science and Law.

Fang, G. & Wang, G. (2007) "The Pitfall of Sport Globalization and Its Influence on Chinese Traditional Sports". *Journal of Chengdu Sport University* (05).

Feng, W. (1950) "Discussions on People's Sport". *New Sports*(03).

Feng, X. & Yin, B. (2004) "The Integration of Chinese School Sport and Modern Olympic Culture". *Journal of Physical Education* 11(04).

Fox Sport. (2011) *Highlights of Portland Trail Blazers vs. Indiana Pacers*. Available at: http://www.nba.com/pacers/video/2011/02/04/BOMANinterviewPACERSwmv-1547260/index.html(accessed: 2011-2-5).

Fu, Y. (2007) *The History of Sport in China(1949—1979)*, Beijing: People's Sport Press.

Gao, L. & Wang, B. (2007) "An Exploration of the Modernization of Chinese School Sport under Globalization". *Journal of Sports and Science*(03).

Giddens, A. (1990) *The Consequences of Modernity*, Cambridge: Polity.

Gilmour, C. & Rowe, D. (2012) "Sport in Malaysia: National Imperatives and Western Seductions". *Sociology of Sport Journal* 29(04).

Giulianotti, R. (2004) "Between Colonialism, Independence and Globalization: Football in Zimbabwe". In Armstrong, G. and Giulianotti, R. (eds) *Football in Africa: Conflict, Conciliation and Community*. Basingstoke, England: Palgrave Macmillan.

Giulianotti, R. & Robertson, R. (2006) "Glocalization, Globalization and Migration: the Case of Scottish Football Supporters in North America". *International Sociology* 21(02): 171 - 198.

Giulianotti, R. & Robertson, R. (2007a) "Forms of Glocalization: Globalization and the Migration Strategies of Scottish Football Fans in North America". *Sociology* 41(01).

Giulianotti, R. & Robertson, R. (2007b) "Recovering the Social: Globalization, Football and Transnationalism". *Global Networks* 07(02): 166 - 186.

Giulianotti, R. & Robertson, R. (2007c) "Sport and Globalization: Transnational Dimensions". *Global Networks* 07(02).

Giulianotti, R. & Robertson, R. (2009) *Globalization and Football*, Thousand Oaks, California: Sage Publications.

Giulianotti, R. & Robertson, R. (2012) "Glocalization and Sport in Asia: Diverse Perspectives and Future Possibilities". *Sociology of Sport Journal* 29(04).

Gratton, C. & Jones, I. (2004) *Research Methods for Sport Studies*, London and New York: Routledge.

Graziano, A. M. & Raulin, M. L. (2004) *Research Methods: A Process of Inquiry*, Boston: Allyn & Bacon.

Green, M. & Houlihan, B. (2005) *Elite Sport Development: Policy Learning and Political Priorities*, London and New York: Routledge.

Grix, J. (2002) "Introducing Students to the Generic Terminology of Social Research". *Politics* 22(03).

Grix, J. (2010) *The Foundations of Research*, Basingstoke, England: Palgrave Macmillan.

Guo, H. (2012) "The Diffusion of Taekwondo and Its Cultural Influence in China". *School of Sport and Physical Education.* Master thesis: Shanxi Normal University.

Guo, J. (2009) "Globalization and Sport Management in China". *Journal of Shenyang Sport University*(06).

Han, J. & Li, X. (2007) "Globalization and the Challenges and Opportunities of China's Sport System". *Guizhou Sports Science and Technology*(01).

Hao, Q. (2008) *The History of Sport in China (1980—1992)*, Beijing: People's Sport Press.

Hao, Q. & Ren, H. (2003) "The Relationship between 'Juguo Tizhi' and the Olympic Strategy: A Study on the Demand of New Olympic Strategies". *Sports Culture Guide* 12(32): 6.

Hargreaves, J. (2002) "Globalisation Theory, Global Sport, and Nations and Nationalism". In Sugden, J. and Tomlinson, A. (eds) *Power Games: A Critical*

Sociology of Sport. London and New York: Routledge.

He, J. (2012) "Positioning Basketball in the History of Dongguan". *Dongguan Daily*, 2014-4-6.

He, P. (2005) "A Historical Analysis on the Professionalization of Baseball in China". *Journal of Tianjin University of Sport*(03).

He, Y. (2011) "The Development of Chinese Martial Arts in Post-Olympic Era". *Journal of Capital Institute of Physical Education*(04).

Held, D. (1999) *Global Transformations: Politics, Economics and Culture*, Palo Alto, California: Stanford University Press.

Held, D. (2000) *A Globalizing World?: Culture, Economics, Politics*, London and New York: Routledge.

Held, D. & McGrew, A. (2001) "Globalization". In Krieger, J. and Crahan, M. E. (eds) *The Oxford Companion to Politics of the World*. Oxford: Oxford University Press.

Held, D. & McGrew, A. (2002) *Globalization/Anti-Globalization: Beyond the Great Divide*, Cambridge: Polity.

Henry, I. P. & the Institute of Sport and Leisure Policy. (2009) *Transnational and Comparative Research in Sport: Globalisation, Governance and Sport Policy*, London and New York: Routledge.

Hinchman, L. P. & Hinchman, S. (1997) *Memory, Identity, Community: The Idea of Narrative in the Human Sciences*, Albany, New York: State University of New York Press.

Hong, F. (1999) "Not All Bad! Communism, Society and Sport in the Great Proletarian Cultural Revolution: A Revisionist Perspective". *The International Journal of the History of Sport* 16(03).

Hong, F. (2008) China. In Houlihan, B. and Green, M. (eds) *Comparative*

Elite Sport Development: Systems, Structures and Public Policy. Oxford: Elsevier.

Hong, F. & Hua, T. (2002) "Sport in China: Conflict between Tradition and Modernity, 1840s to 1930s". *The International Journal of the History of Sport* 19 (02 – 03).

Hong, F. & Huang, F. (2013) "China". In O'Boyle, I. and Bradbury, T. (eds) *Sport Governance: International Case Studies*. London and New York: Routledge.

Hong, F. & Mangan, J. A. (2002) *Sport in Asian Society: Past and Present*, London and New York: Routledge.

Hong, F. & Xiaozheng, X. (2002) "Communist China: Sport, Politics and Diplomacy". *The International Journal of the History of Sport* 19(02 – 03).

Hong, F. & Zhouxiang, L. (2012) "From Barcelona to Athens (1992—2004): 'Juguo Tizhi' and China's Quest for Global Power and Olympic Glory". *The International Journal of the History of Sport* 29(01).

Hong, M. (2010) "Globalization and Its Challenges on Chinese Martial Arts". *Sports World Scholarly*(11).

HoopChina. com. (2011) HoopChina Sports Research Report: Yao's Impact on China's Sports Industry. Beijing: HoopChina. com, (accessed: 2012-7-19).

Horne, J. (2006) *Sport in Consumer Culture*, Basingstoke, England: Palgrave Macmillan.

Houlihan, B. (1997) "Sport, National Identity and Public Policy". *Nations and Nationalism* 03(01).

Houlihan, B. (2009) Mechanisms of International Influence on Domestic Elite Sport Policy. *International Journal of Sport Policy* 01(01).

Houlihan, B. (2012) "Sport Policy Convergence: A Framework for Analysis". *European Sport Management Quarterly* 12(02).

Houlihan, B. & Green, M. (2012) *Comparative Elite Sport Development*, London and New York: Routledge.

Houlihan, B. , Tan, T. -C. & Green, M. (2010) "Policy Transfer and Learning from the West: Elite Basketball Development in the People's Republic of China". *Journal of Sport & Social Issues* 34(01).

Hu, L. & Bai, T. (2011) "Suggestions on the Development of Chinese Martial Arts in Post-Olympic Era". *Shanxi Sports Science & Technology*(01).

Hu, X. (2002) "The Reformation of Juguo Tizhi". *Journal of Physical Education* 09(01).

Hua, T. (2004) "Football Hooligans and Football Supporters' Culture in China". In Horne, J. and Manzenreiter, W. (eds) *Football Goes East: Business, Culture and the People's Game in China, Japan and South Korea*. London and New York: Routledge.

Huang, F. (2008) "Diffusion and Impacts of the NBA in China". *Sports Culture Guide*(08).

Huang, F. (2013) "Glocalisation of Sport: The NBA's Diffusion in China". *The International Journal of the History of Sport* 30(03).

Huang, H. , Zhang, Y. & Zhao, Z. (2007) "A Comparative Study between Chinese Short Weapon and Japanese Kendo". *Journal of Beijing Sport University* (08).

Huang, Y. & Ma, G. (2001) "Rethinking the Cultural Influence of Sport Globalization". *Journal of Shandong Institute of Physical Education and Sports* (02).

Humphreys, B. R. & Howard, D. R. (2008) *The Business of Sports*, Westport, Connecticut: Greenwood Publishing Group.

Jarvie, G. (2006) *Sport, Culture and Society: An Introduction*, London and

New York: Routledge.

Jay, K. (2006) *More Than Just a Game: Sports in American Life Since* 1945, New York: Columbia University Press.

Jefferson, P. (2003) "Slam Dunk, Sports Manga, and Japanese Culture". *Fukuoka University Review of Literature & Humanities* 35(03).

Ji, D. (2006) "The Status Quo of Tennis in Universities in China". *Journal of Capital Institute of Physical Education*(02).

Jiang, H. & Zhang, H. (2010) *Annual Report on Development of China's Sports Industry(*2008—2010*)*, Beijing: Social Science Academic Press.

Jiang, X. (2009) "Globalization and the Future of Chinese Martial Arts". *Journal of Physical Education*(10).

Jin, X. (2011) "A Study on the Status Quo of Kendo in China". *School of Sport and Physical Education.* Master thesis: Yanbian University.

Jin, Y. (2012) "A Comparative Study between the Moral Character in Martial Arts and the Etiquette in Taekwondo". *Graduate School.* Master: Jilin Institute of Physical Education.

Jones, R. (2004) "Football in the People's Republic of China". In Horne, J. and Manzenreiter, W. (eds) *Football Goes East: Business, Culture and the People's Game in East Asia.* London and New York: Routledge.

Jordan, M., Stern, D. J., Hubbard, J. & Association, N. B. (2000) *The Official NBA Encyclopedia,* New York: Doubleday.

Jozsa, F. P. (2004) *Sports Capitalism: The Foreign Business of American Professional Leagues,* Farnham, England: Ashgate Publishing.

Jozsa, F. P. (2006) *Big Sports, Big Business: A Century of League Expansions, Mergers, and Reorganizations,* Westport, Connecticut: Greenwood Publishing Group.

Jozsa, F. P. (2011) *The National Basketball Association: Business, Organization and Strategy*, Singapore: World Scientific.

Kaplan, S. & Langdon, S. (2012) "Chinese Fandom and Potential Marketing Strategies for Expanding the Market for American Professional Sports into China". *International Journal of Sports Marketing and Sponsorship* 14(01).

Kirchberg, C. (2007) *Hoop Lore: A History of the National Basketball Association*, Jefferson, North Carolina: McFarland & Company.

LaFeber, W. (2002) *Michael Jordan and the New Global Capitalism*, New York: W. W. Norton & Company.

Lane, D. C. (2004) "From Mao to Yao: A New Game Plan for China in the Era of Basketball Globalization". *Pacific Rim Law & Policy Journal* 13(01).

Langhorne, R. (2001) *The Coming of Globalization: Its Evolution and Contemporary Consequences*, Basingstoke, England: Palgrave Macmillan.

Lanteigne, M. (2005) *China and International Institutions: Alternate Paths to Global Power*, London and New York: Routledge.

Larmer, B. (2005a) "The Center of the World". *Foreign Policy*(150).

Larmer, B. (2005b) *Operating Yao Ming: The Chinese Sports Empire, American Big Business, and the Making of an NBA Superstar*, Westminster, London: Penguin Group.

Lavelle, K. L. (2006) "Yao Ming and Masculinity in Middle America: A Critical Discourse Analysis of Racial Representations in NBA Game Commentary". *Graduate School.* Doctor thesis: Wayne State University.

Lechte, J. (2003) *Key Contemporary Concepts: From Abjection to Zeno's Paradox*, Thousand Oaks, Cafifornia: Sage Publications.

Lentze, G. (1995) "The Legal Concept of Professional Sports Leagues: The Commissioner and an Alternative Approach from a Corporate Perspective". *Marq.*

Sports LJ(06).

Li, D. (1999) Speech on the 1998—1999 Jiaji League Review Meeting. Beijing: Chinese Basketball Association.

Li, F., Wen, F. & Dong, E. (1991) *A Development History of Chinese Basketball*, Wuhan: Wuhan Press.

Li, J., Wang, X., Zou, J. & Zhang, Z. (2008) "The Evolution of Chinese Traditional Martial Arts Culture". *Journal of Shanghai University of Sport*(02): 58-62.

Li, L. (2004a) "Sport Globalization and Chinese National Minority Sports". *Tibet's Science and Technology*(12).

Li, L. & Zhou, M. (2002) *The Son of Sport: Rong Gaotang*, Beijing: Xinhua Press.

Li, Y. (2004b) "Speech on the 2004 National Routine Meeting for Basketball". Beijing: Chinese Basketball Association.

Li, Y. (2005a) Speech on the 1st Chinese Basketball Culture Forum. Chinese Basketball Culture Research Center: Digital Database(Internal Document).

Li, Y. (2005b) Speech on the 2005 CBAL Club Owners Summit. Beijing: Chinese Basketball Association.

Li, Y. (2005c) Speech on the Chinese Sports Roundtable, the 2005 Global Fortune Forum. Beijing: Chinese Basketball Association.

Li, Y. (2007) Speech on the 2nd Chinese Basketball Culture Forum. Chinese Basketball Culture Research Center: Digital Database(Internal Document).

Li, Y. (2011) Speech on the 3rd Chinese Basketball Culture Forum. Chinese Basketball Culture Research Center: Digital Database(Internal Document).

Li, Y., Bao, M., Ren, H., Lu, Y., Wang, D., Xiong, D., Luo, Y. & Hu, L. (2003) "A Study on the Maintainance of' Juguo Tizhi' in Chinese Elite

Sports". *China Sport Science and Technology* 39(08).

Li, Z. (2010) "A Study on the Profit-seeking Model of the NBA". *Graduate School.* Doctor thesis: Beijing Sport University.

Liu, F. , Yang, Z. & Bai, L. (2005) "The Cultural Connotation of the China Baseball League". *China Sport Science and Technology*(04).

Long, P. (2002) "Reformation and Marketization of Chinese Traditional Sports". *Journal of Xi'an Physical Education University*(04).

Lou, Z. , Yuan, X. & Wang, Z. (2008) "Globalization and the Inheritance of Chinese Traditional Sports". *Journal of Physical Education*(12).

Lowe, B. , Kanin, D. B. & Strenk, A. (1978) *Sport and International Relations*, Champaign, Illinois: Stipes Publishing Company.

Lu, Y. (2007) Speech on the 2nd Chinese Basketball Culture Forum. Chinese Basketball Culture Research Center: Digital Database(Internal Document).

Lu, Y. (2008) "The Selection, Acceptance and Variation to Basketball of Chinese Culture". *Sports Culture Guide*(04).

Lu, Y. (2011) Speech on the 3rd Chinese Basketball Culture Forum. Chinese Basketball Culture Research Center: Digital Database(Internal Document).

Luo, S. (2005) *The Olympics Came to China*, Beijing: Tsinghua University Press.

Luo, S. (2008) "International Communication of Sport in Post-reform China". *Journal of Wuhan Institute of Physical Education* 42(01).

Luo, S. & Huang, F. (2013) "China's Olympic Dream and the Legacies of the Beijing Olympics". *The International Journal of the History of Sport* 30(04).

Ma, G. (2012) Speech on the 30th China International Sporting Goods Show 2012. Chinese Basketball Culture Research Center: Digital Database (Internal Document).

Ma, W. (2008) "Cultural Globalization and the Development and Pedagogy of School Martial Arts in China". *Graduate School.* Doctor thesis: Shanghai University of Sport.

Maguire, J. (1993) "Globalisation, Sport and National Identities: 'The Empires Strike Back?'" *Loisir et Société/Society and Leisure* 16(02).

Maguire, J. (1994) "Sport, Identity Politics, and Globalization: Diminishing Contrasts and Increasing Varieties". *Sociology of Sport Journal* 11(04).

Maguire, J. (1999) *Global Sport: Identities, Societies, Civilizations,* Cambridge: Polity.

Maguire, J. A. (2005) *Power and Global Sport: Zones of Prestige, Emulation and Resistance,* London and New York: Routledge.

Manzenreiter, W. & Horne, J. (2007) "Playing the Post - Fordist Game in/to the Far East: The Footballisation of China, Japan and South Korea". *Soccer & Society* 08(04).

Marczyk, G. R., DeMatteo, D. & Festinger, D. (2005) *Essentials of Research Design and Methodology,* Hoboken, New Jersey: John Wiley & Sons.

Marsh, D. & Furlong, E. (2002) "A Skin not a Sweater: Ontology and Epistemology in Political Science". In Marsh, D. and Stoker, G. (eds) *Theory and Methods in Political Science.* Basingstoke, England: Palgrave Macmillan.

Mason, J. (1996) *Qualitative Researching,* Thousand Oaks, California: Sage Publications.

Matthews, B. & Ross, L. (2010) *Research Methods: A Practical Guide for the Social Sciences,* Upper Saddle River, New Jersey: Pearson Education.

Maxwell, J. A. (2009) "Designing a Qualitative Study". In Bickman, L. and Rog, D. J. (eds) *The Sage Handbook of Applied Social Research Methods.* Thousand Oaks, Califonia: Sage Publications.

May, T. (2001) *Social Research: Issues, Methods and Process,* Maidenhead, England: Open University.

McCune, Z. (2011) "Slam Dunking in Beijing: How America's National Basketball Association Used Global Media Networks to Serve Ping-Pong and Become China's Favorite Sport". *Department of Sociology.* Master thesis: University of Cambridge.

Menefee, W. C. (2009) "Globalization in Professional Sport: a Comparison of Chinese and American Basketball Spectators". *Parks, Recreation and Tourism Management.* Doctor thesis: North Carolina State University.

Merkel, U. (2012) "Sport and Physical Culture in North Korea: Resisting, Recognizing and Relishing Globalization". *Sociology of Sport Journal* 29(04): 506 – 525.

Miller, T. , McKay, J. , Lawrence, G. & Rowe, D. (2001) *Globalization and Sport: Playing the World,* Thousand Oaks, California: Sage Publications.

Morris, A. (2002) "'I Believe You Can Fly': Basketball Culture in Postsocialist China". In Link, E. P. , Madsen, R. and Pickowicz, P. (eds) *Popular China: Unofficial Culture in a Globalizing Society.* Lanham, Maryland: Rowman & Littlefield.

Moses, J. & Knutsen, T. (2007) *Ways of Knowing: Competing Methodologies in Social and Political Research,* Basingstoke, England: Palgrave Macmillan.

Mouton, J. & Marais, H. C. (1988) *Basic Concepts in the Methodology of the Social Sciences,* South Africa: Human Sciences Research Council Press.

Mu, Y. (2008) "A Brief History of Rock Climbing in Chinese Universities". *Graduate School.* Master thesis: Beijing Sport University.

NBA China. (2011a) History of Global Outreach(1946—1989). Beijing: International Media Distribution Department, NBA China.

NBA China. (2011b) History of Global Outreach(1990's). Beijing: International Media Distribution Department, NBA China.

NBA China. (2011c) History of Global Outreach(2000—Present). Beijing: International Media Distribution Department, NBA China.

NBA. (2011a) *Department Overview*. Available at: http://www.nba.com/careers/department_list.html#s(accessed: 2011-10-10).

NBA. (2011b) *Inaugural NBA China Games* 2004 *to Tip Off in October*. Available at: http://www.nba.com/allstar2004/china_games_040214.html (accessed: 2011-7-8).

NBA & NBPA. (2005) Collective Bargaining Agreement 2005. National Basketball Association and National Basketball Players Association.

Nelson, M. R. (2009) *The National Basketball League: A History*, 1935—1949, Jefferson, North Carolina: McFarland & Company.

Noll, R. G. (2003) "The Organization of Sports Leagues". *Oxford Review of Economic Policy* 19(04).

O'Sullivan, S. (2003) *Economics: Principles in Action*, New Jersey: Prentice Hall.

Oates, T. & Polumbaum, J. (2004) "Agile Big Man: The Flexible Marketing of Yao Ming". *Pacific Affairs* 77(02).

Ouyang, L., Zhou, X. & Yang, M. (2004) "Internationalization and Localization of Chinese Sport in the Early 21st Century". *Journal of Physical Education* (01).

Polumbaum, J. (2002) "From Evangelism to Entertainment: The YMCA, the NBA, and the Evolution of Chinese Basketball". *Modern Chinese literature and culture* 14(01).

Prakash, A. & Hart, J. A. (2000) *Coping with Globalization*, London and

New York: Routledge.

Qin, L. & Li, H. (2013) "A Study on Tourists' Staying Time during the Formula 1 Grand Prix in Shanghai: A Survival Model Analysis". *Journal of Tianjin University of Sport*(01).

Qin, X., Wang, J. & Lu, C. (2010) "A Comparative Study on the Equalization Environment between Western Countries and China". *Journal of Beijing Sport University*(02).

Qu, J. (2002) "Sport Globalization and Chinese National Minority Traditional Sports Culture". *China's Ethnic Groups*(09).

Quinn, K. G. (2008) "Player Drafts in The Major North American Sports Leagues". In Humphreys, B. R. and Howard, D. R. (eds) *The Business of Sports: Perspectives on the Sports Industry*. Santa Barbara, California: ABC-CLIO.

Ren, H. (2005) "Globalization and Its Challenges to Chinese Traditional Sports". *Sport Science Research*(04).

Ren, L. (2010) "Sport Globalization and Chinese National Minority Traditional Sports Culture". *Gansu Social Sciences*(01).

Riessman, C. K. (2004) "Narrative Analysis". In Bryman, A. and Liao, T. F. (eds) *The Sage Encyclopedia of Social Science Research Methods*. Thousand Oaks, California: Sage Publications.

Ritzer, G. (1998) *The McDonaldization Thesis: Explorations and Extensions*, Thousand Oaks, California: Sage Publications.

Ritzer, G. (2002) *Mcdonaldization: The Reader*, Thousand Oaks, California: Pine Forge Press.

Ritzer, G. (2003) "Rethinking Globalization: Glocalization/Grobalization and Something/Nothing". *Sociological Theory* 21(03).

Ritzer, G. (2007a) *The Blackwell Companion to Globalization*, Hoboken, New

Jersey: Wiley-Blackwell.

Ritzer, G. (2007b) *The Globalization of Nothing* 2, Thousand Oaks, California: Sage Publications.

Ritzer, G. (2010) *The McDonaldization of Society* 6, Thousand Oaks, California: Sage Publications.

Ritzer, G. (2011) *Globalization: The Essentials*, Hoboken, New Jersey: Wiley-Blackwell.

Rob, R. , Carpenter, H. & Williams, R. (2009) *James Naismith: The Man Who Invented Basketball*, Philadelphia: Temple University Press.

Robertson, R. (1992) *Globalization: Social Theory and Global Culture*, Thousand Oaks, California: Sage Publications.

Robertson, R. (1995) "Glocalization: Time-Space and Homogeneity-Heterogeneity". In Featherstone, M. , Lash, S. and Robertson, R. (eds) *Global Modernities*. Thousand Oaks, Califonia: Sage Publications.

Robinson, W. I. (2008) "Theories of Globalization". In Ritzer, G. (ed) *The Blackwell Companion to Globalization*. Hoboken, New Jersey: John Wiley & Sons.

Rong, G. (1987) *The History of Contemporary Chinese Sport*, Beijing: China Social Science Press.

Rosen, C. (2008) *The First Tip-Off: The Incredible Story of the Birth of the NBA*, New York: McGraw Hill Financial.

Rosenau, J. N. (2007) "Three Steps Toward a Viable Theory of Globalization". In Rossi, I. (ed) *Frontiers of Globalization Research*. New York: Springer, 307-315.

Rosner, S. & Shropshire, K. (2011) *The Business of Sports*, Burlington, Massachusetts: Jones & Bartlett Learning.

Rossi, I. (2007) *Frontiers of Globalization Research: Theoretical and Method-*

ological Approaches, New York: Springer.

Sage, G. H. (1998) *Power and Ideology in American Sport: A Critical Perspective*, Champaign, Illinois: Human Kinetics.

Sang, Q. (2007) "A Cultural and Sociological Analysis on the Development of Leisure Sports in Contemporary China". *Sports Culture Guide*(12).

Sarmento, M. R. (1998) "The NBA on Network Television: A Historical Analysis". *Graduate School.* Master thesis: University of Florida.

Schirato, T. & Webb, J. (2003) *Understanding Globalization*, Thousand Oaks, California: Sage Publications.

Scholte, J. A. (2005) *Globalization: A Critical Introduction*, Basingstoke, England: Palgrave Macmillan.

Schumacher, M. (2008) *Mr. Basketball: George Mikan, the Minneapolis Lakers, and the Birth of the NBA*, Minneapolis: University of Minnesota Press.

Schwarz, E. & Hunter, J. (2012) *Advanced Theory and Practice in Sport Marketing*, London and New York: Routledge.

She, P. (2012) "A Study on the Training Models of Chinese Professional Golf Athletes". *Graduate School.* Master: Beijing Sport University.

Shi, C. (2009) "A Study on the Path-independence of Chinese Professional Basketball Leagues". *Graduate School.* Doctor thesis: Shanghai University of Sport.

Shi, J. (2010) "The Advantages of Developing National Minority Sports in Middle and Primary Schools". *Wushu Science*(10).

Shor, E. & Galily, Y. (2012) "Between Adoption and Resistance: Grobalization and Glocalization in the Development of Israeli Basketball". *Sociology of Sport Journal* 29(04).

Shu, S. (2006) "A Historical Overview on Globalization and Sport in China". *Journal of Physical Education*(05).

Shu, S. , Huang, J. , Ding, J. & Wang, M. (2006) "Globalization and the Sociocultural Values of the Olympics". *Journal of Physical Education Institute of Shanxi Teachers University*(03).

Shu, S. & Shen, J. (2011) "A Figurational Analysis on National Interest under the Globalization of Elite Sports". *Journal of Shanghai University of Sport* (04).

Silk, M. L. , Andrews, D. L. & Cole, C. L. (2005) *Sport and Corporate Nationalism*, London: Bloomsbury Publishing.

Silk, M. L. & Manley, A. (2012) "Globalization, Urbanization & Sporting Spectacle in Pacific Asia: Places, Peoples & Pastness". *Sociology of Sport Journal* 29(04).

Silverman, D. (2001) *Interpreting Qualitative Data: Methods for Analysing Talk, Text and Interaction*, Thousand Oaks, California: Sage Publications.

Song, H. (2010) "Modernity and Chinese Traditional Sports". *Sports Culture Guide*(06).

Song, H. & Zhou, A. (2006) "Sport Globalization and the Cultural Identity of Chinese Traditional Sports". *Sports Culture Guide*(02).

SPCSC. (1958) "The Ten Years' Guidelines for Sports Development". *New Sports*(04).

SPCSC. (1982) *Policy Documents for Sport(1949—1981)*, Beijing: People's Sport Press.

SPCSC. (1993) *The Statistics of Sport and Physical Education of China*, Beijing: State Physical Culture and Sports Commission.

SPCSC. (1995) *Fourth Survey on the Statistics of China's Playground*, Beijing: State Physical Culture and Sports Commission.

SPCSC. (2006) "Decisions about the Reform of Sports System (Draft, 1986)". In Hao, Q. (ed) *History of Sport*. Beijing: People's Sport Press.

Sport Business. com. (2012) *Media, Brands & Marketing and Major Events: Essential Revenue Streams for the Business of Sport*. Available at: http://sncrsports. weebly. com/uploads/1/0/2/8/10283396/sportbusiness_ media_ data_ free_ download. pdf(accessed: 2011-10-10).

Sun, F., Meng, X. & Huang, F. (2010) "The NBA's Diffusion in China". *Sports Culture Guide*(07).

Tan, H. (2005) *A History of Sport*, Beijing: Higher Education Press.

Tan, T. -C. (2008) "Chinese Sports Policy and Globalisation: The Case of the Olympic Movement, Elite Football and Elite Basketball". *School of Sport, Exercise and Health Sciences*. Doctor thesis: Loughborough University.

Tan, T. -C. & Bairner, A. (2010) "Globalization and Chinese Sport Policy: The Case of Elite Football in the People's Republic of China". *The China Quarterly* 203(2010).

Tan, X. & Jiang, X. (2011) "Sport Law: A Global Perspective". *China Sport Science*(11).

The Economist. (2011) *Why China Fails at Football: Little Red Card*. Available at: http://www. economist. com/node/21541716(accessed: 2013-8-6).

Tian, Y. & Liu, Q. (2008) "Challenges and Opportunities of Chinese Professional Tennis". *Journal of Chengdu Sport University*(02).

Tsang, E. Y. -h. (2010) "Vanguards of Consumption, Laggards in Politics? The Emergence of a New Middle Class in South China". *School of Government and Society*. Doctor: University of Birmingham.

TzuHsuan, C. (2012) "From the 'Taiwan Yankees' to the New York Yankees: The Glocal Narratives of Baseball". *Sociology of Sport Journal* 29(04).

Walliman, N. (2006) *Social Research Methods,* Thousand Oaks, California: Sage Publications.

Wang, B. , Zhang, J. & Qiu, H. (2008) "Suggestions on the Culturalization of Chinese Tennis". *Sports Culture Guide*(05).

Wang, C. M. (2004a) "Capitalizing the Big Man: Yao Ming, Asian America, and the China Global". *Inter-Asia Cultural Studies* 05(02).

Wang, G. (2004b) "Sport Globalizationand the Development of Chinese Traditional Sports". *Sports Culture Guide*(01).

Wang, G. & Qiu, P. (2006) "Chinese Martial Arts: Challenges and Countermeasures". *Journal of Sports and Science*(04).

Wang, J. (2007) Speech on the2nd Chinese Basketball Culture Forum. Chinese Basketball Culture Research Center: Digital Database(Internal Document).

Wang, J. (2011) Speech on the 3rd Chinese Basketball Culture Forum. Chinese Basketball Culture Research Center: Digital Database(Internal Document).

Wang, K. & Dong, Q. (2008) "An Cultural Analysis on the Four Major Tennis Opens". *Journal of Xi' an Physical Education University*(06).

Wang, M. (1982) "The Report to the 1980 National Sports Conference". In SPCSC(ed) *Sports Policy Documents (1949—1981).* Beijing: People's Sport Press.

Wang, M. & Shu, S. (2006) "A Review on the Researches on Chinese Extreme Sports". *Journal of Jilin Institute of Physical Education*(04).

Wang, Q. & Fang, X. (2010) "A Cross-cultural Discourse: Challenges and Opportunities in the Internationalization of Chinese Traditional Sports". *China Sport Science*(06).

Waters, M. (2001) *Globalization,* London and New York: Routledge.

Wei, F. , Hong, F. & Zhouxiang, L. (2010) "Chinese State Sports Policy:

Pe-and Post-Beijing 2008". *The International Journal of the History of Sport* 27 (14—15).

Wei, P. & Dong, X. (2009) "A Comparative Study on the National Legal Support for NGOs between Western Countries and China". *Sports Culture Guide* (10).

Wen, Y. (2009) "Globalization and the Reformation of China's Collegiate Sport System". *Journal of Sports and Science*(06).

Wen, Z. , Li, Y. & Zhang, D. (2006) "The Transformation of ' Juguo Tizhi' ". *Journal of Beijing Sport University* 29(06).

Wolff, A. (2010) *Big Game, Small World: A Basketball Adventure,* New York Grand Centeral Publishing.

Wolfram, M. & Wang, B. (2003) "Globalization and Japanese Footbal". *Journal of Physical Education*(04).

Wong, B. , Chen, J. , Han, S. , Chen, Z. & Lian, J. (2004) "Globalization and Chinese Sports Industry". *Sports Culture Guide*(10).

Wu, J. & Li, D. (2012) "Suggestions on the Development of Chinese Golf". *Journal of Wuhan Institute of Physical Education*(10).

Wu, S. (1999) *The History of Sport of the PRC,* Beijing: China Books Press.

Wu, Y. , Yang, S. & Ye, J. (2007) "A Comparative Study on the Football Player Transferring System between European Countries and China". *Journal of Wuhan Institute of Physical Education*(09).

Wu, Y. & Zhang, W. (2009) "A Comparative Analysis on Sport Law: Perspectives from the UK, America and France". *Journal of Nanjing Institute of Physical Education(Social Science)*(05).

Xie, Y. & Li, J. (2012) "Globalization and Pedagogy of Martial Arts in China". *Journal of Shandong Institute of Physical Education and Sports*(06).

Xin, J. (2008) "The Developmental Status Quo of Taekwondo in China". *School of Sport and Physical Education.* Master: Southwest University.

Xin, L. (2009) Speech on the 2008—2009 CBAL Season Review Meeting. Beijing: Chinese Basketball Association.

Xin, L. (2010) Speech on the 2009—2010 CBAL Season Review Meeting. Beijing: Chinese Basketball Association.

Xinhua News. (1979) "The NBA All-Star Team Will Visit China Soon". *China Youth Daily* 04—08.

Xu, C. (1999) Speech on the 1999 National Routine Meeting for Basketball. Beijing: Chinese Basketball Association.

Yang, B. (1994) Speech on the 1994 National Rountine Meeting for Basketball Beijing: Chinese Basketball Association.

Yao, M. (2011) Speech on the 3rd Chinese Basketball Culture Forum. Chinese Basketball Culture Research Center: Digital Database(Internal Document).

Yao, M. (2012) Speech on the 30th China International Sporting Goods Show 2012. Chinese Basketball Culture Research Center: Digital Database (Internal Document).

Ye, X. (2007) "Globalization and the Cultural Identity of Chinese Martial Arts". *Journal of Wuhan Institute of Physical Education*.

Yin, R. K. (2003) *Case Study Research: Design and Methods*, Thousand Oaks, California: Sage Publications.

Yin, R. K. (2010) *Qualitative Research from Start to Finish*, New York: Guilford Publications.

Yu, H. (2009) *Media and Cultural Transformation in China*, London: Routledge Chapman & Hall.

Yu, J., Liu, G., Yang, X. & Qiu, Z. (2005) "A Study on the Marketing of the NBA China Games". *Journal of Beijing Sport University*(11).

Yu, J. & Nie, D. (2008) "A SWOT Analysis on the Professionalization of Tennis in China:. *Journal of Physical Education*(08).

Yu, X. (2005) "A Strategical Analysis on Chinese Golf Clubs". *School of Sport and Physical Education.* Doctor thesis: Ji' nan University.

Zhang, B. (2012a) Speech on the 30th China International Sporting Goods Show 2012. Chinese Basketball Culture Research Center: Digital Database(Internal Document).

Zhang, H., Liu, D., Li, F. & Zhuang, Y. (2006) "Yao Ming Phenomenon". *Sports Culture Guide*(01).

Zhang, J. (2012b) "A Study on the Five Major Football Leagues in Europe". *Sports Culture Guide*(11).

Zhang, M. (2012c) "The Construction of Global Vision in Chinese Sport". *Journal of Guangzhou Physical Education Institute*(06).

Zhang, S. (2007) "Globalization, Inequality and their Challenges to Chinese Sport: The Future of Chinese Sport in Post-Olympic Era". *School of Sport and Physical Education.* Master thesis: Sichuan University.

Zhang, S. (2012d) "A Comparative Study between Chinese Daoyin Exercises and Indian Yoga". *School of Sport and Physical Education.* Master: Southwest University.

Zhang, S. & Zhang, C. (2006) "Globalization, Inequality and the Development of Chinese Traditional Sports". *Journal of Shijiazhuang University* 08(06).

Zhang, T. & Cong, M. (2012) "Globalization, Media and the Transformation of Elite Sport: A Case of the NBA". *Journal of Sports and Science*(03).

Zhang, X., Zhang, Y., Shi, B. & Zhang, K. (2000) "The Internationalization of Sport Agency and the Countermeasures of Chinese Market". *Journal of*

Wuhan Institute of Physical Education(06).

Zhang, Z. (2006) "Rethinking the Development of Chinese Elite Sports under' Juguo Tizhi' ". *Sports Culture Guide*(01).

Zhao, Q. (2008) "The Proliferation of Yogan in China". *School of Sport Studies*. Master: Soochow University.

Zhao, Q. (2010) "Mass Media and the Transformation of English Football Culture". *Graduate School*. Master thesis: Beijing Sport University.

Zhao, Y. (2011) *The Secret of Basketball*, Beijing: China Youth Press.

Zheng, Y. (2006) "An Economic Analysis on Glof Facilities in China". *Graduate School*. Doctor thesis: Beijing Sport University.

Zhong, T. (1989) *A History of Basketball in China*, Beijing: People's Sport Press.

Zhou, J. (2007) "The Developmental Status Quo and Countermeasures of Rock Climbing in Chengdu's Universities". *School of Sport and Physical Education*. Master thesis: Sichuan University.

Zhu, D. (1950) "Speech on the All-China Sport and Physical Education Congress". *New Sports*(01).

Zhu, J. , Cheng, H. , Wang, Z. & Wang, X. (2010) "Globalization and the Inheritance of Chinese National Minority Traditional Sports: An SWOT Analysis". *Journal of Nanjing Institute of Physical Education(Social Science)*(02).

Zhu, Z. , Ding, S. & Kang, Q. (2009) "A Historical Analysis on the Integration of Western Sport and Chinese Sport". *Journal of Nanjing Institute of Physical Education(Social Science)*(05).

Acknowledgement

I am deeply beholden to a number of people who have helped me on the road to completing this thesis. First, I would like to thank my supervisor, Professor Fan Hong, for her guidance. I would also like to say thanks to all the staff and to my fellow research students in the School of Asian Studies at University College Cork for their support and encouragement.

I am grateful to the staff in the School of Sport Studies at Soochow University, who made it possible for me to have incredibly deep access to a wide range of official documents. I am also indebted to all those individuals interviewed for their time and willingness to participate in the study. This thesis could not have progressed without their full cooperation.

My special and deep gratitude goes to the China Scholarship Council, which offered me the valuable opportunity to undertake my doctoral studies in Ireland. I would also like to express my sincere gratitude to the John F. Kennedy Fund and to Prof. Chris Curtin with the School of Political Science & Sociology, National University of Ireland, Galway, for their generous financial support of my studies in relation to American professional team sports.

Finally, I am indebted to my parents, my sisters, and Ms Huijie Zhang for their support, forbearance, and love. I would have never come so far in life without their support. This thesis is therefore dedicated to them.